THE **O**THER

SIDE

OF

PSYCHOLOGY

THE OTHER SIDE OF PSYCHOLOGY

DENISE D. CUMMINS, PH.D.

WITHDRAWN

ST. MARTIN'S PRESS ❧ *NEW YORK*

THE OTHER SIDE OF PSYCHOLOGY. Copyright © 1995 by
Denise D. Cummins. All rights reserved. Printed in the
United States of America. No part of this book may be
used or reproduced in any manner whatsoever without
written permission except in the case of brief quotations
embodied in critical articles or reviews. For information,
address St. Martin's Press, 175 Fifth Avenue, New York,
N.Y. 10010.

Library of Congress Cataloging-in-Publication Data

Cummins, Denise D.
    The other side of psychology : what experimental
psychologists learn about the way we think and act /
Denise D. Cummins.
        p.   cm.
    "A Thomas Dunne book."
    ISBN 0-312-13577-7
    1. Psychology, Experimental.   I. Title.
BF181.C74   1995   95-8789
150'.724—dc20   CIP

First Edition: September 1995

10 9 8 7 6 5 4 3 2 1

FOR ROB

Contents

Foreword

T ry this the next time you're at a cocktail party: When people ask you what you do for a living, tell them you are an experimental psychologist. Hearing this, some people will launch immediately into a description of their difficulties with their kids, others will corner you near the punchbowl and whisper to you about their sex problems, and still others will ask you if you know their "shrink," who is the "best in town." In each case, say, "I'm not that kind of psychologist."

This reply will elicit a variety of reactions. Some people will look at you blankly, some will wander off in search of more hospitable chatter, and some will ask if this means you don't really have a degree. Eventually, someone will blurt out, "Then what kind of psychologist *are* you? What *is* an experimental psychologist?"

Perhaps you're asking that question right now. Here's the answer. Experimental psychologists are scientists (not psychotherapists) who study human and animal minds. They don't do psychotherapy. They are not trained for it, and (usually) they have no interest in it. Instead, they are trained (and receive PhDs) to conduct scientific research on the matter of the mind. Here are a few examples of the types of questions they address:

- How could the Holocaust have occurred?
- Are we are born capable of making sense of our visual inputs or must we learn to see?
- Why are kids so attached to their parents?
- There are millions of species of creatures on earth. Why do only humans have language?
- Why do we dream? Is it biologically necessary?
- What determines whether creative insights will or won't occur?

This is the world of the experimental psychologist. I know because I am one.

Interest in psychology seems to be a pretty stable and reliable phenomenon. According to the *U.S. National Center for Education Statistics,* psychology is the seventh most popular major in American colleges and universities. From personal experience, I know that Introductory Psychology enrolls more students at Yale and the University of Arizona during any given semester than any other introductory level course (an average of 1,000 students *each semester* at the University of Arizona).

It has always bothered me that despite all of this hunger for knowledge about the mind, *there are virtually NO books on experimental psychology written for the general audience.* When it comes to informing people about what makes us tick, the psychotherapists have led the way, filling shelves with books of the self-help variety. Books on scientific psychology, however, are typically written as textbooks for college courses. These large, cumbersome tomes make for great bedtime reading because it's almost a sure thing you'll fall asleep within the first few pages.

Given this state of affairs, I decided to write a book, based on courses I taught at Yale University, that would satisfy the intelligent reader's hunger for scientific knowledge about the mind. This is it. I hope you enjoy it, and I hope it will stop people from telling me about their sex problems at cocktail parties . . .

Acknowledgments

Many thanks to Richard Gerrig, Mahzarin Banaji, Peter Salovey, and Paul Bloom for sharing their notes with me and for being great colleagues. Thanks also to Karen Wynn and John Kihlstrom for reprints and preprints of their work. Special thanks go to Katya, Masha, Harry, Sheila, Caine, Jasper, Kirby, Austen, Emily, Smokey, Ceili, Clarence, and, of course, Rob. They know why.

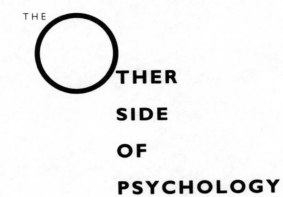

THE **O**THER

SIDE

OF

PSYCHOLOGY

Prologue: The Science of Psychology

Take a prism and let a ray of sunlight pass through it. What happens? The white light entering the prism is split into a spectrum of brilliant colors. Do you find this frightening? Controversial? Shocking? Many people did when Sir Isaac Newton used this demonstration to develop his theory of color.

For centuries, people believed that light was the purest of all essences, nondivisible and whole. When it came in contact with objects, a substance or substances within the objects *degraded* the pure light and produced colors. Newton's scientific demonstration that this "purest of all essences" was in fact itself a compound made up of many colors frightened and repulsed many people. The idea that things are not as they seem, that nature could lie to us, and that our powers of perception could be so misled was very threatening indeed. The German poet and scientist Goethe, for instance, was so enraged by this demonstration that he set out to prove that Newton was a fraud. He railed against and sneered at Newton's experimental approach to the study of color. As one writer put it, Goethe believed that "Just as a genuine work of art cannot bear retouching by a strange hand, so [Goethe] would have us believe Nature resists the interference of the experimenter who tortures her and disturbs her; and, in revenge, misleads the impertinent kill-joy by a distorted image of herself."[1] To study white light, the purest of all essences, experimentally in a laboratory was, to many, aberrant, ludicrous, and misleading.

This very simple fact about white light is far from threatening or controversial to us today. In fact, Goethe's concerns seem somewhat reactionary and childish to us. Yet, while people got used to the idea of scientifically studying light, the idea of scientifically studying *the mind* was—and frequently still is—met with the same type of emotional resistance. The mind is our "white light," the purest of essences, inviolable and sacred. Studying it scientifically in a laboratory is considered by many to be aberrant, ludicrous, and impossible.

For centuries, there has been a great deal of skepticism that a science of psychology could even exist. René Descartes introduced the notion that the mind and body were separate entities, and that the mind was inherently a nonphysical and hence nonmeasurable thing. Immanuel Kant believed that because of the inherently private nature of psychological events, "Psychology can, therefore, never become anything more than a . . . natural description of the soul, but not a science of the soul, or even a psychological experimental doctrine."[2] He believed there was no objective way of measuring mental events, so there could be no science of psychology.

In the late 1800s, however, some things occurred that challenged this view of the mind as an immeasurable ghost or holistic "pure essence." First, Hermann von Helmholtz, a physicist and physiologist, measured the speed of neural transmission in humans by requiring them to push a button whenever a stimulus was applied to their legs. He found it to be between 165–330 feet per second.[3] This was a disturbing result for most scientists at the time because it was generally believed that mental events and acts of will occurred instantaneously. The idea that it took time for a thought to be formed and acted on was truly revolutionary, and many people reacted in much the same way that Goethe did to Newton's spectrum demonstration!

Another scientist, named F. C. Donders, picked up on Helmholtz's method and measured an even more "mental" phenomenon.[4] He measured the time it took people to respond to a single stimulus and the time it took them to respond to the same stimulus in the context of another. By subtracting the two times, he obtained a measure of how long it takes a human being to discriminate between two stimuli, a very mental process.

As mild as this all seems to us today, it was very controversial at the time because these experiments suggested that mental events could be measured objectively. The mind was becoming a legitimate object of scientific study like any other object. It held no special status in the grand scheme of things. Eventually, enough people got interested in questions about the nature of mental and emotional events that a laboratory was established in Leipzig in 1879 by Wilhelm Wundt to study them exclusively. Thus, the field of *experimental psychology* was born. This is the "other psychology," the one few people know about.

The psychology that is more familiar to people is *clinical psychology*, the discipline that explores abnormal psychology, behavior that has gone wrong. While there are researchers who study abnormal behavior in a scientific way, the majority of psychologists in this area are therapists. They assist people whose coping skills have broken down to find their way through their pain and to function again as whole persons. To use an analogy with the medical arts and sciences, a clinical psychologist is like a medical doctor, and an experimental psychologist is like a biologist. Psychotherapists and medical doctors use the knowledge derived from clinical and experimental studies (as well as their own experience and judgment) to treat patients. Sometimes, a psychotherapist or medical doctor will also be involved in research, but his or her primary concern is the care of patients. In contrast, experimental psychologists, like biologists, spend most of their time doing research. Their research participants can be people or animals. As a rule, they do *not* do psychotherapy or see patients. They are not trained for this. They are trained to do research.

The clinical side of psychology owes its existence almost exclusively to one person: Sigmund Freud. In the late 1800s (about the same time that mental events were beginning to be measured), a few doctors began noticing that many seemingly physical ailments could be cured with hypnosis. The ailments in question were called hysterical ailments because they seemed to have no physical basis at all. This is in contrast to psychosomatic ailments, where there really is something wrong with the body (e.g., an ulcer), but the cause of the ailment is mental or emotional (e.g., psychological stress). In a hysterical ailment, there is nothing wrong with the body, but the patient behaves as though there were. For example, he or she may be unable to walk, yet there is nothing wrong with the legs or the nervous system.

In 1895, a medical doctor named Josef Breuer reported a case of a woman named Anna O. who developed a persistent cough while caring for her dying father.[5] The cough had no physical origin, yet was a very real physical symptom. Breuer cured Anna through hypnosis. He then spoke about it to the young Dr. Freud, who became intrigued with such cases. Freud soon found that many hysterical ailments were the manifestations of very deeply repressed psychological traumas. He developed a theory in which psychodynamic forces produced hysterical ailments. His theory met with great resistance, in part because people found it very difficult to accept the idea that the mind—that abstract, metaphysical entity—could so affect the body. Particularly threatening was Freud's notion of the unconscious—the idea that part of your mind is not open to introspection. In fact, for centuries, the notion that one could have an idea in the mind and not be conscious of it was considered a contradiction. As John Locke put it in 1690: "I do say a man cannot think at any time, waking or sleeping, and without being sensible of it."[6] Many people also had a difficult time accepting the almost central role of sexuality in Freud's theories of normal and abnormal psychological development. Nonetheless, the idea that psychological disturbances could be treated through psychotherapy techniques was eventually accepted and blossomed into the fields of clinical psychology and psychiatry.

A great many books are written on psychotherapy today, but few on the experimental side of psychology. Experimental psychology is indeed "the other psychology," the one only people who have taken Introductory Psychology seem to know about. This is unfortunate since contemporary experimental psychologists study phenomena far more interesting and complex than the simple perceptual discrimination tasks that so interested Donders and his contemporaries. Today, experimental psychology is a broad discipline that comprises many subdisciplines.

Each subdiscipline is full of fascinating experimental results, results that answer questions about how it is that human beings come to think, act, perceive, remember, and dream the way they do.

Some people respond to research questions such as these just as Goethe did to Newton's investigations of light, believing that scientific study of the mind degrades the mind and misleads us. Others are receptive to the body of facts that are emerging from such research, and see how such facts can be used to better understand ourselves and others. In the chapters that follow, you will be taken into the world of the experimental psychologist, and will learn how it is that we perceive, learn, remember, think, scheme, love, and dream.

CHAPTER 1

Minds in Groups: How Others Influence Our Behavior

Human beings are social beings. In the United States alone, there are literally thousands of associations, professional societies, churches, and street gangs. Clearly, we as a species tend to seek out and band together with others like ourselves.

From a psychological viewpoint, the social side of human nature presents an intriguing paradox: People behave differently in groups than they do when they're alone. Ordinary folks find themselves performing acts of epic heroism or base debauchery when cheered on or egged on by peers—acts that would never even occur to them to try when alone. For this reason, a good deal of research in scientific psychology is aimed at identifying exactly *how* group dynamics bring about changes in individual behavior.

Consider, for example, the Holocaust. How could ordinary, decent human beings stand guard over the death camps? How could an entire nation stand by while six million of their citizens were sent to die in death camps and gas chambers? While countless volumes have been written on the topic, perhaps it is the *Milgram experiments* that shed the most light on the psychology of those ordinary soldiers and bystanders.

Imagine you've signed up to participate in a psychology experiment on learning. You arrive at the laboratory at a major Ivy League university. A middle-aged man wearing a white laboratory coat greets you and introduces himself as Dr. Milgram. He escorts you to a brightly lit, well-furnished room and asks you to be seated. A few minutes later, another person shows up. He, too, as it turns out, is a volunteer participant. Dr. Milgram explains that he has been conducting research on learning for a number of years, and is an expert in the area. He is developing a new technique for improving performance on memory tasks. The technique is based on punishment. One participant will serve as the "teacher," who will read a list of unrelated word pairs (e.g., bank-hat) to the other participant, who will serve as the "learner." The learner must learn the word pairs perfectly so that when the teacher says one member of the pair (e.g., bank), the learner responds with the other member (e.g., hat). Whenever the learner responds incorrectly, the teacher is to administer an electric shock to the learner. At this point, Dr. Milgram shows you the electric shock generator, and administers a brief 45-volt shock to each participant's arm. It hurts mildly, and is very unpleasant. He shows you a piece of equipment about the size and shape of a stereo receiver. It has thirty switches on it which are labeled with voltage ratings ranging from 15 volts to 450 volts. Underneath the voltage ratings are verbal labels ranging from "Slight" to "Danger: Severe Shock" to an ominous-looking "XXX." He says that the teacher must increase the voltage of the shock with each error. He tells you that normally very few errors are committed, and that the shock level usually does not rise above moderate. He then asks if you both still agree to participate in the study, and you both do. You draw lots to see who will be the teacher and who will be the learner. To your relief, you see that you will be the teacher. You accompany Dr. Milgram and the learner into another room, and assist him in strapping the learner into his chair and attaching the electrodes. You are then seated in front of the shock generator in an adjacent room, where you can't see the learner. The two of you communicate via an intercom.

You soon begin to worry that something very wrong is happening. The learner has made so many mistakes that you are now all the way up to 120 volts. The learner is shouting that the shocks are too painful. You turn around and ask the experimenter if you should continue, and he says that you should.

The learner continues to make mistakes, and you are told to continue increasing the voltage of the shocks. What do you do?

If you are like the 65 percent majority of people who participated in the studies of Stanley Milgram at Yale University during the early sixties, you will continue administering shocks right on up through the "XXX" rating level.[1] Things would go something like this: At 150 volts, the learner would demand to be let out of the experiment. At 180 volts, he would cry that he could no longer stand the pain. At 300 volts, he would begin pounding on the wall and scream that he would no longer answer any questions. After 330 volts, there would be nothing but an ominous silence. Ninety-five percent of Milgram's "teachers" delivered shocks to the learners up to the 300–volt level, and 65 percent went the entire distance.

Perhaps you are one of the 65 percent who administered all of the shocks. When you are finished, Dr. Milgram takes you to the learner's room. When he opens the door, you are surprised to see the learner sitting comfortably in an easy chair. "Seated" in the strapped chair is a tape recorder playing his prerecorded responses. You are immensely relieved to find out that you were not in fact shocking anyone. Dr. Milgram explains that the learner is really his research assistant, and the lot drawing was rigged. He explains that the real purpose of the experiment was to investigate obedience to authority. The three of you discuss the implications of the study, its purpose and its ethics. You fill out a questionaire on your feelings about the study. Some weeks later, you are contacted again by Dr. Milgram to see how you are doing—whether you are suffering any negative aftereffects of participating in the study.

Studies that employ this much deception and carry this much emotional "threat" could not be carried out today because it would be nearly impossible for them to pass the regulations imposed by scientific regulating committees instituted at all universities. And perhaps this is a good thing. In fact, it was the outrage many people felt when reading about these studies that led to the creation of guidelines and committees governing the use of human participants in scientific research. Nonetheless, it is interesting to note that although people who read about these studies were appalled by them, few of the randomly selected people who actually participated in the research felt that way. Eighty percent of those who participated said they were happy to have been in the studies, 15 percent were neutral, and fewer than 1 percent were at most unhappy about participating.

These important matters aside, what did the Milgram experiments tell us about ourselves? If we were to divide the participants into two groups, those who obeyed and those who did not, what would be the critical difference between the two? What determines who will obey a malevolent authority and who will not?

Milgram investigated a large number of variables, but the results of the experiments point to a single, crucial factor: *Blind obedience occurs when people shift the responsibility for their actions onto someone or something else.* This was the critical difference. Once a shift in accountability is made in one's mind, blind obedience follows.

Let's see how Milgram came to this conclusion: First, when Milgram asked his participants why they continued to obey (even though they were not threatened in any way), the most common responses given were: "It didn't seem immoral or wrong because the professor said it was okay," "The professor wouldn't let me," and "I was only following his orders." (The last response is chillingly identical to the reason given repeatedly by the Nazis tried for war crimes and atrocities at Nuremberg following World War II.) These responses seem to imply that the participant did *not* feel responsible for his or her actions.

Second, he found that high levels of obedience occurred only when the orders to shock came from a legitimate authority. If an "ordinary person," that is, another participant (who was a confederate of the experimenter) gave the orders, the percentage of people who obeyed to the "XXX" stage dropped from 65 percent to 20 percent. The same drop from 65 percent to 20 percent was observed when the learner was the one giving the orders, demanding that the teacher continue to shock him whether the teacher wanted to or not. In these cases, the orders to deliver the shocks did not come from a legitimate authority, and the participants were less likely to obey.

On the other hand, if two authorities were present, but they contradicted each other (one said do it, the other said not to), *no one* went all the way since it was not clear which authority to obey.

Third, factors that "diluted" one's feelings of responsibility increased the percentage who "went all the way." For example, when the participant served as an "assistant" to someone in delivering the shocks, 92 percent went the distance. Contrast this with the condition in which it was entirely up to the teacher to choose which level of shock to deliver after each wrong answer. In this case, only 2 percent of them went the distance. It was nearly impossible in this latter condition for the teacher to shift responsibility onto someone else.

Fourth, the proximity of the victim mattered a good deal. When the "teacher" could not see or hear the victim, 65 percent obeyed. When they could hear the victim's cries, 63 percent obeyed. But when the victim was in the same room, and could be seen and heard, obedience dropped to 40 percent. Finally, if the teacher had to touch the victim by holding his hand down onto a shock plate, the figure was reduced still further to 30 percent. As it became harder to avoid facing the direct consequences of one's behavior, it became harder to shift responsibility for one's actions elsewhere.

We might ask whether the *victim* had any control over what happened to him. The answer seems to be no. When the learner announced prior to the experiment that he had a heart condition, 65 percent of the teachers still obeyed the authority's orders to deliver the full range of shocks. When the learner agreed to ·participate *only* under the condition that he be let out when he wanted to be let out, 40 percent of the teachers ignored this verbal contract and shocked him up to the "XXX" level anyway. When asked afterward whether there was anything the learner could have said that would have made the teacher stop, the typical obedient teacher's response was "no." Milgram also noticed that the participants who obeyed tended to devalue the victim, saying things such as "He was so stupid, he deserved to be shocked." Sometimes this devaluation occurred *as a consequence* of shocking the victim.

What if the authority served as the learner? Would the teacher obey this "victimized" authority when he asked to terminate the lesson? The answer was unequivocally yes; none of the teachers continued to shock him. But if one authority served as the learner and another ordered the shocks, the percentage of teachers who obeyed shot back up to 65 percent. The lesson seems to be "Do as the authority figure says, even to another authority figure!" Authority figures seem to lose their authority when they themselves become the victims of other authority figures.

In each case, it is clear that the teachers were more likely to deliver shocks up to the "XXX" level if there was some way they could shift the responsibility for their actions onto someone else. When an authority was giving the orders, one could easily point to him and say, "He told me to. It wasn't my idea. I was only following orders." If a nonauthority tried to give the orders, it was more difficult to shift responsibility for one's actions since the person giving the orders had no more power, knowledge, or authority than the teacher did; hence, people were much less likely to obey. If the teachers were only "assisting," their sense of responsibility was also lessened, just as it was when they couldn't directly see the results of their actions. In these cases, obedience increased.

A few individual differences among participants were also found to reduce obedience. For example, participants who were in the legal, medical, or teaching professions were less obedient than those who were in engineering, the physical sciences, and the military. Of those in the military, the longer the military career, the more obedient. In contrast, other characteristics such as gender, political affiliation, religious convictions, and years of education, had little effect on obedience rates.

So what have we learned from the Milgram experiments? Perhaps the most unsettling thing is that, contrary to Freudian doctrine, this kind of brutality does not seem to stem from anger or aggressive impulses. Indeed, other experiments have frustrated and angered their participants prior to allowing them to shock their frustrators, and the effects of this manipulation were minuscule compared to the effects observed under conditions of obedience.[2]

Milgram's results seem to convey something more dangerous and unsettling, namely a human propensity to abandon our humanity and defy our consciences rather than defy an authority—even a malevolent authority. As long as the orders come from a legitimate authority, a substantial percentage of us will obey, and will become focused on *how* to obey the orders rather than *whether* to obey them. If you embed this propensity in a framework where the victim has been devalued and the participants have been strongly indoctrinated in obedience to authority, you have the making of an atrocity.

During the reign of the Nazi Party in Germany, more than six million people were murdered in death camps. We know that the German economy was crumbling, the people were frightened, and the Nazis gave them an easy scapegoat for Germany's problems: German Jews. We also know that there were deep-seated prejudices against the Jewish people in Europe (not just Germany). The Nazis fanned the flames of this prejudice by openly and repeatedly vilifying and dehumanizing Jews. Even so, it is clear that the Nazi Party could not on its own have carried out the Holocaust. What was needed was the obedience of countless thousands—from the people who stood by while Jewish neighbors were taken away, to the soldiers who operated the death machines. Obedience was a crucial variable since many Germans did not agree with the "final solution," but did nothing to resist it. This blind obedience to authority is not, of course, limited to the German people. Following the My Lai massacre during the Vietnam War, 51 percent of Americans surveyed said they would follow orders if commanded to shoot *all* of the inhabitants of a Vietnamese village—even the children.

But Milgram's results also give us reason for hope. There was one crucial condition in which the overwhelming majority of people refused to obey the malevolent authority's orders to harm an innocent human being: When the "teacher" was accompanied by *two peers who defiantly refused* to continue the experiment, the obedience rate plummeted to 10 percent. Perhaps the lesson to be learned here is that we each can act as catalysts for conscionable resistance to malevolent authority.

Authority figures are not the only people who can strongly influence our behavior. Sometimes the presence of others is in itself a strong influence on our behavior. In this case, it is the power of *conformity* that controls us.

Imagine you've signed up for another psychology experiment. You arrive at the assigned room on time, and notice a lot of other people sitting around a table. Fortunately, there are still a few empty seats and you take one. The experimenter announces that the experiment will begin shortly, but while you are waiting for others to arrive, you will be asked to make a few simple perceptual judgments. He then displays a pair of cards. The first card, card A, has a vertical line on it that is about three inches long. The second card has three lines, which respectively measure one inch, three inches, and five inches. You are to call out which of the three lines on card B you think is equal in length to the line on card A. Each participant is to indicate his or her judgment by calling them out in turn. This procedure will continue for a dozen or so pairs of cards.

This seems like an easy task because it is so apparent that the second line on card B matches the line on card A. So you are very surprised when the first participant calls out, "One" in response to the pair above. You are even more surprised when the next participant agrees. Now it is your turn. What do you do?

This is a description of one in a series of experiments conducted by Solomon Asch in the late fifties and replicated numerous times since.[3] There is just one more thing about the design that must be told: In each group session, there was only one real participant. The others were all confederates, and the seating arrangements were such that at least one confederate would call out his or her response prior to the real participant's turn. (Several groups were run in each experiment in order to get a reasonably large sample size.) The results were surprising: 74 percent of the participants conformed to the confederates' responses at least once, and 32 percent conformed on every trial. In contrast, participants rarely called out wrong responses when alone. When there is social pressure, we don't believe our own eyes—or at least won't admit to it out loud.

Behavior such as this is called *conformity* as opposed to obedience because there is no authority figure to obey. Instead, we feel pressured to go along with the majority, to conform. Asch explored the factors that influence conformity. He found that the more ambiguous the situation, the more conformity increases. For example, if the length of the lines were all nearly the same, the incidence of conformity increased. Group size influenced conformity as well, but perhaps not as one would predict. Conformity tended to increase as the group size increased from one to about three, but remained fairly stable after that.

In contrast, conformity dropped substantially when the group was *not* unanimous. Even if just one confederate said "Two" to the above, conformity dropped to 6 percent. Having just one other dissenting voice reduced conformity dramatically. This was true even if the dissenter did not agree with the participant (e.g., said "Three" in answer to the above). And the earlier the dissension occurred, the more likely the participant was to dissent as well (a phenomenon familiar to anyone who has sat on committees).

Why do we conform so readily? Perhaps it's because (James Dean notwithstanding), we tend to like conformers more than nonconformers. For example, some researchers asked several groups of six participants and three confederates to debate a case of a juvenile delinquent and decide what should be done about him.[4] The three confederates listened to the debate for a while and then assumed one of three roles. The first (modal) took a position that conformed exactly to the group average. The second (deviate) took a position exactly opposite to the group. The third (slider) at first agreed with the deviate, and gradually shifted to the modal's view. After a decision was made, each group member was asked to rate how well they liked the other group members. The results indicated that the modal (conforming) confederate was liked the best, followed by the slider; the deviate, who held out against the group's position, was the least liked.

Although we may not like nonconformists, we seem to benefit from their dissension. People exposed to minority opinions (dissension) have been found to use more strategies to solve problems, find more correct solutions, and produce more unusual solutions.[5] They also scored higher on measures of creativity. The lesson seems to be that although we may not like the James Deans among us, we benefit from their rebelliousness.

Our propensity to conform can sometimes have disastrous consequences. On March 27, 1964, the *New York Times* carried the following story:

For more than half an hour, 38 respectable law-abiding citizens of Queens watched a killer stalk and stab a woman in three separate attacks in Kew Gardens. Twice, the sound of their voices and the sudden glow of their bedroom lights interrupted him and frightened him off. Each time, he returned, sought her out, and stabbed her again. Not one person telephoned the police during the assault; one witness called after the woman was dead.

How could a crime of such brutality occur with so many witnesses? It would seem that with so many people present, the probability that at least one person would call the police or try to intervene ought to be fairly high. Subsequent laboratory work by social psychologists suggested, however, that such bystander apathy occurs not in spite of the large number of witnesses but because of it. In fact, bystander apathy is a type of passive conformity.

A classical study by Bibb Latané and Judy Rodin investigated the relationship between crowd size and helping behavior in the following way:[6] A young female experimenter greeted research participants, asking them to be seated and to fill out questionnaires. After telling them she would be right back, she disappeared into an adjoining room. She could be heard dragging a chair across the room and climbing onto it. This was followed by a scream, a loud crash of chairs and a bookcase falling, and a thud, as though someone had fallen. The experimenter began to moan in pain, calling out, "Oh my God! My ankle! I can't move it! I think it's broken!" She continued in this way until one of the participants came to her aid, or until one minute had transpired if no one came. (Again, this experiment contained elements of deception. The experimenter, of course, had not fallen nor broken her ankle. In this as in the above studies, the deception was explained in detail to the participants before they left the laboratory.)

The results were quite striking. Seventy percent of the participants offered help when they were alone. When there were two participants waiting, however, the experimenter got help in only 40 percent of the sessions, a 30 percent drop! An even more dramatic drop was observed when the participant waited along with a passive confederate who did nothing to offer help. In these cases, the real participant went to the "victim's" aid only 7 percent of the time.

The results of this experiment clearly indicate that the likelihood of a victim receiving help decreases as the number of witnesses increases. This result has been replicated repeatedly in a variety of different settings. For example, in one experiment by John Darley and Bibb Latané, people were asked to participate in a group discussion about college life with either one, three, or five other persons.[7] The participants were seated in individual cubicles that prevented them from seeing the other group members. They communicated with each other via an intercom system. Again, there was only one real participant in any particular group session; the rest were tape recordings. The discussion began as one of the tape-recorded confederates described some of his personal problems, including a tendency to have epileptic seizures when stressed. When he began to speak again during the second round of discussion, he began to suffer a seizure and gasped for help. Did the real participant try to help (by seeking out the experimenter and reporting the seizure)?

On 85 percent of the occasions when the real participant thought he or she was the only other discussant, the "seizure" was reported to the experimenter. When the real participant thought he or she was in a three-person group, the percentage of attempts to obtain help dropped to 62 percent, and in a six-person group, the percentage dropped even further to 31 percent. Clearly, the larger the group size, the less likely the victim was to receive help.

Why should group size matter? Why are we less likely to help when more people are present? By examining the reasons participants gave for their unresponsiveness and by manipulating certain variables in subsequent research, social psychologists identified two factors that become operative when people are not alone in witnessing an emergency situation. The first is *pluralistic ignorance: By their very presence, everyone in the group misleads everyone else into defining the situation as a nonemergency.* The idea is that people believe "things like this" don't happen in broad daylight with so many people around. It is a form of conformity. We look around, see all those other people there doing nothing, and we do nothing ourselves. The unresponsiveness of others misleads us into "not believing our own eyes," that is, not believing that the situation really is an emergency that requires our intervention. This is a little like the Asch experiments where the real participant conforms to the other "participants' " responses (or, in the present case, lack of response) and behaves accordingly.

The second factor is *diffusion of responsibility: No one person feels responsible for responding to the emergency.* Because other people are there, we assume someone else will help or already has helped. As in the Milgram experiments, we no longer feel responsible for our own behavior (or lack thereof). When we are alone, we know no one else can help the victim, hence it is more difficult to "pass the buck" or avoid our responsibility to come to the aid of another. For example, in a variation of the "seizure" experiment above, the participant was as likely to help in larger groups as when he or she was alone *if* the other group members were believed to be in a remote building too far to help.[8] On the other hand, if the participant was led to believe that one of the other group members was a medical student, he or she was less likely to try to help the seizure victim.[9] In this case, it was far easier to "pass the buck" to the medical student, assuming that given his greater expertise, he ought to be the one to help the victim.

There are two lessons that can be drawn from this work. The first is how to "devictimize" yourself. Even though *you* are the victim in need of help, you must help bystanders to define your situation as an emergency. Don't just scream—cry "Help!" Describe your situation to help clarify it for the bystanders. For example, cry out, "Call the police! I'm being attacked!" Assign responsibility. Point to someone and say, "You, call the police."

The second lesson is that if you are a bystander, don't look around to see what the other bystanders are doing—ACT! Don't let the presence of so many other people define the situation as a nonemergency for you. Get help. The worst you can do is suffer some embarrassment if you're wrong, and you may save a life if you're right.

While these admonitions may seem strange, a personal anecdote reported by one experimental psychologist underscores their importance.[10] He was involved in a rather serious car crash in which both he and the other driver were seriously hurt. The other driver was unconscious, slumped over his steering wheel, while the psychologist managed to stagger out of his car, bleeding, onto the road. The accident had occurred in the center of an intersection in full view of other drivers waiting for the light to turn. When it did turn, the cars began to roll slowly by, with their drivers and passengers gawking at him through their windows. The psychologist immediately recognized what was happening: diffusion of responsibility. He pulled himself up so he could be seen clearly, pointed to the driver of the nearest car and said, "Call the police!" He pointed to two other drivers and said, "Pull over, we need help!" The responses of the drivers were instantaneous. The police were called, and an ambulance arrived shortly. The other drivers also used their handkerchiefs to blot the blood away from his face, put a jacket under his head, and volunteered to serve as witnesses to the accident; one even offered to drive him to the hospital. Other drivers also stopped to help the injured man. As the psychologist pointed out, the trick was to get the ball rolling in the direction of aid. The "spells" of pluralistic ignorance and diffusion of responsibility needed to be broken so that potential helpers could become actualized ones. A more cynical way of putting it is that if you are a victim, it is crucial that you get the human propensity to conform working to *your* advantage: Define the behavior of getting and giving you help as that to which bystanders must conform.

Other people influence not just our behavior but our beliefs as well. I always feel some qualms when talking about the body of research that reveals how people come to change their beliefs and attitudes because the knowledge embodied by this research can be used either to manipulate or to enlighten. I always precede these talks by telling people that they should use this knowledge defensively to protect themselves from being manipulated by people who use these techniques, and not offensively to manipulate others. With that in mind, let's see how people can be brought to change their beliefs. As you might suspect, the most powerful techniques have little to do with reason and more to do with saving face.

During the Korean War, many captured American soldiers were held in prisoner-of-war camps run by the Chinese Communists. Psychologists were particularly interested in these POWs because of the unsettling success the Chinese achieved in getting them to change their beliefs about their own country's role in the war. They came to believe, for example, that the U.S. had engaged in germ warfare and had been the initial aggressors in starting the war. There was also an extremely high rate of collaboration with the enemy on the part of the POWs, ranging from benign activities such as running errands voluntarily to serious behaviors such as turning in fellow prisoners who tried to escape.

The surprising thing about these belief changes and collaborations is that they occurred despite the absence of severe coercion. In contrast to the North Koreans, who favored brutal interrogation techniques, the Chinese camps followed a "lenient policy" in which violent measures were used far less often. This policy was extremely successful. Nearly all of their POWs are said to have collaborated with the enemy in one way or another.[11] As Edgar Schein, a principal American investigator of the Chinese indoctrination program in Korea, put it, "When an escape did occur, the Chinese usually recovered the man easily by offering a bag of rice to anyone turning him in." How did the Chinese achieve this?

Subsequent research suggested that the surprising key to the POWs' belief changes and collaborations is hidden in that last statement, namely, *the paltriness of the reward given for behaving in a way that is inconsistent with one's beliefs.* Let's see how this works. One tactic used by the Chinese was to hold political essay contests. The prizes were kept exceedingly small—a few cigarettes, a bit of fruit—but the contests and prizes were sufficient to evoke interest from prisoners living in such desolate circumstances. In order to win the prize, the essay had to contain elements of a pro-Communist stand, even a token nod in that direction. In this way, the winning POW would obtain the prize only by providing support—however small—for the enemy's cause. While salting an essay with a few token statements in favor of communism might have seemed harmless to the POW under the circumstances, the important thing was that it was there in black-and-white and in his own handwriting. He could hardly deny having written it later. So how does he justify his behavior when the essay is trotted out later and shown to his fellow prisoners, his family, or the American press? By appealing to the cigarette or piece of fruit he was offered in return? Does such a paltry inducement justify "aiding" the enemy in their propaganda campaign?

And there you have it. The contradiction between your beliefs on the one hand (e.g., communism is "bad" and democracy is "good") and your actions on the other (e.g., writing that communism is good) causes unpleasant uneasiness in your mind. Something has got to give, and since you cannot take back your actions, you change your beliefs. Psychologist Leon Festinger called the discomfort that most people feel in the face of such inconsistency "cognitive dissonance," and he attributed the belief change that follows to a desire on the part of the individual to reduce these feelings of discomfort.[12]

As social psychologist Robert Cialdini puts it, "The Chinese withheld large prizes in favor of less powerful inducements [because] they wanted the participants to *own* what they had done. No excuses, no ways out were allowed. . . . A prisoner who salted his political essay with anti-American comments could not be permitted to shrug it off as motivated by a big reward [or severe punishment]. . . . It was not enough to wring commitments out of their men; those men had to be made to take inner responsibility for their actions."[13]

As Cialdini goes on to say, we accept inner responsibility for our behavior when we think we have *chosen* to perform it in the absence of strong outside pressures. A strong reward or threat of punishment constitute such strong outside pressures. This implies that in order to change people's beliefs, you must accomplish two things. First, you must get them to behave in a way that is inconsistent with their beliefs. Second, you must make them take responsibility for their behavior. *Faced with an inconsistency between their beliefs and their actions, most people will change their beliefs to bring them in line with their actions.*

As unintuitive as this theoretical framework seems, it has been successfully tested repeatedly in the laboratory. This work shows quite clearly that attitude shifts like this occur under everyday circumstances, not just in highly aberrant situations such as captivity or maltreatment.

Participants in one study were preselected on the basis of their attitudes toward controversial topics, such as the legalization of marijuana.[14] They were asked to write an essay that gave arguments in favor of the opposing view, and were later again queried about their real beliefs about the issue. Consistent with cognitive dissonance theory, only poorly paid participants who were led to believe that their essays would be shown to other people displayed changes in their positions. Those who were paid well or who thought no one would see their essays showed little change. Both components had to be there—the uneasiness caused by knowing others would find out about their behaving inconsistently with their true beliefs, and the lack of a justifiable reason (e.g., a large reward) for behaving that way.

Attitude shifts like these have also been observed in more benign circumstances. Leon Festinger and James Carlsmith, for example, asked their participants to perform exceedingly boring tasks for payment.[15] The tasks included such things as packing spools into a tray, and turning pegs on a board one-quarter turn. The tasks took an hour to perform, and had been rated previously by a test group of students as extremely boring. When the participants were done, some were sent immediately to another experimenter, who asked them to rate how much they enjoyed performing the task. The rest were asked to engage in a little deception: They were asked to tell another person who was waiting to participate in the study that the tasks were fun, interesting, and enjoyable. As an inducement, half of these "deceivers" were offered one dollar to deceive while the other half were offered twenty dollars. Then they were taken to the other experimenter, who asked them to rate how much they actually enjoyed the tasks.

The control group (those who were not asked to deceive) disliked the tasks immensely, rating them as extremely boring. Since participants were randomly assigned to groups, we can assume that this group gave a true picture of how *all* the participants felt about the tasks immediately upon completing them. But the attitudes of the people who were subsequently paid to deceive others appeared to undergo a dramatic change. Those who were paid twenty dollars for deceiving others reported feeling *neutral* toward the tasks. But even more striking was the fact that those who were paid only one dollar reported that they really did find the tasks enjoyable. Consistent with cognitive dissonance theory, these participants underwent the greatest attitude change, bringing their professed beliefs more in line with their unjustified deception.

Similarly, in the spring of 1959, there was a riot on the Yale campus and the New Haven police were called in. Accusations of police brutality followed. The overwhelming majority of students on campus believed that the actions taken by the police were totally unjustified. One professor asked his Introductory Psychology students to go around campus and ask people to write a strong and forceful essay entitled "New Haven Police Actions Were Justified." Some students were offered ten dollars to write the essays, others were offered five dollars, others one dollar, and still others only fifty cents. After writing the essay, the student was asked to give his or her own opinion about the police actions. Other students were asked to give their opinions without having to write an essay at all.

The results of this demonstration were quite clear. Those who were paid the least tended to agree more with the police (relative to the control group, who wrote no essay at all) than those who were paid the most. In fact, sympathy for the police rose systematically across the groups as payment *decreased* from ten dollars to fifty cents.

Attitude shifts can also be produced by manipulating the threat of punishment rather than the promise of reward. In a study using children, seven- to nine-year-old boys were individually brought into a room and shown an array of five toys.[16] Four of the toys were rather boring (a cheap plastic submarine, a baseball glove without a ball, an unloaded toy rifle, and a toy tractor); the fifth, a toy robot, was really interesting. The experimenter told the boy that he had to leave the room for a few minutes, and that he was free to play with any of the toys—except the robot—while he was gone. He stressed that it was wrong to play with the robot. But there was one important difference. He told half of the boys, "If you play with the robot, I'll be very angry and will have to do something about it." He didn't threaten the other half with punishment. He then left the room and observed each boy through a one-way mirror. Only one boy out of twenty-two in each group played with the robot while the experimenter was out of the room.

The more interesting result, however, took place six weeks later, when each of the boys was brought back to the room by a different experimenter. This new experimenter made no comment about any connection to the first experiment or the first experimenter. She gave each boy a drawing test, and then told him that he was free to play with any of the toys he chose while she scored the test. Of the boys who had received a threat of punishment six weeks previously, 77 percent played with the robot. Of those who had not received the threat, only 33 percent played with the robot. Why this dramatic difference?

The results are readily interpretable using cognitive dissonance theory. Boys in the first group didn't play with the toy during the first session because they had been threatened with punishment. They didn't *own* their behavior, the person who threatened them did. Therefore, there was no contradiction between their beliefs (the robot is the best but I'll get punished if I play with it) and their actions (not playing with it). When the threat of punishment was removed during the second session, their attitude toward the robot emerged and was found to be intact— they still believed the robot was the most fun to play with.

The boys in the second group, however, present a different picture. They didn't play with the robot either, but why not? They were not threatened with punishment. They willingly chose not to play with the robot. They owned their actions in a way that the other boys did not, and these actions contradicted their belief that the robot was the preferred toy. During the second session, their attitude toward the robot emerged and was found to have undergone significant change: The robot was not the toy most preferred to play with. Unlike the boys in the first group, these boys had internalized the idea that there was something wrong about playing with the robot.

To summarize, this body of research indicates that people often will change their beliefs when they behave in a way that is inconsistent with them and they have no justifiable reason for the inconsistency. This is especially true if they are aware that their apparent inconsistency will be made known to others. In essence, we often sacrifice our beliefs in order to save face.

Fortunately, not all of our interactions with others are of the negative variety. We don't just conform, obey, and manipulate. We also seek out fun, companionship, and romance. These interactions have also been the subject of a good deal of research, and the results might surprise you.

Which variable do you think best predicts whether you will again contact a person you took on a blind date? While people invariably respond to questions like these with answers such as the person's "warmth," "sense of humor," or "intelligence," the real answer seems to be physical attractiveness. In one study conducted at the University of Minnesota, students were randomly paired by a computer for attendance at a dance.[17] The experimenters asked the students to fill out questionnaires concerning their dates after the dance. The only variable that reliably predicted whether the person saw his or her partner again was physical attractiveness. In fact, if an attractive man had been paired with an attractive woman, the relationship was most likely to continue.

Physical attractiveness also influences how we react to another person's treatment of us. In one experiment, a naturally attractive female confederate posed as a graduate student in psychology and interviewed male participants.[18] For half of the participants, she appeared as her own attractive self. For the other half, she made herself appear unattractive by using bad makeup, dumpy clothes, and a frizzy wig. At the end of the interview, she gave an evaluation of the participant. For half of the participants, this prearranged evaluation was positive; for the other half, it was negative. The participants were then asked to fill out a questionnaire in which they were asked, among other things, how much they liked the interviewer. The results indicated that when the interviewer was attractive, the men were very much affected by her evaluation. They liked her a good deal when she gave them a positive evaluation, and hated her a good deal when she gave them a negative evaluation. They also expressed a strong desire to see her again when she gave them a bad evaluation, presumably to get another shot at winning her approval. In contrast, they didn't seem to much care about her evaluation when she was unattractive. They felt neutral about her regardless of her evaluation, and expressed no particular desire to see her again.

Attractiveness also influences more serious decisions about others, such as the fate of defendants. When a group of participants was asked to decide the fate of two defendants in identical mock cases of college cheating, the attractive defendant was better liked, judged less guilty, and received less punishment than the unattractive defendant.[19] More disturbing is the fact that a defendant's attractiveness also significantly influences the severity of sentences imposed in real-life court cases.[20]

As we all know, prejudice also influences how people judge us and how we judge others. It is interesting to see how people's weighing of factors such as gender has changed over the years. In 1974, a study was conducted in which participants were told of an anticipated influx of women into predominantly male professions, such as medicine and engineering.[21] The prestige ratings for these professions dropped (relative to ratings from another group who were told that the same male-female ratios were expected in the future). In another study, raters were told that an influx of men was expected in predominately female professions, such as nursing and social work.[22] The prestige ratings for these professions shot up (relative to ratings from a group who were told that the ratios were not going to change).

In 1986, however, these studies were tried again, and no differences were observed.[23] The professions were rated as equally prestigious regardless of whether an influx of women or men was expected or not. Participants in this study also were given a description about a (fictitious) new profession called "information recovery analyst," and were asked to rate the prestige of this new and unknown profession. The same prestige ratings were observed regardless of whether the description said the profession was predominantly female or predominantly male. Results such as these suggest that both men and women are becoming more comfortable with the idea of women in positions of authority and power.

We saw at the beginning of this chapter how readily we obey people in positions of authority, and I'd like to end this chapter by returning to this theme. Our search for the ideal leader in real life (e.g., Reagan, Thatcher, Gandhi, Hitler) and fantasy (e.g., Jean Luc Picard, Murphy Brown, Marcus Welby, Rambo) is never ending. Given our fascination with power and our propensity to follow authority, we might want to know what sort of leadership style brings out the best in us.

When researching this question, one always runs across a rather famous landmark study in which the behavior of groups of ten-year-old boys were observed under autocratic, democratic, and laissez-faire adult leaders.[24] The leaders were trained in one of these leadership styles, and they rotated every six weeks so that there was ample time to observe the effects of the various styles on the boys. The autocratic leader determined the goals of the group, dictated how the goals were to be achieved, assigned tasks, and remained aloof from the group. The democratic leader allowed the group to determine policy, offered suggestions for how to achieve goals, allowed the boys to choose their own tasks, and participated in the group tasks. The laissez-faire leader allowed the group complete freedom to do as it chose, and did not participate himself. The tasks the groups were to accomplish included things such as making masks and building objects.

While one might want to exercise caution in generalizing to adults the outcome of a study based on children, the results themselves were indeed intriguing. There are two questions we can ask: The first is how leadership style affected the working climate within the groups. These results were unequivocal: Under the autocratic style of leadership, the boys were thirty times as hostile and eight times as aggressive as they were under the democratic leadership style. There was frequent scapegoating in the autocratic climate; in fact, two scapegoats left the group entirely. In contrast, scapegoating was not observed in the democratic situation. Experimentally induced frustrations wreaked havoc under autocratic leadership, but under democratic leadership they produced organized responses.

Of particular interest was what happened when there was a change of leader. When a change from autocratic to laissez-faire leadership occurred, the incidence of hostile aggression shot up dramatically for a short period and then decreased to a moderate level. This result is consistent with the idea that there was a great deal of frustration and anger building under autocratic leadership; once the "lid was off," this anger manifested itself. This pattern of unleashed aggression is uncomfortably similar to that observed following the overthrow of autocratic rulers throughout history.

The second question of interest is how leadership style affected productivity. The results were not as clear here. The boys worked longer and turned out more products under autocratic leadership, but the products turned out under democratic leadership were of better quality. Moreover, the boys worked consistently on their tasks whether their democratic leader was in the room or not. In the autocratic situation, work decreased significantly (and even stopped) whenever the leader left the room.

In a related study, groups were found to be more productive with autocratic leaders when they worked under stressful conditions.[25] When stressors were not present, they were more productive under democratic leadership. This result also parallels patterns observed in real life. For example, when a business is on the rocks, it is not unusual for an autocratic, take-charge type of leader to be hired to put the company back in the black again. Once that goal is achieved, however, the autocrat cannot seem to maintain the company. Instead, he antagonizes middle-management, workers, and stockholders alike.

I have seen this in academia, where hot-shot chairs are hired to build programs in certain disciplines, and they succeed amazingly well. After the honeymoon is over, however, the faculty members begin to resent the autocrat, and deep-seated hostilities begin to grow. Eventually, things blow up, and the faculty becomes an incoherent jumble of disjointed factions. Seeing the department in chaos, the administration of course . . . hires a new autocrat to put things right, starting the whole cycle over again!

2

The Mind
in the Brain

The ultimate goal of scientific psychology is to explain the relationship between brain activity and mind activity. We are corporeal beings, and our thoughts, feelings, and actions are all rooted in bits of neural activity. A viable brain is vital to being who we are. When the brain is damaged, we no longer behave the way we used to. If the brain is damaged severely enough, we are no longer the person we were. And the cessation of brain activity is typically taken as the surest sign of death.

If one is to understand the mind, one must also understand the brain. The nature of the mind is, in a very real sense, a reflection of brain structure and function. That is why heart transplants are logically possible, but brain transplants aren't. After a heart transplant, the same person awakes from anesthesia. After a brain transplant, someone else wakes up. You couldn't have a brain transplant and still be you. Your body would now house a different person.

In this chapter, I will give a gross overview of brain structures and function in order to give you a pretty good grasp of what goes on where in your head. The most important thing to keep in mind in this and subsequent chapters on the human mind is that the brain engages in an enormous amount of computing. Even the seemingly simplest task is rendered simple precisely because our brains are so good at certain types of computing.

Take a simple example, hitting a baseball. Major League hitters notwithstanding, hitting a baseball is objectively one of the most improbable events on earth. Why? Because a Major League pitcher throws a baseball at a speed that is faster than the human eye can track. It is physically impossible for the hitter's eye to follow that ball. And yet a good Major League batter will hit that ball—and put it in fair territory—one out of three or four times on average.

How is this possible? Research on this skill shows that the batter's eyes focus on the ball for a split second just as the ball is leaving the pitcher's hand.[1] In that split second, the batter's brain has picked up enough information about the rotation and speed of the ball to compute the ball's trajectory. The batter's eyes can't track the ball, but his brain can compute where the ball is going to be a second or so later, and it directs his eyes to look there and his arms to move such that the bat will be there, too. If you watch the batter's eyes on slow-motion camera film, you can see the point at which the eyes are tracking the ball and the point at which they switch to another place in visual space. For a good batter, that place will be just where the ball later appears. His arms will also have begun to move to meet the ball in that visual space as well. All of this will have happened in a fraction of a second without his conscious awareness. So your Little League coach's admonitions to "keep your eye on the ball" may have been okay at that level, but once you're in the Major Leagues, it's a physical impossibility.

Here is a simpler example. Have a friend move a pencil slowly or quickly in front of you, and try to grab the pencil at any point. You'll be able to do this with ease. It will seem trivially simple. Congratulate yourself. You have just accomplished something that has so far almost completely eluded the field of robotics: tracking and grabbing a moving object. As simple as it seems to you and cheetahs, pouncing on a moving object is an extremely difficult coordination task.

If you were to build a machine that could hit a baseball or grab a moving object, what would you need? Well, you'd need a camera-like component to scan the environment and pick up visual information, and mechanical limbs of some sort for moving about and manipulating the environment. You'd also need something that could process that visual information to make sense of it, e.g., distinguish real objects from shadows, and the object to be grabbed from among all the other objects. This "something" would also need to compute the object's trajectory, and to control the movements of the machine's limbs in order to close the distance between the object and itself. It would need to compute the exact moment when the distance was optimal for one of its limbs to be put forth, opened, and closed in order to grasp the object.

That's a whole lot of computing going on. When you look around the workshop for the sort of machine component that could possibly do all that, a computer would be your likely choice. When you look around the organic environment to see what has evolved in real creatures that could be capable of doing all this computing, the only likely candidate is the brain.

The average human brain weighs about three pounds; its volume is about three pints. If you mounded up the contents of about three pint-size containers of cottage cheese, you'd have something that is about the same size, volume, and consistency as the average human brain.

The brain constitutes only about 2 percent of your total body weight, but it accounts for 20 percent of the body's total oxygen consumption. When you take a breath, the lion's share of your oxygen intake goes to your brain. When you drink soft drinks, the lion's share of the sugar goes to your brain as well.

Brain events are slow compared to the average computer's. Brain activity can be measured on the order of milliseconds (1/1,000 of a second). Computer activity, in contrast, must be measured on the order of nanoseconds (1/1,000,000,000 of a second).

Brains are convoluted, with layers of cells folded in on themselves to form ridges. You can pack a lot more cells and a lot more surface area into a small space that way. If you were to line up the brains of animals on the basis of their place on the phylogenetic scale (from, say, mice to humans), the brains would get more wrinkled and convoluted the further up their place in the scale. This has nothing to do with size. An elephant brain is bigger than a human brain, but it is far less wrinkled and convoluted. This suggests we can pack a lot more knowledge in our brains than elephants can in theirs.

Brains are made up of cells called neurons, glial cells, and a few stem cells that give rise to neurons and glial cells. As far as we currently know, neurons do all of the computing and the glial cells feed and nourish them. There are about a trillion neurons in the average human brain.

Unlike cells in other parts of the body, neurons do *not* regenerate. You're born with a certain number, and they die off at an astonishing rate. When a neuron dies, it's gone; others are not formed to replace it. That is why strokes are so traumatic. The patient cannot regenerate more neurons to replace the ones damaged by the stroke. He or she can only hope that other neurons will be able to take on the functions of the damaged ones. There are two exceptions to this state of affairs. The first is fetal neurons. These cells *do* regenerate and multiply. That is why some doctors want to use brain cells from aborted fetuses to treat certain forms of brain damage and disease. The second exception is that if you put a substance known as epidermal growth factor (EGF) into a culture dish with stem cells, they will multiply and develop into neurons.[2] This is a relatively recent discovery, and its impact on the treatment of stroke and other brain damage is still unknown.

For our purposes, we need to know only one thing about neurons: They are instruments of communication in that they receive, integrate, and send signals. They are like clerks with "in" and "out" baskets. They take things from their in baskets, process them, and put their results in their out baskets, or more accurately, put them in other clerks' in baskets. The signals they process are electrochemical. A neuron sends a signal by secreting chemicals into the gap (called a synapse) between itself and other neurons. These chemicals change the permeability of the other neurons' skins. That allows positive ions to flow into these neurons, and this movement of ions creates an electric current. (Yes, there is electrical activity in your head. That's what brain wave, or EEG, machines measure.) Lots of neurons are typically sending these kinds of signals to any given neuron, and when enough current converges, the neuron "fires," meaning that it, too, sends a signal to its neighbors by secreting chemicals into the synapses between itself and others. In this way, the signal is propagated through the brain.

So what have we got so far? We have a mass of gray mush made up of things that receive, process, and send signals. This flurry of electrochemical activity constitutes our thoughts, dreams, and plans for action. And here is the strangest part: Learning constitutes nothing more than modifying synapses to make neurons more or less likely to fire when certain signal patterns come in. Whether you're learning to walk, solve differential equations, or read sixteenth-century French poetry, the exact same thing occurs in your brain—synapses get modified.

The brain is a mass of gray mush, but it is not an amorphous mass of gray mush. It has very clear and well-defined structures. Because of this, the brain is a really a committee. There are many ways to describe the committees, many ways to divide up the brain. The first is from an evolutionary standpoint. If you were to take a cross section of the brain, the first thing you would notice is that there is a white part of the brain that is covered with the gray "mush" we've already noted. The white part of the brain evolved earlier than the gray part. The gray is almost like frosting on a cake.

If we start from the base of the brain, where it meets the spinal cord, and move up to the top of the head, it appears that we have three brains. Evolution just put one on top of the other. This is depicted in Figure 1, on the next page. The first "brain" we encounter is the brain stem, a primitive structure that we have in common with animals as low on the phylogenetic scale as, for example, lizards. It consists of the medulla and the cerebellum. The medulla controls functions such as breathing, heart rate, and certain reflexes. It is here that the nerve pathways cross over so that the left side of the brain ends up controlling the right side of our bodies and vice versa. Damage to this part of the brain endangers life itself, since such vital functions as heart rate and breathing are disrupted.

The cerebellum is almost a brain in itself. It controls coordination of motor movements, e.g., moving the arms and legs for things such as walking and jumping. Animals that are very graceful, such as gazelles, have very large cerebellums. (It makes

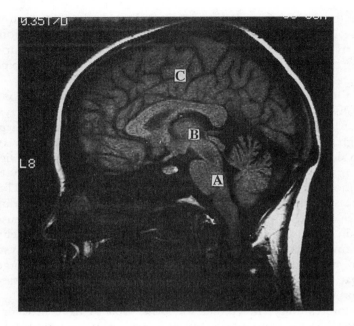

Figure 1. A view of the "three brains" that make up the human brain. When you look at this picture, you're looking at the evolution of the nervous system. (A) The brain stem (where the spinal cord meets the brain) and the cerebellum (the spongy structure to the right of the brain stem) evolved first. They regulate basic processes such as breathing, heart rate, and coordinating movement. (B) The middle structures in the center of the brain (old brain) evolved next, and are involved in the processing of emotions and certain aspects of memory. (C) The convoluted structures that surround the old brain (cerebral cortex) evolved last, and are the seat of perception, sensation, thought, and language. (Reprinted with permission from Watson, C. [1991] *Basic human neuroanatomy* [4th ed.] fig. 67, p. 120. Boston: Little, Brown & Company.)

one wonder about Baryshnikov's.) Damage to this part of the brain results in "herky-jerky" robotlike movement and a loss of fine coordination of movements. In a sense, the smooth execution and coordination of simple movements, such as reaching out your hand, is so complex that we have a "subbrain" devoted almost entirely to it. I say "almost" because recent work has implicated the cerebellum in other more "cerebral" functions, such as learning.[3]

As we move up from the brain stem, we encounter the midbrain, or, as it is sometimes called, the old brain. Structures in the midbrain are involved in the initiation and regulation of activities that satisfy basic needs, such as sleeping, eating, drinking, and sex, as well as basic emotional and cognitive experiences, such as pain, fear, memory, and learning.

One of the more interesting functions of the midbrain is the transmission of pain signals. There are two pain pathways in the brain.[4] The first is a "fast" pathway through which pain signals pass with lightning-fast speed. The second pathway is so slow that it can take upwards of two seconds for a pain signal from the foot to reach the brain. Signals on this pathway take a more circuitous route to the brain through numerous old brain areas, during which emotional, motivational, and other subjective aspects of painful stimulation are added to the basic sensory pain signals. This system is well developed even in vertebrate animals very low on the phylogenetic scale, while the fast system does not appear until much higher on the scale. This suggests that the fast system is a much more recent evolutionary development.

Interestingly, morphine and other opiates have little or no effect on the fast system, but have very powerful blocking actions on the slow system. There are also neurons in the slow pathway that control the amount of pain information that reaches the brain. These neurons can be stimulated by the brain itself to control the amount of pain input that it receives from the body via the nerve paths in the spinal cord. This means, in theory anyway, that we have the power to limit the amount of pain we feel.

Another interesting structure in the midbrain is the hypothalamus. This structure regulates metabolism, body temperature (including fever), and four of our favorite activities, namely, eating, drinking, sex, and aggression. If you knock out the center part of the hypothalamus via surgery in rats, chickens, or monkeys, you get very, very fat rats, chickens, and monkeys.[5] The animals will increase their food intake until they reach a certain level of obesity. Then they will regulate their intake to maintain the new level of weight. Humans who have tumors in this area also tend to be very obese.[6] In contrast, if you damage the lateral (side) parts of the hypothalamus, you end up with very, very thin rats, chickens, and monkeys.[7] They will stop eating and drinking until their weight level drops dramatically below their normal level. (Sometimes they must be force-fed or force-watered or they will starve or dehydrate themselves to death.) Once a certain level of weight is attained, however, they usually maintain at this new emaciated level.

How the hypothalamus regulates eating is not completely understood, but one theory is that it is involved in metabolizing fat.[8] Normally, animals use some of their food intake as fuel and store some as fat. According to this theory, damage to the middle of the hypothalamus disrupts this burn-store ratio so that almost all of the food intake is stored as fat. This, of course, leaves the animal with nothing to live on, nothing to burn as fuel. It probably feels constant hunger as a result, and increases its food intake considerably in an effort to stay alive. In support of this theory is the fact that rats with damage to the middle of the hypothalamus produce more fat than normal rats even when both groups are fed the same amount of food.

More will be said in chapters 4 and 6 about the role the hypothalamus and other midbrain structures play in our capacities to feel emotions, remember events, and express our sexuality. For now, suffice it so say that having these structures intact is crucial to our ability to engage in such activities.

Surrounding the old brain is the new brain—the cerebral cortex. Evolutionarily speaking, this brain is much younger than its brethren beneath it. The cerebral cortex is the gray matter that surrounds the other levels, the frosting on the brain cake or the rind on the brain orange. For the linguistic scholars among us, *cortex* means tree bark. So the cortex is the bark, frosting, rind, or outer layer of the brain.

Our ancestors weren't very impressed with the cortex. The ancient Egyptians thought it so useless that they removed it through the nose with tweezers and discarded it during the process of mummification. With all of its convolutions and wrinkles, the cortex looks like a radiator, and that's what Aristotle thought it was—an organ whose purpose was to cool the body. And in a sense, he was right. Because of all of those ridges, heat loss through the head is tremendous. That's why your mother always admonished you to wear a hat in cold weather. And that is why many hospitals put woolen hats on newborn babies—the hats prevent them from losing a lot of heat through their bald heads.

Despite its unattractive appearance, the cortex is of immense importance to us. It is the seat of consciousness—everything we are aware of resides here. All sensation is here. All voluntary movement. All thought and language.

The cortex itself is made up of different parts, and it can be divided up in different ways. The first way is down the middle, dividing it into two hemispheres, as shown in Figure 2. In a

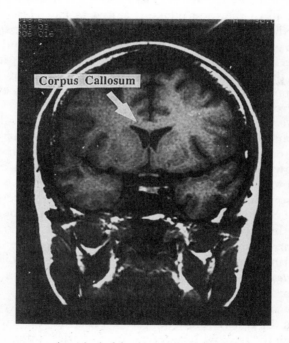

Corpus Callosum

Figure 2. The most recently evolved of the three brains shown in Figure 1 (the cerebral cortex) is itself really two separate brains. These two brains can communicate with each other only by sending signals across the thin band of fibers (the corpus callosum) that connect them. The right brain controls the left side of the body, and the left brain controls the right side—with one exception: The retinas are divided so that the left side of each eye is connected to the right side of the brain and the right side of each eye is connected to the left side of the brain. (Reprinted with permission from Watson, C. [1991] *Basic human neuroanatomy* [4th ed.] fig. 83, p. 152. Boston: Little, Brown & Company.)

sense, the hemispheres are really two separate brains. These two brains communicate with each other by sending nerve impulses across a thin band of fibers, called the corpus callosum, that connects them. In chapter 5, I'll discuss the profound effects wrought on human consciousness if this thin band is severed.

The hemispheres are divided into different sections, called lobes, which are schematized in Figure 3. Beginning at the back and the bottom of each hemisphere, there is a lobe called the occipital lobe. These lobes are the visual center of the brain, so in a sense, your grade school teachers really did have eyes in the backs of their heads. Nerve impulses from your eyes are directed here in a rather odd way. Nerves in the individual eye cross over, so that the input from the left half of each eye goes to the right side of the brain and the input from the right half of each eye goes to the left side of the brain.

Curiously, if you suffer some damage to your visual cortex (or your retinas), you often won't notice. There can be a fairly large "hole" (scotoma) in your cortex (or damage in your retina), and you won't see a hole in your visual experience. Careful

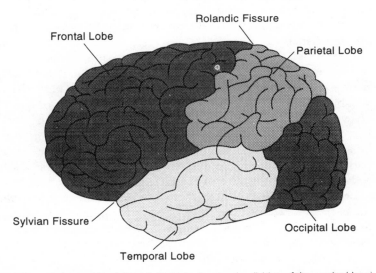

Figure 3. A schematized depiction of the brain showing the division of the cerebral hemispheres into lobes.

testing by your optometrist or ophthalmologist will uncover it, but your visual system does a good job of keeping your visual information whole and seamless, even though it's operating at reduced capacity.

Essentially, we see with our brains and not with our eyes, and accordingly, there are several strange syndromes associated with damage to the visual cortex.[9] The first is visual agnosia, and it is caused by tumors or other damage to certain areas of the visual cortex. Patients with this type of damage can see properly but cannot identify what they see. For example, they can copy a drawing of a flower, and they can tell you what a flower is. But when asked what the object is that they just copied, they can't tell you.

Another syndrome is "blindsight," which is also caused by damage to the visual cortex. Patients with this type of damage can still maneuver around furniture, reliably distinguish between X's and O's or squares and triangles, and locate a pinpoint of light in visual space. Yet they insist that they are blind. They appear to have no awareness of a visual sensation. They report instead having a prickly feeling, or of feeling "gunfire at a distance" when they look at things. They have perceptual experiences in response to visual stimulation, but these perceptions are not visual.

In contrast, there is another syndrome associated with damage to the visual cortex called "blindness denial," in which the patient is indeed blind but denies that this is the case. These patients will bump into furniture and then explain that the room is rather crowded or that they are clumsy. They will claim that the doctor is wearing a brown tie and holding up two fingers when in fact he is wearing no tie at all and is holding up four fingers. These patients don't seem to be deliberately lying; they seem instead to be genuinely unaware of the fact that they cannot see.

Leaving the visual cortex, there is another pair of lobes called the parietal lobes, just on either side of the midline of your head. Sensations of heat, cold, touch, and pain are experienced here, as is body awareness. For example, patients with right parietal tumors or other damage tend to ignore events that occur on the left side of the body.[10] This is called hemineglect. These patients will attempt to dress only the right side of their bodies, will eat food only on the right side of a plate, read only the right side of the newspaper, draw only the right side of figures, and point to the middle of the right half of their bodies if asked to point to the middle of their bodies. The patient may recognize her wristwatch, but be surprised and annoyed to find it on a "foreign" arm (her own left arm).

Just on the other side of the Rolandic fissure (see Figure 3, on page 38) are the frontal lobes, which extend toward your forehead. All commands to move muscles initiate in the frontal lobes, and all forms of higher cognition, such as thought, reasoning, and language, occur here. Finally, just below the parietal lobes (about where your ears are) are the temporal lobes. Audition is processed here, as well as some emotions.

Although the lobe structures of each hemisphere look pretty much the same (frontal, parietal, temporal, and occipital), there are some interesting functional differences between those on the left and those on the right. For example, damage to certain sections of the left hemisphere severely impairs the ability to understand and speak a language, and to organize sequenced actions; corresponding damage to the right hemisphere does not. On the other hand, damage to certain parts of the right hemisphere disrupts body awareness and impairs the ability to produce coherent drawings. Overall, the left hemisphere appears to be specialized for processing *organization in time* whereas the right is specialized for processing organization in space.[11]

You may be wondering at this point just how we know all of this very detailed information about the relation between mind and brain. There are several interesting techniques that have been used to obtain this information.

In 1950, a neurophysiologist named Wilder Penfield used electrical stimulation to explore the brains of patients suffering from epilepsy.[12] By doing so, he produced a good "map" of the motor and sensory parts of the cortex. The technique was rather interesting. The patients were undergoing exploration of their brains prior to a surgical operation whose purpose was to alleviate seizures. Since everyone's brain is a little different, it is a good idea to map out certain areas of the brain for an individual patient to ensure that certain important areas (like the speech area) don't get tampered with. (Now, much of this can be done noninvasively with other techniques, which will be discussed later.) To do this, Penfield applied a local anesthetic to the skull and removed a portion of it. Then he stimulated portions of the brain with a mild electric current. He could do this because the brain has no pain receptors for itself, only for other parts of the body. He could stimulate a patient's brain while the patient was still awake and conscious without causing him or her undue discomfort.

When Penfield stimulated the sensory and motor sections of the parietal and frontal lobes, his patients reported feeling sensations and movement in parts of their bodies. The extraordinary thing was that the lion's share of these sections were devoted to the face and hands. That's why we can produce so many expressions with our faces and so many fine and intricate movements with our hands and fingers (like picking up a pin). Communication and manipulation of the environment were, evolutionarily speaking, crucial for survival of humans as a species. Hence, a lot of brain is devoted to them.

A more benign procedure, positron emission tomography (PET), has been developed in recent years. The key to understanding this technique is recalling that the brain is a hog where oxygen and nutrients are concerned. Neurons themselves live on glucose—the sugarlike fluid that your body creates out of the food you eat. In PET scanning, a safe level of radioactive tagging substance is mixed with glucose and the fluid is then injected into the bloodstream. Within a few minutes, nearly all of the glucose will make its way straight to the brain. The radioactive tagging substance can be picked up by a scanner, and its output can be fed into a computer. The computer then generates a color-coded map of glucose consumption. The different colors represent different levels of glucose consumption. As neurons work, they consume glucose, so the greater the consumption, the greater the likelihood that that particular part of the brain is working at the moment. By looking at the patterns of color, the researcher can tell which part of the brain is working the hardest.

When performing a visual task, the brain's occipital lobes become very active. When performing a language-intensive task, the left hemisphere becomes active, particularly the right frontal lobe. Auditory tasks activate the temporal lobes, and reasoning tasks "light up" the frontal lobes. But perhaps most intriguing is this: When a memory task is performed, a great deal of the brain "lights up." Memories seem to be distributed rather widely across the cortex and the "old brain," rather than being stored in a particular place. Memories, it seems, are everywhere in the brain.

Recent PET work has shown that the amount of effort the brain exerts on a task depends on the person's level of expertise and intelligence. When we are first learning a new task, the brain is very active. But with time, as the skill becomes learned, the brain becomes more efficient in its functioning, and less activity is observed. Similarly, people who score higher on tests of intelligence also tend to show less activity in their task–related PET scans than those who score lower on these tests.[13]

An easy way to bring together everything presented so far about "what happens where" in the brain is to spend a few minutes playing neurologist. In his book *Brain Matters,* neurologist Bruce Dobkin describes in some detail the kinds of non-invasive preliminary tests neurologists use when examining patients with suspected brain abnormalities.[14] It is a little like playing detective. The patient's performance on various tests provides clues as to which brain structure is damaged.

The patient is a middle-aged executive who is suffering from intense headaches and bouts of forgetfulness. Because of the patient's complaints of forgetfulness, Dobkin begins by testing his memory capacity. He calls out a string of seven random numbers and asks the patient to repeat them both forwards and backwards. The patient gets it right in both directions. Dobkin then recites the phrase "peaches, newspapers, and Chestnut Street." Although Dobkin has to repeat it several times before the patient seems to grasp it fully, the patient can recall the phrase flawlessly ten minutes later. Dobkin then asks him to recall current events and newspaper headlines from the past few years, and he can do this as well, with minimum errors. Conclusion: The patient's memory processes seem to be functioning properly but rather slowly. This means the damage is probably not in the old brain areas that are involved in the formation and retrieval of memories. If anything, there seems to be something wrong with the patient's higher cognitive abilities, which suggests a problem with the frontal lobes, but it's too early in the examination to tell.

Dobkin then tries to pinpoint whether the damage is in the right or left brain. Because the right brain is specialized for processing organization in space, the best way to test for damage there is by having the patient copy interlocking geometric figures. The patient does this without difficulty, so Dobkin tentatively rules out a problem in the right brain. Certain aspects of language are located in the left brain, and Dobkin goes on to test whether these areas are damaged. He asks the patient to name uncommon objects, such as the parts of a wristwatch, and to generate a list of ten animals. The patient does all this without difficulty. Conclusion: The damage is probably not in the language areas of the left brain.

Dobkin then moves on to the frontal lobes, which is where higher reasoning processes take place. He asks the patient to interpret several proverbs. The patient does so, coming up with their appropriate, abstract meanings. But he does so slowly and rather apathetically. He is then asked some higher-reasoning questions, such as explaining how a cat and mouse are alike. The patient replies to such questions with complete indifference, and his responses are rather "shallow." For example, in response to the cat-mouse question, he replies that they're both white rather than, for example, that they are both animals. Conclusion: The patient's barely adequate responses to the reasoning tasks suggest a problem in the frontal lobes, the brain areas most actively involved in higher cognition. But which frontal lobe, the one in the right brain or the one in the left?

To address this question, Dobkin asks the patient to hold his arms out in front of him, palms up. He does so, but his right arm rotates slightly inward and droops, as though he can't hold it up properly. The elbow reflex is much brisker in the right arm as well. This strongly suggests that the damage is in the left frontal lobe (the left brain controls the right arm).

The next stage in the exam is to do a CAT scan to verify Dobkin's diagnosis. A CAT scanner produces pictures of the brain in "slices." Looking for brain damage using a CAT scan is a little like looking for a raisin baked somewhere in a loaf of bread by slicing the loaf thinly and examining each slice to see if the raisin is there. That is why the preliminary "detective" work is so important: It gives the neurologist some idea of which CAT scan slice to examine most closely.

Dobkin watches with increasing anticipation as each new "slice" of the patient's brain shows up on the CAT scan viewing screen, beginning at the base of the brain near the spinal cord and moving slowly up to the top of the head. Each new slice looks normal; there is nothing odd until the third-to-last sweep near the top of the head. Dark fluid appears across the left frontal lobe, the kind that accompanies a tumor. The second-to-last slice shows a thick gray-white mass pressing against the brain, pushing it away from the skull. But it's not a tumor; it's a blood clot, a hematoma. Dobkin breathes a sigh of relief because although hematomas are extremely dangerous—they can increase intercranial pressure and ultimately cause death—they can also be surgically removed. A neurosurgeon is called and the patient is prepared for surgery. Dobkin explains the diagnosis, and the patient remembers hitting the top of his head on the doorframe of his car as he was getting out of it several days ago. That blow apparently tore a few tiny veins in the brain and caused swelling in that part of the brain. The swelling is pressing down onto the left frontal lobe, disrupting its normal operation. The surgery is a success, and the patient is fine. His brain recovers quickly now that the hematoma is gone, leaving no noticeable trace in his thought or behavior.

CHAPTER 3

Why Things Look, Sound, and Feel the Way They Do

Scientific psychologists study sensation and perception for many reasons, but the most intriguing reason is this: What we experience inside of our heads is not always identical to what is actually "out there." You can prove this to yourself using nothing more than a flashlight or a camera photoflash. Get a good afterimage by flashing the camera photoflash or shining the flashlight in your eyes. Immediately face a wall. You'll see a bright spot on the wall, which is really the afterimage produced when the light bleached out a portion of your retinas. Now slowly lean in and then back away from the wall, back and forth a good distance.

The important thing to remember is that the spot on your retina does *not* change size; it remains the same until your retinal cells recover. But that's not what you'll see. Instead, the spot on the wall will appear to change size: It will appear to shrink as you lean closer to the wall and grow as you lean farther away. What you experience visually is not really what's "out there."

What's happening is that you are getting a firsthand, direct experience of your brain *interpreting* the input it receives from your eyes. You are actually seeing your brain's best guesses about what is out there. Your brain can't tell the difference between what is on the retina and what is out there because the only visual information it gets comes from the retinas themselves. It then must interpret that information to figure out what it means. In this case, it interprets the spot on the wall as an object in space, but a rather odd one. Normally, when you get closer to something, the retinal image gets bigger, and so objects appear bigger as we get closer to them. But in this case, the retinal image doesn't get bigger as you get closer. Instead, it remains the same size. The only way that could happen with a real object is if it shrunk as you got closer to it. And so that is what you experience: You "see" the spot get smaller as you get closer. The opposite happens as you move away from the wall. Normally, as we move away from an object, the retinal image gets smaller, and so the receding object appears smaller. But this time, the retinal image remained constant as you moved away. The only way that could happen with a real object is if it *got bigger* as you moved away. And so that is what you see— a growing object.

This simple demonstration brings home a crucially important point, that our brains construct our inner experiences from bits of information gotten from our senses. Every visual experience we have, from the time we open our eyes in the morning until we close them at night, is exactly like the photoflash demonstration. What we "see" in our mind's eye is the best guess our brain has come up with as to what is out there. Every minute our eyes are open, the brain receives ambiguous two-dimensional patterns of light from retinas, and it uses them to construct an unambiguous three-dimensional visual experience.

A number of simple but elegant studies have made this point clear.[1] When people were asked to report the color-letter combinations of a series of letter trios presented to them very briefly (less than one-quarter of a second), they often made mistakes. But the nature of the mistakes were intriguing. For example, if they saw a blue X, a green T, and a red O, they might report seeing a blue T, a green O, and a red X. Why? Because when we look at a scene, completely different parts of our visual system extract color information and shape information. The information from these separate subsystems is integrated later to form our visual images. But if the visual input is turned off before this process is completed, the information can be integrated the wrong way, producing incorrect images of what was out there.

Another more striking effect can be gotten by presenting jumbles of angles and lines like those in figures 1a and b. When jumbles like Figure 1a were presented very briefly to people, they rarely reported seeing triangles. But when small circles were added to the jumble, as in Figure 1b, they often reported seeing triangles. Why? Because a triangle is a *closed* geometric figure that has slanted lines and angles. Figure 1a has only two of the necessary features—slanted lines and angles. But Figure 1b has all three—slanted lines, angles, and "closed." The last feature, "closed," is provided by the small, closed circles. Again, separate parts of our visual system extract these features, and then they are put together later. When they're put together, the slanted-line extracter reports, "There were slanted lines out there," the angle extracter reports, "There were angles out there," and the closure extracter reports, "There were closed figures out there." Your perceptual system tries to reconstruct the input from that information, and finds it has the definition of "triangle." And so that is what you see.

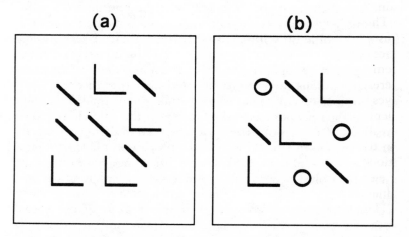

Figure 1. When the jumbles in (a) were flashed to people, they rarely reported seeing triangles, but when the jumbles in (b) were flashed, they typically reported seeing triangles. See text for an explanation of why. (After Treisman, 1960)

Another way to put it is that our eye-and-brain visual system is not like a videocam, faithfully recording what is out there. Instead, it is more like a computer graphics program that digitizes input from the videocam (our eyes) and constructs pictures using a lot of internal computing (by our brain). And like a computer graphics program, the pictures this eye-and-brain perceptual system ends up producing depends a good deal on how the system is designed or "wired," and on what the system "knows."

The effect of innate "wiring" is apparent even in our basic sensations. At the very root of our perceptual experiences are sensory systems that act as transducers, that is, they take one type of physical energy and turn it into a different type. Microphones and loudspeakers are common types of transducers. A microphone takes sound energy and turns it into electrical energy. A loudspeaker does the reverse, taking electrical energy and turning it into sound energy. Our senses behave the same way. They take light energy, sound waves, and airborn molecules, and turn them into electrical nerve cell activity. These patterns of nerve cell activity are then interpreted higher up in the brain as perceptual experiences of light, color, sound, smell, pain, and pressure.

The decoupling of external reality and internal experience begins very early in the game because of the particular characteristics of our senses. For example, if I wanted to make a room seem twice as bright to you, I would have to make a ninefold increase in the light intensity in the room. Our visual systems (eyes and brain) scale down changes in light intensity; consequently, there is not a one-to-one correspondence between what is really happening to the light intensity and what we experience. On the other hand, our senses scale up changes in pain stimulation. For example, even very small increases in the intensity of electric shock produce really big changes in perceived painfulness.

These differences in scale factors make a good deal of sense. Since electric shock is potentially damaging to the body, you would want even very small changes to produce very big responses in the organism. Our perceptual systems magnify even minor pain stimulation in order to get our attention. On the other hand, consider the fact that the light intensity outside on a sunny day is one thousand times greater than the light intensity in a normal room. If our visual systems didn't scale down our sensations of brightness, we would be overwhelmed every time we went outside on a sunny day.

Another source of information that our perceptual systems modify comes from our own movements.[2] If you've ever scanned a scene a bit too quickly with a videocam, you've probably found to your chagrin that the recorded image was just a fast blur. Yet you move your eyes and heads around more quickly than that every minute of the day. Why don't you see a fast blur every time you move your eyes? Because your brain ignores or compensates for the inputs it receives when it tells your eyes or head to move. You can prove this yourself: Cover one of your eyes and move your other eye with your finger by pushing gently at the corner. Your brain didn't send any commands to that eye to move, so it doesn't ignore the signals that eye sends back to it. As a result, you see the world blur.

The same things happens in clinical cases where the eye muscles or their nerve supply have been damaged or paralyzed. When these patients try to move their eyes, they see the world move in the direction their eyes should have moved. (Physicist Ernst Mach [1838–1916] got the same effect by surrounding his eyes with putty so that they were immobilized and then trying to move them.) This is because the brain has told the eyes to move, and is prepared to compensate for the change in the visual image once the muscles indicate that they're moving. But when the muscles or their nerves are damaged, no such signals are sent back to the brain. Only the unchanging visual input is received. So the commands to move the eyes combined with a stationary visual image are interpreted as a movement *in the world*. In other words, it's as though your brain is saying, "I told the eyes to move, so I'm expecting a sweep in the visual image. No such sweep occurred. The only way that could happen is if the world moved at the same speed and in the same direction as the eyes moved. So I've got to create a perceptual experience of the world moving in the direction that the eyes moved." And that's exactly what these patients see.

Again, our visual experiences are not mere recordings of what is out there. They are images that are *constructed* by the brain. The nature of our visual experience depends as much on how we are designed to interpret our visual inputs as on what is really out there.

Perhaps the most striking example of this is the fact that we appear to be "wired" from birth to treat faces as very special stimuli. Newborns (no more than a few minutes old) respond preferentially to faces over other types of designs. For example, they move their eyes to follow a head shape bearing normal features, but tend to ignore the same shape whose features are arranged randomly.[3] This special "wiring" can be selectively damaged by injury to a particular section of the brain, the right parietal region (about midway between your right ear and the top of your head). A tumor or injury here produces facial agnosia, that is, an inability to recognize faces. One particular case was described in detail by Oliver Sacks in *The Man Who Mistook His Wife for a Hat*.[4] The man had otherwise normal vision, but could not recognize faces, such as his wife's face. He would compensate for this deficiency by using other visual cues such as her glasses or hat. If these articles were put on someone else, he would think that person was his wife. It seems that faces are special, and a special subpart of the brain is devoted to processing and remembering them consciously.

A simple example of the special way our brains treat faces is the mask illusion. If you take pictures of a mask while it rotates, some of the pictures will show the outside of the mask (the side that faces the world when you put it on) and some will show the inside of the mask (the part that fits over your face when you put it on). We all know that the outside of a mask has normal, convex contours. If the mask were hanging on a wall, face outward, the nose would project out toward you. We also know that the inside of a mask has reversed, concave contours. If you turned the hanging mask around so it faced the wall, the nose would project inward, toward the wall. But that is not what you'll see when you look at the pictures.[5] The pictures of the outside of the mask will look like a normal face, but so will the pictures of the inside of the mask. They will look like pictures of a normal, convex face with all the normal contours. In fact, it is *impossible* to see the pictured face as concave. Your brain "insists" that there are no such things as concave faces, and so you cannot see these faces as being anything else than convex. Noses project out, not in!

To get a particularly eerie illusion, look at the picture of Margaret Thatcher in Figure 2.[6] Notice that although the picture is upside down, the face appears normal. But if you look closely, you'll see that her eyes and mouth have been inverted. Now turn the page upside down, and you'll get quite a shock. The face you'll see is not something that ought to occur in nature, and your brain will do a good job of sending an alarm signal through your body. Try rotating it slowly and see if you can detect just when the "horrific" effect takes place. It doesn't occur gradually; it's very much all or nothing.

Figure 2. The Margaret Thatcher illusion. Notice that the eyes and mouth are inverted. Turn the picture upside down, and you'll get quite a shock. (Courtesy Dr. T. E. Parks, University of California-Davis)

We are born with other special types of knowledge about perceptual events, particularly knowledge about which types of events tend to go together. For example, newborns move their heads in the direction of sound.[7] This simple response shows they can localize the source of sounds, and know that if they move their eyes in that direction, they'll probably see something of interest. Four-week-old infants appreciate the relationship between what something feels like and what something looks like.[8] This was demonstrated by allowing a group of them to explore by mouth one of two objects, a small, smooth sphere or a small, nubby one, and then showing them a short time later larger versions of the two objects. Those infants who had explored the smooth one by mouth spent more time looking at the large, smooth sphere than the nubby one; those who had explored the nubby one by mouth spent more time looking at the large, nubby sphere than the smooth one. It seems they knew what "feels smooth" and "feels nubby" should *look* like.

Similarly, four-month-old infants were demonstrated to appreciate the relationship between sight and sound by a study in which they were shown two movies simultaneously.[9] In one, a woman repeatedly covered and uncovered her face with her hands while saying, "Peekaboo!" In the other, a hand held a stick and rhythmically struck a wooden block. The sound track that accompanied the movies had either a woman's voice saying, "Hello, baby! Peekaboo!" *or* the sound of a drumbeat. The infants were observed to spend more time looking at the movie that was coordinated with the sound track. If they heard the "peekaboo" sound track, they looked at the movie of the woman. If they heard the drumbeat, they looked at the movie of the hand and the wooden block. Clearly, they could integrate their visual and auditory inputs. They had a pretty good idea of what something should look like given what it sounded like, and vice versa.

Not all of the knowledge our brain uses to construct perceptual experiences is innate. In fact, oftentimes what we see or feel depends a good deal on what we've *learned* about the world. Consider, for example, the Müller-Lyer line drawings in Figure 3. Jot down what you estimate their lengths to be. If you now measure them with a ruler, you'll find that they are the same

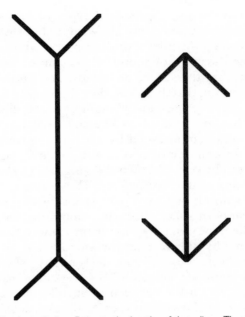

Figure 3. The Müller-Lyer illusion. Estimate the lengths of these lines. Then measure them.

length. Why do they look so different? The answer lies in our visual experiences. Take a look at Figure 4, which shows typical room and building corners. Notice that the Müller-Lyer arrows are embedded in the corners. From experience, you know that if the lines were the same length, then the walls on the left must be bigger than the walls on the right. When you look at the Müller-Lyer arrows, your visual system quite literally shows you what it has learned from experience with room corners, namely, that the left arrow *must* be longer than the right arrow. That is what you see.

We know this illusion stems from acquired as opposed to innate knowledge for two reasons. First, it turns out that these arrows look different only to people who live in environments with straight lines and corners. People who live in environments that don't have them (such as the African Zulus, who live in round huts on open plains) do not appear to suffer this illusion; they estimate the lines to be of equal length.[10] Second, decades

Figure 4. The Müller-Lyer illusion in real life.

of work aimed at creating artificial systems (robots) that can see has made us aware that systems that do *not* fall prey to illusions like these can't see properly. A system that is not subject to the Müller-Lyer illusion can't tell which way a room corner is oriented (concave or convex) or which corner is closer.

A good deal more evidence exists that the quality of our perceptual experiences depends in part on how we are designed and in part on the nature of our sensory experiences with the world. Our brains are born with the capacity to make sense of the world, but if our senses or the world doesn't cooperate to provide quality sensory experiences, we can lose these abilities. In a very real sense, we learn to see through a very careful interaction of neural predispositions and environmental stimulation.

This point can be best appreciated by considering a question posed to philosopher John Locke in a letter from his friend

Molyneux in the year 1690: "Suppose a man born blind, and now adult, and taught by his touch to distinguish between a cube and a sphere of the same metal . . . Suppose then the cube and sphere placed on a table, and the blind man made to see; query whether by his sight, before he touched them, he could now distinguish and tell which is the globe and which the cube?"[11]

Molyneux believed he would not be able to because the visual sensations would make no sense to him. Locke agreed. So did Berkeley. They thought the man would need time to learn what the visual experience meant. Were they right?

Consider the case of S.B., a legally blind man who at the age of fifty-two had his deformed corneas surgically replaced.[12] Could he see? It depended on what he was looking at. In fact, it seemed *he could see what he already knew by touch*. He could recognize capital letters by sight, but not lower case—presumably because he had learned upper case in school (via wooden blocks) but not lower case. He never did learn to read visually although he was proficient at braille. He could accurately judge the distance of objects he knew by touch (e.g., a pencil held a certain distance from him) but he thought he could touch the ground outside his window if he hung from the sill by his hands. In fact, the distance to the ground was at least ten times his height.

The most striking thing about S.B.'s visual capacities is that they seemed to be so much worse than the perceptual capacities of newborn infants. Unlike S.B., newborns can distinguish between objects they have not yet explored by touch, such as triangles and rectangles. Why couldn't S.B.? Perhaps the answer lies in recognizing that S.B. spent years in visual deprivation. For the majority of his life, the parts of S.B.'s brain that would normally receive visual input (the occipital lobes at the back of the head) had been deprived of any input at all. This suggests the tantalizing possibility that innate visual knowledge is like many other things in life—if you don't use it, you lose it.

This poses both a research question and an ethical dilemma: To resolve this dilemma, we need to deprive a newborn's visual system of quality visual input and observe the effects. Whether right or wrong, whenever scientists are faced with dilemmas of this nature, they turn to other species to resolve it.

The visual systems of cats and monkeys are very similar to that of humans. By sinking electrodes into various cortical neurons, it is possible to record activity painlessly in these neurons in living animals. (Remember that the brain has no pain receptors for itself.) The results of research by physiologists and psychologists using this type of procedure are intriguing.

Remember that S.B.'s cataracts prevented much light from entering his eyes, meaning that his brain got very little if any visual information. If kittens and monkeys are raised in darkness, thereby preventing their brains from receiving visual input, they behave as though they are blind—they do not respond to visual stimulation *and neither do their brain cells.*[13] If one eye is patched for a period of time soon after birth, few if any brain cells respond to the input to that eye. All of the visual cortex switches over and becomes devoted to processing the inputs of the other eye.[14] But if adult cats who have spent most of their lives receiving quality visual input have one eye covered, this switchover does not occur; the cats see normally after the patches are removed.

Together, this pattern of results present an intriguing picture. They suggest that depriving the visual brain of input early in life prohibits the development of normal vision. The part of the brain that normally processes visual input apparently becomes devoted to processing other types of information. And that is probably what happened to S.B. When his cataracts were finally removed, his brain no longer had the capacity to process the information his eyes sent it.

Further research on the visual systems of cats and primates has given us an even more complete picture of just how our early visual experiences affect our brain cells. It turns out that there are cells in the visual cortex that respond most strongly to lines of certain orientations. For example, some cells fire strongly only when there is a vertical line in their visual fields (the areas of the retina from which they receive input), while others fire strongly only when there is a horizontal line. Still others respond strongly only to lines that are tilted at 15 degrees, 30 degress, 63 degrees, and so on.[15]

The interesting part is that these preferences are not as sharply defined at birth as they are after the animal has spent some time looking around its world.[16] Although initially any given cell responds somewhat to all line orientations, cells show slight preferences for lines of particular orientations. After the animal is given normal visual experience with the world, the cells' preferences become much more defined. Now some respond strongly only to vertical lines and hardly at all to lines of other orientations. Others respond strongly only to horizontal lines, others to lines of 45-degree orientation, and so on. Normal visual experience "fine-tunes" or sharpens the initial preferences of visual brain cells.

This "plasticity" of brain cells is what makes quality early visual experience so important. Plasticity means that our brain cells are modified by their inputs. In other words, they learn about the world. If they do not receive quality information about the world, what they learn can be quite skewed. For example, the visual inputs of kittens can be restricted by having them wear wide collars that prevent them from seeing their own bodies, and then raising them in environments whose walls are painted with stripes of a certain orientation. When the brain cells of kittens reared in environments like this were tested, it was found that they responded strongly only to lines that matched the orientation of the lines on the wall of their environments.[17] In other words, their visual brain cells changed their initial preferences in order to optimally process the visual environment in which the kittens found themselves. Moreover, the kittens *behaved* as though they were blind to all but the line orientation they were exposed to. Like S.B., they could see only what they knew something about.

The results of another experiment bring us even closer to fully appreciating just how much our explorations of the world shape the brain's ability to make sense out of what the eyes tell it.[18] Here, kittens were yoked together as depicted in Figure 5. The kitten in the gondola received exactly the same visual experience as the one who could move about freely. When they were not yoked together, they were kept in a darkened room. The kittens who were free to move about when yoked developed normal vision. But those who were in the gondola did not. They did

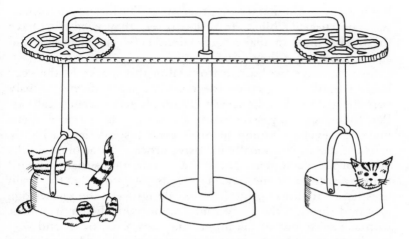

Figure 5. A method for investigating whether perceptual learning can take place in a passive animal. The active kitten's brain has a chance to connect the visual information it receives with information from the other senses and with the motor commands it sends to the body. The passive kitten's brain doesn't. After sufficient exposure to this situation, only the active kitten is found able to perform visual tasks. (After Held and Hein, 1963)

not blink when objects were thrust near their faces, nor did they raise their paws defensively. They took longer to learn a "paw to prong" task in which the kitten is lowered onto a Y-shaped object and must learn to put its paws onto the branches of the Y in order to stand stably. If they were put on a platform and coaxed to move onto a "visual cliff" (a glass platform over a steep drop), they would walk onto it without hesitancy. Normal kittens will not walk onto glass platforms like this. Their depth perception tells them it might be dangerous.

These kittens, therefore, appeared to be deficient in their visual processing. It is as though their eyes received inputs and sent them onto the brain, but their brains never came to make sense of them. Since the visual input was never correlated sensibly with any other sensory input (e.g., touch) or with any motor commands (i.e., voluntary paw and leg movements), it never became meaningful to the kittens. Their brains seemed to treat all that input in the way we respond to the "white noise" between radio stations on the tuning dials—it's definitely input, but it carries no signal worth processing. The kittens, in a sense, were functionally blind. In order to see, they needed to have the opportunity to make connections between what they did and felt and what they saw.

So what have we learned from all of this work? At the very least, I think we've come to appreciate what an enormously complicated process the seemingly simple act of seeing really is. Perceiving is not a passive process, not a simple matter of opening one's eyes or tuning in one's ears. Instead, it is a highly active and computationally intensive process. Your brain works very hard to make sense out of the myriad inputs that bombard it every second of the day. To do its job properly, the brain uses its innate knowledge (nature's design) and the knowledge acquired through the body's interaction with the environment to make sense out of the inputs our eyes, ears, nose, and skin are sending it. Our perceptual experience is the culmination of an enormous inferential process. What should amaze us most is that despite the number of things that could go wrong along the way, our brain's best guesses are so often right on the money. We navigate through the world just fine. Most of us rarely hallucinate, or anyway, not for long . . .

As a closing note, I'd like to point out that our visual system is not the only sensory system that seems to have built-in interpretations for things. Have you ever wondered why we hate the sound of fingernails scraping on blackboards so much? Why does that sound drive us right up the wall? One set of researchers took a sound very similar to that (a rake scraping on metal), digitized it, and had a computer compare the pattern to thousands of other digitized sounds that occur in nature.[19] To their surprise, the nail-scraping pattern most closely matched . . . the warning cry primates give when they spot a predator in the wild.

CHAPTER 4

How We Remember

In a very real sense, we are what we remember. Our ability to form memories enables us to develop a "personal history" that provides continuity to our sense of self, our lives, and our identity. For this reason, the study of memory is a core component of scientific psychology.

Creatures with brains—no matter how rudimentary—have the power to form memories. That is because brain tissue, unlike other types of tissue, has a very special property: It is capable of learning. Every act of perception, cognition, or movement modifies our brain tissue, thereby leaving behind a memory trace of the event. In fact, there is a good deal of evidence that this occurs whether or not we have any conscious recollection of it.

Consider the following study: Volunteers were shown a series of ten irregular, solid-black octagons on a white background.[1] Each octagon was flashed so quickly (for 1 millisecond, or 1/1,000 of a second) that most participants were not even sure they saw anything at all. Then another series of ten pairs of octagons was displayed at a slower rate (1 second per pair), a rate that allowed the volunteers time enough to see each pair clearly and to answer questions about them. The important thing about these pairs is that each one consisted of an "old" octagon taken from the very quick series just presented and a "new" octagon that hadn't been presented before. The volunteers were asked to indicate which member they had seen before, and which they liked better. They were also asked to indicate how sure they were of their decisions.

Not surprisingly, the volunteers found the old/new recognition task to be nearly impossible to do and performed at chance levels (50 percent correct). After all, they were barely aware of having seen anything. But a very different picture emerged on the "like better" task: Despite the fact that the volunteers couldn't reliably tell which octagons were old and which were new, they showed a small but reliable preference for the octagons they'd seen before, choosing them more than 60 percent of the time. The difference was even greater for the preferences they felt most confident about, with old octagons selected more than 70 percent of the time on these occasions.

These results suggest that the volunteers had developed a clear emotional bias in favor of octagons they had no conscious memory of having seen before. (The difference in preferences couldn't be attributed to something special about the first series because two series were used, series A and series B. Half the volunteers saw series A first, followed by A-B pairs, and the other half saw series B first, followed by A-B pairs. It also couldn't have been due to choosing only right- or left-hand members of the pairs because the octagons were randomly paired. And half of the volunteers did the old/new test first while the other half did the "like better" test first, so it couldn't be due to something special about their first or second responses.) The volunteers' emotional reactions showed that something had in fact been retained from the experience, even if their cognitive decisions didn't.

The same dissociation between cognitive and emotional experiences has been observed using more objective response measures, such as galvanic skin response (GSR) and event-related potentials (ERP). GSR is a measure of the drop in the electrical resistance of the skin, and is a good measure of emotional, stressful, or general arousal reactions to stimuli. It is one of the types of responses lie-detector tests measure. ERPs are spikes or peaks seen in EEG (brain wave) activity shortly after a stimulus event occurs. GSRs and ERPs tend to be consistently larger for words already studied than for words presented for the first time—even when people cannot reliably indicate which words were shown to them before.[2]

This doesn't mean that people lie under these circumstances or try to hide their emotions. Instead, these results point to a fundamental division in our memory system called *explicit and implicit memory*.[3] Explicit memories are those that we consciously recall, such as facts (e.g., "John Kennedy was assassinated in 1963") and personal episodes (e.g., "I remember hearing the announcement of his assassination in school during recess"). Typically, explicit memories for episodes have the self as the agent or experiencer of the event, and include at least some of the context in which the event occurred. Explicit memory is the kind of memory most of us mean when we use the term "I remember."

In contrast, implicit memories cannot be consciously recalled, but are retained by our brains nonetheless. The implicit memory system is most typically involved in skill learning (such as playing tennis), habit formation, and emotional learning. The important thing is that implicit memory is expressed through performance or emotional reactions rather than through conscious recollection. The emotional preferences of the volunteers in the above studies indicate that their implicit memory systems remembered what was shown to them even if their explicit systems didn't.

These separate memory systems are affected by entirely different factors. For example, suppose I were to ask you and a friend to study a list of common words like TABLE. While you're studying the words, I ask you questions about the meaning of each word; while your friend studies the words, I ask her to decide whether or not each word contains a particular letter. Then I give you a stem–completion task and an old/new recognition task. In stem completion, you are given part of a word (e.g., TAB__) and asked to complete it. In old/new recognition, you are shown a list of words and asked to indicate which ones were presented before.

It has been shown repeatedly that conscious recollection, such as old/new recognition, benefits from thinking about the *meaning* of the words; but implicit memory, such as stem completion, is unaffected by attending to meaning.[4] Instead, implicit memory is affected by changes in surface characteristics, such as modality or font. For example, suppose I were to read a list of words to you and then ask you to do an old/new recognition task or a stem-completion task. The catch is that I switch modalities on you. You *heard* the words, but the memory tests are presented *visually*. This switch won't matter at all on the recognition task— you'll recognize as many old items as you would if I tested you aurally. But it will matter very much to the stem-completion task. You'll be much faster if the mode of presentation doesn't change.[5] The same is true if I change from upper- to lower-case letters (or vice versa).[6] Implicit memory is very much affected by changes in the surface aspects of the event; explicit recollection is hardly affected by these changes at all.

These results might seem like interesting curiosities, but they are really much more than that. They suggest that there are two very different memory systems residing in our brains, an idea that is supported biologically. PET scanning (see chapter 2) and ERP measurement studies consistently show different parts of the brain to be active during conscious recollection tests and implicit memory tests.[7] The time course of the events differ as well for the two systems, with explicit memories taking longer to retrieve (500–800 milliseconds) than implicit (400–500 milliseconds).

So it seems that we have two memory systems operating in tandem every minute of our lives. These systems attend to different aspects of the environment and each has its own time course. This division appears to be present in all healthy functioning mammalian brain systems; it allows us to learn things from our life experiences, whether or not we are aware that we've learned anything. But because our memory systems are intact, we usually don't notice the dissociation. We identify with the memories we can consciously recollect, and refer uneasily to the workings of the implicit system in terms of hunches, intuitions, or gut reactions. But when certain types of brain damage occur, the separate functioning of these two distinct systems can become shockingly apparent.

PET scanning has shown us which parts of the brain are active during conscious recall. If these areas are damaged by a stroke or injury, a very strange syndrome appears: These patients can see, hear, think, and speak normally, but they can't seem to form any new memories. They can remember things from their past just fine, but can't remember, for example, what happened during the round of golf they just finished playing.[8] This is called amnesic syndrome.[9]

If amnesics can't remember anything, then you'd think it was a sure bet that they can't learn anything new, either. In fact, for decades this was exactly what doctors thought—even though there were curious cases reported of apparent memories for certain types of experiences. Amnesics, for example, can be conditioned to blink in response to a tone if the tone has been paired repeatedly with a strong puff of air to the eye (see chapter 7).[10] They prefer melodies they've recently heard over new ones.[11] When shown hard-to-find illusory figures in pictures, they can spot them again later.[12] With repeated presentations, they also get better at tracing paths through mazes and putting jigsaw puzzles together.[13] In one rather amazing case, an amnesic successfully learned to program a computer.[14]

The fact that amnesics can learn is astonishing enough, but even more incredible is the fact that they evidence no conscious memory of ever having learned anything. In the reports above, the amnesics tested had no conscious memory of having heard the melodies before, or of having seen the hidden-figure pictures, or of having interacted with the mazes or jigsaw puzzles. The computer programmer amnesic insisted he had never worked with a computer. When shown the conditioning apparatus (a tube that delivered a puff of air to the eye along with a tone) ten minutes after learning, the amnesics could not explain what the apparatus was for. They didn't even remember using it.[15]

These results are less befuddling if you see them in terms of explicit and implicit memory. Amnesics have no explicit, conscious memory of events, but their implicit system seems to be still intact. In fact, the division that is apparent in the performance of normal participants on explicit and implicit memory tests shows up in high relief among amnesics. For example, amnesics fail miserably on tests of conscious recall and recognition. If you ask them to use word stems to try to *recall* words they saw just a few minutes ago, they cannot use them successfully. But if you ask them just to *complete* the stems with the first words that come to mind, they do just fine—as well as normals, in fact. The catch is that they treat the tasks as guessing games or puzzles. They are completely unaware of the fact that they are completing the stems with words they saw just a few minutes before.[16]

Perhaps the most striking effects reported come from a study in which amnesics and normals were asked to perform a reaction-time task.[17] They placed their index and middle fingers on the 3, 5, 7, and 9 keys on a computer keyboard and watched as an asterisk suddenly appeared on the screen above one of these keys. Their task was to press the key below the asterisk as quickly as they could. They did this for eight blocks of one hundred trials. Unbeknownst to the volunteers, in half of the blocks, the asterisk appeared in a patterned sequence of ten moves (e.g., right index finger, left index finger, right middle finger, left middle finger, etc.). This pattern repeated ten times within the block. In the other half of the blocks, the asterisk appeared randomly across the four positions.

The interesting thing is that *all* of the volunteers picked up on the pattern—*even the amnesics!* Although the amnesics were slower overall than the normals, they got quicker on the patterned trials just as the normals did, anticipating where the next asterisk would appear. Nobody got quicker on the random trials, so the improvement wasn't a simple matter of getting more familiar with the task.

When the two groups were questioned about the pattern after the study ended, however, a very different picture emerged. All of the normal volunteers said they detected the pattern, and reported what it was, but none of the amnesics did. The amnesics not only couldn't report the pattern, they insisted they hadn't detected any pattern at all. But their performance told otherwise. Their implicit memory system dutifully noted and recorded the sequence, producing a dramatic improvement in performance over time.

Perhaps the most celebrated case of amnesic learning is that of H.M., a man who had his hippocampus surgically removed in a daring attempt to control his intractable epilepsy.[18] The hippocampus is a structure in the "old brain," that is, in the brain matter that lies underneath the cerebral cortex. It is intimately involved in the formation of new memories. After he recovered from the surgery, it became apparent that H.M.'s memory processes were severely impaired: Although he could remember things from the past quite well, he could no longer acquire new memories. He seemed to forget things as soon as they happened. He couldn't remember what he had for lunch, or his way to the bathroom in the hospital, or new people he had met.

Or perhaps we should say he had no *conscious* memory of any of these things. In order to study the extent of H.M.'s deficits, researchers required him to learn to perform a series of tasks. One of them was called "mirror tracing." In this task, a drawing of a simple object (such as a star) is placed in front of a mirror and the person is asked to trace the object with a pencil by watching his or her hand in the mirror. Try it. It's actually quite difficult because everything is reversed in the mirror. People generally get better at this with time, learning to countermand their usual responses to the visual information their brain is receiving. Each time H.M. was asked to try the mirror-tracing task, he professed to having never done such a thing before. Nonetheless, he got better at it over time; across a series of trials, the amount of time he required to trace the objects systematically decreased.[19] Clearly he was learning something, but he was unaware of it. H.M. also got better at playing certain games, such as the Tower of Hanoi, that require players to remember sequences of moves. In each case, he could not consciously recall ever playing the game before, but his implicit memory system accumulated knowledge nonetheless. In contrast, his explicit memory system was left untouched by the experience.

The explicit memory deficits suffered by H.M. and stroke victims are also seen in Alzheimer's disease. This disease is characterized in part by severe memory impairment. But again, Alzheimer's patients can typically remember things from the past quite well (and can regale you with stories from their youths in the 1930s, etc.), but they cannot remember what they had for lunch or anything else that happened recently. In short, their memories seem very much like H.M.'s The only explicit memories they have are ones that were formed before the disease knocked out the explicit memory system. As the disease progresses, they are left with only the implicit system. Physiologically, Alzheimer's disease does its dirty work by isolating the hippocampus from the rest of the brain. The cells that connect it to other brain structures deteriorate, and eventually it becomes an island unto itself.[20] As a result, the patient can experience the present, but he or she cannot form new conscious memories because the structure that is intimately involved in building new memories is isolated from the rest of the brain where such memories are typically stored.

What does all this mean? We now understand that amnesic syndrome occurs when the explicit memory system is damaged. Fortunately, nature is kind, having given us another system that works in parallel with the explicit system. If the explicit one is damaged, we can still make our way through life, learning from our experiences even if we can't remember them. The key player in all of this is the hippocampus. According to one theory, it is needed to temporarily bind together the numerous areas of brain activity that together make up a whole memory.[21] When the hippocampus is damaged or isolated, these separate memories can't come together to produce a conscious recollection. Instead, we can only *unconsciously* remember certain aspects of our experiences.

The fact that the explicit memory system is so easily damaged suggests that it is, evolutionarily speaking, a younger system. The durable implicit system seems to be a more primitive system that evolved first and now operates simultaneously with its more sophisticated counterpart. This conjecture is supported by the fact that the explicit system also takes longer to emerge in infanthood.[22] The hippocampus, for example, is not fully developed at birth in many species (including humans). In rats, the period of hippocampal development corresponds to a period when they have difficulty learning various tasks. In humans, the hippocampus requires the first two years of life to fully develop and grow pathways to other brain structures. And that is probably why we have no conscious memories of this period of our childhoods.

While the advantages of conscious memories might seem apparent to us, the evolution of this memory system seems to have yielded some rather odd characteristics. Retaining conscious memories seems to require more resources than even our considerable brains can manage. For this reason, separate components of the explicit memory system retain information at different stages and for different lengths of time. For example, suppose I were to flash the following array of letters on a wall for 50 milliseconds (1/20 of a second):

EPMG
BQNZ
VTOM

How many letters do you think you would consciously recall seeing? None? Five? Ten? The entire array? In fact, you would retain a memory of the *entire* array for an extremely brief period of time—about a quarter of a second. After that, you would be able to retain, on average, about five to nine letters. This phenomenon was first discovered in 1960 by an experimental psychologist at Bell Laboratories named George Sperling.[23] Sperling flashed series of letter and number arrays like these to groups of volunteers and asked them to report the entire array each time as soon as the slide was extinguished. Under these circumstances, the volunteers could reliably report only about seven items from the three-by-four arrays. They had already forgotten the rest. Then he tried a different technique. He told his volunteers to report the items in the top, middle, or bottom row depending on whether a tone they heard was high, medium, or low. The important thing is that the tone was played *after* the slide was extinguished; Sperling's volunteers didn't know which row they would be asked to report until after the display had disappeared. Under these conditions, a very different picture emerged: They now could reliably report the *entire contents of any row* in the display. If too much time intervened between extinguishing the slide and the sounding of the tone, the volunteers went back to not being able to remember very much of the array.

This means that for a very brief period of time, we are in possession of a complete, veridical image of a visual display. Sperling called this form of memory *iconic memory;* it is a "photograph of the world." The phenomenon of iconic memory has been replicated numerous times using larger arrays and various techniques.[24] For a very brief period of time—on the order of milliseconds—the explicit memory system retains a "photograph" of what the eyes have seen. But, just as rapidly, the image decays. (A similar type of memory exists for audition, called echoic memory.[25])

Iconic memory serves a very important purpose. If it were not for the iconic image, the world would disappear every time we blinked our eyes. Our view of the world would be constantly interrupted by brief periods of blackness. With iconic memory, the world appears to us as a continuous, seamless visual experience, unhampered by random interruptions.

What happens after the icon disappears? It turns out that most of us can reliably retain somewhere between five and nine items (letters, words, sentences, etc.) for a few minutes before forgetting them. Other researchers had noticed this phenomenon as well, as shown by this tongue-in-cheek introduction to a paper published by Dr. George Miller in 1956:

> My problem is that I have been persecuted by an integer. For seven years, this number has followed me around, has intruded in my most private data, and has assaulted me from the pages of our most public journals. This number assumes a variety of disguises, being sometimes a little larger and sometimes a little smaller than usual, but never changing so much as to be unrecognizable. The persistence with which this number plagues me is far more than a random accident. There is, to quote a famous senator, a design behind it, some pattern governing its appearances. Either there really is something unusual about the number or else I am suffering from delusions of persecution.[26]

What was this menacing number? The title of the article tells it all: "The Magical Number Seven, Plus or Minus Two: Some Limits on Our Capacity for Processing Information." Once the iconic image has decayed, it seems we can reliably remember only seven plus or minus two chunks of information, on average. The key here is the phrase "chunks of information." A chunk can be a letter, a word, a geometric shape, a phrase, a sentence, a paragraph—any meaningful unit, no matter how large.[27] One long-distance runner was found to be able to recall up to eighty randomly generated, spoken digits by chunking them into meaningful marathon running times.[28]

Retaining conscious memories is an effortful affair, and the explicit memory system is consequently conservative in terms of what it retains. Items that mark the beginning and end of events (such as the beginning and end of a list, advertisement, or letter) are remembered better than items in the middle— unless these middle items are particularly meaningful to you. This is called the primacy-recency effect,[29] and it's a good one to keep in mind if you're a speech writer, teacher, advertiser, or politician. Repeated information also tends to be better retained than unrepeated information—provided that other information intervenes between the repetitions. This is called the spacing effect, and it, too, is a good one to keep in mind.[30] If you want to make sure something is remembered, say it, then say some other things, then say the important thing again. People will be more likely to remember it than if you just say the important thing twice in a row.

Whether and how you retain information over the long haul is inextricably tied to its meaningfulness to you. The results of one study make this point abundantly clear.[31] Volunteers were presented lists of sentences in which an adjective and a noun were underlined, such as "They ate toast and sliced ham for breakfast" or "They ate toast and strawberry jam for breakfast." Their task was to remember the underlined words. Later, they were shown a list of word pairs and asked to pick out the nouns they had seen. Some of the nouns appeared with their old partners (e.g., sliced ham, strawberry jam) and some appeared with new partners. The new partners either maintained the noun's original meaning (e.g., smoked ham, blackberry jam) or gave them new meanings (e.g., radio ham, traffic jam). Surprisingly, the volunteers often failed to recognize the old nouns when they were accompanied by new partners that changed their meaning. Notice what this means. If the volunteers saw "strawberry jam" and were later shown "traffic jam," *they didn't remember having seen the word "jam" before*. It's the same physical stimulus both times, but the *meaning* changed. Our explicit memory systems retain the meaning of the events we witness, not their physical characteristics.

But fortunately, not every meaning is remembered. Why do I say fortunately? Consider the following study:[32] Volunteers were asked questions about famous people, and the time it took them to respond was recorded. Long delays followed by "I don't know" responses were observed for some questions, such as "How old is Bert Parks?" and "Does Ann Landers have a journalism degree?" Why? Because of the associations alluded to in these questions. The study was conducted shortly after Bert Parks had been terminated as host of the Miss America pageant because of his age. There was an association between "Bert Parks" and "age" that most of the volunteers were aware of, and this caused them to search their memories carefully to see if they could retrieve information about his actual age. In the second example, there is an association between Ann Landers and newspapers. Once again, this gave the volunteers pause as they pondered whether they had any knowledge of her credentials. In contrast, they responded "I don't know" extremely quickly when asked, "Does Bert Parks have a degree in journalism?" They were sure they didn't know that one because no association existed between "Bert Parks" and "journalism" in their minds.

Now think of the millions of bits of information you are exposed to every day of your life, and the millions of associations you learn among them. If your brain dutifully recorded each one and tenaciously clung to all of them, you'd be in big trouble. You would quickly be overwhelmed by the sheer volume of information the environment throws at you. And searching through it for needed information would be impossible. It might take you several lifetimes to answer even the simplest question. For this reason, creatures that have the power to remember must also have the ability to *forget*.

CHAPTER 5

Consciousness

In chapter 2, the brain was likened to a computer. There are, however, two very important differences between brains and computers. There are computers today that reason as intelligently as humans in some domains, but *none are conscious and none experience emotions.* Consciousness and emotions seem (so far) to be very special properties of biological, evolved brains, and for this reason, a good deal of psychological research has been devoted to studying them. In this chapter, we'll look at the unique property of consciousness; in the next, we'll explore emotions.

I'll use the following as a working definition of consciousness: Consciousness is awareness of one's own thoughts and feelings, and of what is happening around one. This definition has an internal dimension (i.e., one's own thoughts and feelings) and an external dimension (i.e., awareness of what's going on outside). These two become blended together in a sort of mosaic inside us. This mosaic of thoughts, feelings, and sensations defines who we are at any given moment. It is the "I" that we refer to when we talk about ourselves and our experiences.

It might seem to us that this "I" is a single, nondivisible whole, an immutable core that is ever present and of which we are always aware. In fact, consciousness is a many-layered thing. Consider this simple fact: We've all experienced being in a situation where more than one conversation is going on around us. A cocktail party is a common example. While engaging in conversation within your little group, you're completely unaware of the conversations going on around you. They seem like background noise, a steady hum of indistinguishable sounds. But if someone from another group mentions your name in the course of normal conversation, you certainly hear it. Immediately your attention zooms to the other group as you strain to hear what is being said about you. If you were unaware of what was being said in the numerous groups around you, how did you know your name was mentioned?

At some level, the information from all of those other conversations was getting through, but your brain busily dampened it to allow you to concentrate on the people in your group. A high-priority event like your name, however, is allowed to enter your consciousness. This ability to ignore all stimulation except that which is high priority is vital to our ability to function. Certain disorders, such as autism and certain types of schizophrenia, are characterized by an inability to perform this vital function. Sufferers are literally overwhelmed by the amount of stimulation coming at them—squawking voices, grimacing faces, roaring cars, buzzing insects, humming lights. The world is a riot of color, shapes, and noises. They cannot sort out what is important from what is not. As a result, they cannot function.[1]

The fact that consciousness is a many-layered thing should come as no surprise given our discussion of the brain in chapter 2. The brain is a mishmash of cortical lobes and subcortical structures that each handle separate aspects of incoming and outgoing information. Yet remarkably enough, our subjective experience is one of a cohesive whole.

This cohesiveness may be more of an illusion than a reality. In fact, in his recent book *Consciousness Explained,* philosopher Dan Dennett argues that consciousness is best described as multiple "drafts," that is, as multiple encodings of an event that are distributed throughout the brain. Every time we perceive, think, or act, numerous brain systems are involved, and each of these systems separately records some aspect of the perception, thought, or action. No one "draft" is more correct than another, but they can and do influence one another.

It is easy to show this in the laboratory using a technique called "dichotic listening." In this technique, a listener hears two different messages played simultaneously over a set of head-phones. The right headphone plays one message and the left plays a different one. The listener is asked to "shadow," that is, repeat word for word, only one of the messages, the message that is played through the earphone to one of the ears. The message speed is quite fast on these tapes, so it takes a good deal of concentration to keep up.

After a period of time, the tapes are stopped and the listener receives a "surprise quiz" on the material from the nonshadowed message. Generally, listeners are incapable of reporting very much of the conversation that occurred on the nonshadowed side. In fact, they typically can remember only very surface aspects of the conversation, such as whether the speakers were male or female, whether the voice pitches were low or high, the number of speakers, and very generally what the topic was.[2] But regardless of whether they can *report* the meaning of the nonshadowed message, that meaning does seem to get through. For example, like the cocktail party phenomenon, listeners can reliably report whether their *own* names were mentioned, but not other names.[3]

Even more interesting is the fact that the interpretation of ambiguous words heard in the shadowed ear is influenced by what is played to the nonshadowed ear. For example, if the sentence "They were throwing rocks at the bank" is played to the shadowed ear, the word "bank" is more likely to be inter-preted as a financial institution if the word "money" is simul-taneously played to the nonshadowed ear. Conversely, "bank" is more likely to be interpreted as the side of a river if the word "river" is simultaneously played to the nonshadowed ear.[4] This is true even though the listeners cannot recall having heard either word, and report that they were unaware of processing the meanings of the sounds played to the nonshadowed ear.

Studies like these show just how easily the multifaceted nature of our internal states of consciousness can be teased apart. More striking demonstrations come from more extraordinary circum-stances.

As we saw in chapter 2, the cerebral cortex is really two brains that are joined by a narrow band of nerve fibers called the corpus callosum. The corpus callosum provides the only means these two brains have of communicating with each other. In certain forms of epilepsy, the nerve impulses traveling across the corpus callosum get of control and cause massive brain seizures, so massive that the person is in danger of dying. To alleviate these seizures, surgeons will sometimes cut the corpus callosum. The seizures thereby subside. But think about what's happened. These patients now essentially have two brains in their heads, *and these two brains can't communicate with each other because the communication bridge is gone.* Do these patients notice anything different about their inner lives? Their consciousness?

These patients behave normally in everyday life, and you probably wouldn't know that they are missing corpus callosa. But there are certain strange things that these patients do notice about their internal states. Like the fact that they can't strike a match with their eyes closed. The right hand is being directed by the left brain and the left hand is being directed by the right. When the patient's eyes are closed so that the two brains can't see what the other is doing, the patient has no idea where his hands are relative to each other. The right hand literally knoweth not what the left hand doeth. To get some feel for this, hold a matchbox and have a friend strike a match on it. Now have the two of you try it with your eyes closed. Where's the box? Where's the match? Your two brains each know one-half of the puzzle, and that's not enough. This is the split-brain patient's dilemma.

A still stranger example was volunteered by one patient. She complained that when she was getting dressed in the morning, her left hand would reach in a drawer—seemingly of its own volition—and get out things that she didn't want at all. For example, she might have just put on a pair of shorts, and her left hand would pull a slip out of the drawer.

So many patients voiced complaints like these that two neuropsychologists decided to study them further in the laboratory.[5] The experimental technique they used was quite ingenious. Each patient was seated in front of a rear-projection screen and asked to fixate on a spot directly in the center of the screen. Then a stimulus was flashed on one-half of the screen very, very briefly, say for 100 milliseconds (1/10 of 1 second). Since the patient's eyes were fixated on the center of the screen, the visual stimulus entered only one-half of the visual field—either the right or the left half—meaning that only one cerebral hemisphere (brain) saw what was flashed. (Remember that our retinas are divided so that the images on the right half go to the left brain and images on the left half go to the right brain.) The patients were then asked to do one of several things. In one experiment, they were asked simply to read a word that was flashed up on the screen. If the word was flashed to the left brain, they had no problem reporting the word. (Remember that our language faculty resides in the left brain.) If the word was flashed to the right brain, they had a big problem. Either they would guess at what was there or would report seeing nothing at all. In one case, the word HEART was displayed across the two fields so that the dividing line between the two visual fields was between the "E" and the "A." When asked to report the word, the patients reporting seeing "ART."

You might be tempted to conclude at this point that our consciousness resides in our left brains because coherent responses were obtained only when this brain was queried. But the results of other tasks told otherwise. When the patients were required to reach under the partition with one hand and select the object whose name or picture was flashed on the screen, they were capable of retrieving the correct object regardless of which brain saw the word or picture. But when asked to *name* the object just retrieved, only the left brain could respond appropriately. The right brain didn't know the name of the object retrieved. For example, if the word "spoon" or a picture of a spoon was flashed to the right brain, the patient had no trouble reaching under the partition with the left hand (the right brain controls the left hand), feeling around, and selecting a spoon from among the various objects under there. But when asked to name the object the left hand was holding, the patient couldn't do it. On the other hand (quite literally), when the word or picture was flashed to the left brain, the patient had no trouble selecting the object with the right hand *and* naming it. These results show that the right brain was aware of the meaning of the word or picture it saw. It just couldn't retrieve its name. Names for things are located in the other brain. (As an aside, it is often difficult for people to realize that words are visual objects with names. This research makes that point abundantly clear. The right knows the meaning of words, but not their names.)

These results were startling to researcher and patient alike because they suggested that the surgeon's knife had cut consciousness in two. But this is what our everyday consciousness is like. The two brains in our heads attend to different aspects of an event, and enjoy their own states of consciousness. Normally, the two brains can communicate with each other via the corpus callosum, and we don't notice their disparate states.

But more important, what happened to these patients' personalities? Since they have essentially two disparate brains in their heads, do they have two personalities as well? Perhaps. Consider this anecdote. When the question "Where are you?" was asked of one patient's left and right brains, the same response was given by the patient both times: "Vermont." Then each brain was asked, "What do you want to be?" His left brain replied, "A draftsman." His right replied, "A race car driver." So if you sometimes feel as if you're of two minds about something, you may literally be of two minds about it.

You may be saying to yourself at this point, "Split-brain research is based on the brains of epileptics. Perhaps the disease impairs brains in odd ways. How generalizable are these results to the nonepileptic population?" Good question. Obviously, we can't go around cutting the corpus callosa of healthy people. But there is another less invasive way of answering this question.

In one technique, called the Wada technique. A barbiturate is injected into the carotid artery (in the neck) of volunteers. The volunteer is then asked to raise his or her hand on the side of the body where the injection was made and to count aloud. The barbiturate suppresses the activity in the brain fed by that artery (left artery, left brain; right artery, right brain). Essentially, only one brain is made to fall asleep. When the volunteer's arm drops and the counting stops, this means the brain in question has succumbed to the barbiturate.

It turns out that the Wada technique is a scary business. Volunteers who have undergone this technique could report no coherent memories of what went on.[6] They were totally confused about the whole experience. They didn't remember the paralysis, and their retrospective reports of their emotional reactions (e.g., happiness) didn't match the reactions observed during the procedure (e.g., crying). It seems that it is less traumatic to have our consciousness teased apart into separate streams than it is to completely eliminate one of these streams.

The teasing apart of consciousness seems to be involved in another, more bizarre phenomenon—multiple personalities. Consider the case of Kathy/Katherine: After giving birth to a healthy baby girl, twenty-eight-year-old Katherine seemed to undergo a personality change.[7] According to her husband, she acted like a child, said sex was "bad and dumb" and wanted to die. She responded only to the name Kathy and seemed to be in trance. During therapy, it became apparent that Katherine and Kathy were really two different personalities. Katherine was an adult, while Kathy was a child who was very much afraid of sex.

It emerged during therapy that when Katherine was only five years old, her older brother attempted to rape her at the urging of her older sister. He was unsuccessful, and she didn't understand what it was all about. Two years later, however, he accomplished the deed, raping her both orally and anally. The seven-year-old Kathy was so traumatized that she could not even respond to her father's demands as to why she was late for dinner. Her father punished her severely for her disobedience, and she internalized this as punishment for what had happened to her.

The trauma of this incident was so intense that Kathy's developing personality split apart. "Katherine" emerged as a shy and inhibited personality who successfully blocked out the entire incident. Because "Katherine" had no memory of what had happened, she could continue to interact with the world and grow up. "Kathy," on the other hand, remained locked away in her own world of trauma and grief.

This fledgling personality split was further exacerbated by subsequent events. When Kathy was ten, she saw her twelve-year-old sister gang-raped. At seventeen, she herself was gang-raped. Her father also began making sexual overtures toward her, but she stopped him by telling him he was "dumb and stupid," the words she now used to prevent sex with her husband.

Katherine lived a pretty normal life until she had her baby. When the baby appeared, Kathy realized she was going to have to grow up. The baby needed an adult to look after him. Kathy rebelled, emerging in an attempt to take over Katherine's entire life. Katherine's story has a happy ending, however, because therapy worked for her. Healing these deep-seated wounds healed the painful division of her consciousness as well.

Most cases of multiple personalities involve a background of intense physical and emotional abuse such as this one.[8] The patient's early home experiences are filled with violent and excessive punishment, rape, and emotional torment delivered by a sadistic parent while a pathologically passive one looks on and does nothing to stop it.[9] The emergence of a second or third personality appears to be an attempt on the part of the threatened organism to protect itself from the trauma.

If you have ever been in a severe car accident or the victim of a violent crime, you might have experienced something like the dissociation such patients feel. The violence and carnage seemed to be happening a long distance away to someone else. "You" were floating above somewhere, observing. Your consciousness was certainly "divided"—so much so that your personality temporarily dissociated itself from the horror at hand. My reading of multiple-personality cases puts them in this category. In order to survive, parts of a young, developing consciousness that are associated with life-threatening abuse are split off and isolated from other parts. Other personalities emerge to deal with the world, leaving the traumatized ones frozen in time. That's the only way the young organism can survive in such dire circumstances. The result is a disunited personality, compartmentalized consciousness that, like split brains, cannot communicate with each other.

Up to this point, I have focused exclusively on waking consciousness. But that is not where our consciousness begins and ends. We spend approximately one-third of our lives relinquishing awareness to the necessity of sleep, a time of naturally altered consciousness. When we sleep we become aware exclusively of our internal worlds, a fact that makes us vulnerable to the dangers of the outer world. From an evolutionary standpoint, requiring organisms to remain in this forced state of vulnerability for a third of their lives doesn't make much sense. So then why do we sleep? What is its purpose?

The usual answer is that we need to rest. But if you think that sleep is a time of rest and relaxation, think again. Sleep is *not* a time of quiescence. When we are asleep, our brains are highly active, our hearts beat, our kidneys function, and even orgasms occur. Incidences of angina, hemorrhage, and sudden death all peak around 5–6 A.M, when most of our dreaming occurs.[10] If you were to compare brain wave activity during certain parts of the sleep cycle with brain wave activity during waking hours, you would find them indistinguishable.

Falling asleep is itself a very active process—and a very complicated one. The key to the process is the reticular activating system (RAS), a structure that is part of the old brain. The cortex is the seat of conscious perception and thought, but it cannot by itself maintain a conscious state. A functioning RAS is needed for that. If the RAS is damaged or destroyed, a coma results. If the RAS of a sleeping cat is stimulated via mild electrical current, the cat immediately wakes up.[11] If the RAS is destroyed, the cat falls into a coma. Stimulating the RAS in waking monkeys jolts them into a hyperalert state, causing them to look around expectantly.[12]

Furthermore, sleep is not a single phenomenon but a series of successive states that depends upon the coordination of many systems. The RAS initiates and coordinates the activity of these systems in order to accomplish a crucially important task: *isolating the cortex from other parts of the body*. Cortical isolation is crucial, for two reasons. First, incoming sensory stimulation must be prevented from reaching the cortex in order to shut out the world. The RAS acts as a kind of filter that is set very high during sleep so that external stimulation does not activate the cortex. As a result, you become unaware of the external world and hyperaware of your internal world. Second, the motor cortex is shut off from your musculature so *you can't act out your dreams*. If you were to look at brain wave activity during sleep, you'd see that the sensory and motor cortexes are highly active, particularly during dreaming. But because the cortex is isolated from the rest of the body, the commands to move that are issued by the motor cortex do not reach your muscles, and the stimulation processed by the sensory cortex does not come from the outside world. You are adrift within your own universe when asleep, creating your own virtual reality and moving about in it.

But this doesn't mean that the brain is not still monitoring outside reality. Meaningful stimuli (such as a child's cry) or novel stimuli (such as the ceiling leaking) can still get through. In fact, events like these require less intensity to awaken a person than "meaningless" ones (such as traffic noise, clicks, or flashes of light).[13] A newborn infant's cry need not be much above hearing threshold to awaken her sleeping mother.[14] Even while we are asleep, our brain monitors incoming stimuli, producing a nighttime version of the "cocktail party" phenomenon.

There are five stages of sleep, and we cycle through them all night long.[15] The first four stages are called NREM sleep, or non-rapid eye movement sleep. The fifth stage is called rapid eye movement sleep (REM) because the eyes move rapidly during this stage. Bursts of middle ear muscle activity also occurs during REM sleep.[16]

REM sleep is often called paradoxical sleep because brain activity during it is nearly indistinguishable from waking brain activity, yet it is the most difficult stage to wake people from. Dreaming almost always occurs during this stage. In one study, dreams were reported on 85 percent of the occasions when sleepers were awakened during REM versus 30 percent during NREM sleep.[17] Also, the quality of the dreams reported differed. NREM dreams seemed more like thinking; there wasn't much imagery involved. REM dreams, in contrast, were full of imagery and emotional experiences.

How much time do we spend dreaming during the night? It depends on how old you are.[18] Newborns sleep, on average, seventeen to eighteen hours a day, and spend 50 percent of that time in REM sleep. They also tend to go immediately into REM from the waking state. In fact, the other four stages of sleep are not clearly delineated until babies are about six months of age. In contrast, adults sleep an average of eight hours per day and spend about 25 percent of that time in REM sleep, with most of it occurring during the last few hours of the sleep period. Why newborns spend so much time in REM sleep is not altogether clear, but its seems crucial to the proper development of the brain, especially the visual cortex. Dreaming seems to stimulate the cortex in much the same way that external stimulation does.

Perhaps you've noticed the family dog twitching and woofing softly in his sleep. Is he dreaming? Do animals dream? The answer seems to be yes. REM sleep is not particular to humans; it has been observed in all mammalian species studied so far, and even some bird species.[19] But does the presence of REM sleep necessarily mean dreaming is occurring? It would seem so. If the system that inhibits movement during sleep is damaged in cats, they appear to act out their dreams, stalking and attacking nonexistent objects in their cage.[20] And a gorilla trained to use sign language made up the term "sleep pictures" to describe his nighttime experiences.[21]

What happens if we're deprived of sleep by worries, traffic noise, babies crying, and the like? Well, it depends. Of the various sleep stages, REM and stage 4 (deep) sleep appear to be most critical to our well-being.[22] It is harder to deprive sleepers of stage 4 sleep than REM sleep. The number of awakenings necessary to prevent sleepers from going into stage 4 is far greater than the number needed to prevent them from going into REM. But something interesting happens when they are finally allowed to sleep normally again. The proportion of time spent in REM and stage 4 increases relative to the other sleep stages, but this "rebound effect" is far greater for REM sleep. It is as though the sleepers are trying to make up for lost dream time. As far as the body is concerned, *dreaming is biologically necessary*.

Selectively depriving sleepers of REM sleep also produces some rather marked psychological disturbances.[23] REM-deprived sleepers become extremely cranky and irritable, suffering from fatigue and loss of concentration. They fantasize more during the day. When finally allowed to sleep without interruption, they dream more (REM rebound), and their dreams become more nightmarish with greater periods of deprivation. "Breakthrough dreaming" during waking hours—literally dreaming while awake—has also been reported.

Given that REM and stage 4 sleep are so critical to our physical well-being, it might come as a surprise to you to learn that barbiturates—and their latter-day chemical cousins Valium, Halcion, and Dalmane—*decrease* both types of sleep.[24] That is why people who are addicted to barbiturates never feel fully rested after they sleep, and suffer from nightmares (REM rebound) when they try to sleep without them.

If you suffer from insomnia, drugs may not be what you need. Your problem might not be a sleep problem at all but a shifted circadian rhythm. A certain percentage of the population suffers from delayed sleep phase syndrome (DSPS), a syndrome that is characterized by an out-of-kilter sleep-wake cycle. There is a stage in the daily biological cycle during which sleeping is difficult or impossible. Most people leave this stage at about 10 P.M. and enter it again around 6–7 A.M. Insomniacs have been found to leave this stage after 1 A.M., almost four hours later than noninsomniacs.[25] That might be why you spend hours in bed tossing and turning before finally drifting off to sleep in the wee hours of the morning.

Why do REM and stage 4 sleep matter so much? One theory has it that stage 4 sleep is needed to restore *body* tissues and REM is needed to restore *brain* tissues.[26] Increases in stage 4 sleep usually occur after heavy exercise, such as marathon running,[27] while increases in REM sleep usually occur after intense periods of learning.[28] In fact, if REM sleep is disrupted following learning, memory for the learned material is severely impaired; disrupting other sleep stages has little effect.[29] In contrast, stimulating the RAS of animals with mild electrical current during REM sleep enhances learning; stimulating the same area when they are awake or in non-REM sleep does not produce the same memory-enhancing effect.[30]

Why should REM sleep matter so much to memory and learning? Learning is believed to rely on metabolism of new proteins,[31] and REM sleep is associated with high levels of protein synthesis.[32] If drugs that block or inhibit protein synthesis are injected during the heightened REM period that follows learning, REM sleep is disrupted and learning suffers.[33] Injecting these drugs before or after the REM surge has little effect. REM sleep seems to be intimately involved in forming permanent memories of previous events.

This doesn't mean that we should try to learn while in REM sleep. On the contrary, REM seems to facilitate memory for pre-REM events, not current ones, and not ones that follow too closely after. For example, some researchers played lists of word pairs, such as "tortoise-hare," to sleepers during REM sleep. When tested upon awakening, the sleepers evidenced virtually no memory for the lists (not even implicit memory).[34] Other studies have corroborated this—material learned just after periods of sleep tend to be poorly remembered.[35] The protein synthesis that goes on during REM sleep seems to be devoted solely to consolidating *previous* learning. Sleep appears to be a state of consciousness in which we shut out as much of the external world as possible to consolidate what we've experienced by synthesizing proteins and weaving dreams.

There is one other state of consciousness that most of us experience at one time or another in our lives and that is the state of anesthesia. In the play *Elephant Man,* the hero's doctor delivers a monologue in which he bemoans the lack of a "reliable anesthetic." The anesthetic in common use among surgeons at the time was ether, a decidedly unreliable drug. Sometimes patients under ether would awake *during* the surgical procedure— to the chagrin of surgeon and patient alike. Sometimes, they never awoke at all—even after the procedure was completed and the surgeon tried desperately to revive the patient. It gives one pause to consider that humans have been performing surgery since ancient times, but *reliable anesthetics have been around only since the end of World War II.*

There is a distinction between general anesthetics and analgesics that must be appreciated here.[36] The purpose of both is to render a patient insensitive to pain, but they go about it in entirely different ways. Analgesics work by blocking transmission of pain signals from the body to the brain. When under the effects of analgesics, the patient loses sensation in the place where the analgesic was applied, but retains sensation everywhere else, including vision and audition. In contrast, general anesthetics operate directly on the central nervous system by producing a loss of consciousness and a loss of sensory awareness everywhere in the body. For this reason, the state of anesthesia is sometimes called a state of "controlled coma." The patient becomes oblivious to both the private inner world and the public outer world of stimulation.

Or so we thought. In recent years, numerous reports have been published from controlled experiments showing memory of surgical events among adequately anesthetized patients. In order to fully appreciate when and how these memories occur, it's necessary to fully understand what an anesthetically induced "controlled coma" is and how it is brought about.

Inducing anesthesia is a complicated procedure involving a variety of drugs. The exact combination of drugs differs depending on the surgical procedure involved and the physician's preferences. Despite differences, however, the general technique, called balanced anesthesia, involves the use of sedation, analgesia, and muscle relaxation.

A typical case begins with premedication with a sedative to relieve anxiety.[37] Then, the patient receives an intravenous injection of more sedatives or a narcotic. This injection induces anesthesia—the "controlled coma." While the patient is losing consciousness, an injection of a drug that induces muscle paralysis is administered. Muscle paralysis is necessary to ensure that the patient doesn't move during the procedure, which could be disastrous. The problem is that you use your intercostal (chest) muscles to breathe. After induction of muscle paralysis, the patient can no longer breathe unassisted, so he or she is connected to a ventilation machine. This is done by passing a slender, flexible tube down the throat.

During the surgery itself, the "controlled coma" is maintained by a mixture of oxygen and nitrous oxide (aka "laughing gas"— the stuff dentists used before novocaine became available). Oftentimes, another substance is mixed in; sometimes an intravenous narcotic is used instead. When the last stitch is being tied off, muscle paralysis is reversed using another drug, and the tube is removed from the patient's throat. Then the patient is wheeled into the recovery room.

What this complicated procedure achieves is a patient who is insensitive to pain. More precisely, "controlled coma" includes

(1) the lack of voluntary movement in response to instructions to move, (2) the suppression of involuntary movement to surgical incisions, etc., (3) the absence of awareness of surgically induced pain, both during and after the procedure, and (4) amnesia (lack of memory) for surgical events, including verbal communications among the medical team.

All well and good. But, here lies the rub: While it's pretty clear that patients can't move during surgery and rarely remember having any pain, the last point—amnesia for surgical events—is not so clear. In fact, memory of surgical events, particularly auditory ones, can be reliably demonstrated. Let's take a look at a few. (Informed consent was obtained from all patients prior to including them in the studies below. These volunteers were patients already scheduled to undergo surgical procedures for various ailments.)

One researcher investigated a number of surgical patients who were experiencing a poor course of postoperative recovery.[38] They all seemed to have one thing in common: When hypnotized, they all reported recalling negative statements that had been made about them during surgery by members of the surgical team. One medical team staged a bogus crisis during ten surgeries.[39] Although none of the patients had any conscious memory of the event, a very different picture emerged when they were subsequently interviewed under hypnosis. When hypnotized, four of them reported the anesthetist's comments verbatim, and another four became highly agitated. These results suggest that patients' recoveries may be adversely affected by what is said during anesthesia.

You might feel somewhat uncomfortable with these studies because they rely on hypnosis to uncover the memories in question. But other evidence supports the notion that messages delivered to anesthetized patients do in fact get through. Surgical patients have been shown to recover more quickly if tapes suggesting relaxation and rapid healing are played to them during anesthesia.[40] In one set of studies, researchers played personalized messages to patients during surgery through earphones.[41] The messages included calming music, suggestions for postoperative comfort and rapid healing, *and* a suggestion that a specific response be enacted during a postsurgical interview. These responses included lifting the left index finger or pulling an earlobe when a certain verbal cue occurred during the upcoming interview. Although no patient reported any memory of the contents of the tape, 77 percent of those receiving the "lift finger" suggestion and 82 percent of those receiving the "pull ear" suggestion did so during the postoperative interview in response to the innocuous verbal cue. Clearly these patients were aware, at some level, of the verbal instructions they received.

How can they have memories for things that occurred when they weren't even conscious? The answer, it seems, has to do with the effects of anesthetic drugs on the explicit and implicit memory systems. In chapter 4 on memory, we saw that people often show evidence of implicit memory for events that they cannot consciously recall. For example, they will spontaneously complete word stems (e.g., TAB__) with words they were shown previously but cannot consciously recall. The same sort of dissociation between implicit and explicit memory has been demonstrated under anesthesia. *But*—and this is crucial—demonstrating the dissociation depends on which anesthetic drug is used.

When describing how the anesthetized state of "controlled coma" is maintained, I mentioned that sometimes a substance is mixed in with "laughing gas" *or* an intravenous narcotic is used instead. Patients in one set of studies had either isoflurane gas mixed in with the laughing gas to maintain their controlled comas *or* an injection of fentanyl, a narcotic.[42] During this stage, they were allowed to hear a list of rarely used words, such as *coruscate* and *tergiversation*. Following recovery, they were shown lists of words and asked to circle the words played to them during surgery. They couldn't; they reported having no memory of hearing anything. But when those who had received isoflurane were subsequently asked just to circle words that seemed familiar, they were found to circle words played to them during surgery more often than other words. Those who received the shot of fentanyl showed no preference for the words played to them during surgery. The inhalant isoflurane seems to suppress only the explicit memory system; the narcotic fentanyl seems to knock out both.

Results like these prompted one pair of researchers to propose a new classification system for anesthetics based on their psychological and physiological effects rather than simply on their chemical composition, which is how they are currently classified.[43] Using this system, four classes of anesthetic agents emerge. One class (e.g., halogenated ethers like isoflurane, and barbiturates) simply depresses most physiological functions and explicit memory, but spares implicit memory. A second class (e.g., fentanyl and other narcotics) leaves the heart and musculature alone, but impacts particular central nervous system functions, wiping out *both* explicit and implicit memory for events. A third class (e.g., diazepam and other benzodiazepine sedatives) selectively suppresses certain brain, heart, and muscle functions, along with explicit memory.[44] Finally, the fourth class (e.g., ketamine and etomidate) produces a profound disorganization of EEG and other brain functions while stimulating the heart and musculature.

The point of all this is that consciousness is a very complex phenomenon. Not all parts of consciousness are affected equally by the stimulation our brains receive. Even when impaired by drugs that wipe out our ability to consciously remember things, our nervous system still continues to record events going on around us, albeit in extremely subtle ways.

Plato likened the mind to a wax tablet upon which events left impressions of varying shapes and depths. It isn't a bad metaphor for our nervous systems. All events seem to leave traces of varying degrees, even upon unconscious brains. Perhaps that's because even when anesthetized or asleep, we want to make sure we don't miss anything. . . .

CHAPTER 6

Emotion: Why We Feel the Way We Do

As I pointed out in chapter 5, computers don't feel emotions, but biologically evolved biocomputers—otherwise known as brains—do. When you think about it, the ability to feel emotions gives one a tremendous survival advantage. Why wait for your sluggish reasoning processes to decide whether or not this growling grizzly means us harm when a good, strong fear reaction will mobilize our bodies to race to a safer place in which to carry on your philosophical enquiries? Why depend on conscious memories to tell you who has treated you kindly when a quickly formed emotional attachment will bond us to that person with ease? Our emotional reactions are powerful sources of information about what is safe and what is not safe in the world.

The difficulty, of course, is that sometimes our emotional reactions are at variance with our best interests. Sometimes, fleeing from grizzlies who can easily outrun you may not be a good idea, but curling up in a ball and playing dead is. Try telling that to your emotional brain as the grizzly snorts and paws your "lifeless" body. Romantic relationships with "mean mistreaters" are not such a good idea, but try explaining that to your palpitating heart.

The complexity of our emotional experiences has always been of interest to scientific psychologists, and much research has been undertaken to investigate the nature of our emotional reactions and attachments. The bottom line on this research is that we feel the way we do in part because of the way our brains are innately designed (nature) and in part because of the knowledge we acquire from our interactions with the world (nurture).

The innate side of our emotional life is readily demonstrated by studies of the brain. Different parts of the brain seem to be involved in processing different kinds of emotions. Experiencing sexual pleasure appears to depend of the involvement of the old brain, particularly the hypothalamus.[1] If the front and side portions of the hypothalamus in rats is stimulated with electrodes, the animals behave as though they are experiencing intense pleasure. In fact, if you sink an electrode in this section and allow the rat to self-administer electrical stimulation by pressing a bar, it will press the bar on the order of five thousand times an hour until it drops from exhaustion. When it wakes up, it will immediately start bar-pressing again. Clearly there is something pleasurable going on here. In contrast, if you sink the electrode in the middle back portion of the hypothalamus, the rat will behave as though it has received an intensely painful stimulus when it presses the bar. It will not go near the bar again. So it seems that at a primitive level, pleasure and pain are only a few millimeters apart in the brain.

Similar effects have been observed in humans. If a region near the hypothalamus (the septum) is stimulated in humans (in preparation for certain types of surgery), the patients often report feelings of euphoria and pleasure, and their thoughts will often turn to sexuality.[2] The sexual act itself and its accompanying emotions appear to be organized in the front end of the hypothalamus near the septal region. These regions become active only when they receive the right hormones from their blood supply. Because of their location, they are also extremely vulnerable to head injuries. For this reason, it is not surprising that impotence and a loss of interest in sex is sometimes seen among professional boxers.[3]

Like pain perception, there are two pathways involved in regulating aggressive behavior, and they both pass through the hypothalamus as well.[4] One pathway produces a "cold-blooded killer" response in which animals stalk and kill their prey. (This is the same pathway, incidentally, that elicits eating behavior when stimulated.[5]) Stimulating the other pathway produces a "rage" response, in which the animal behaves as though it were frightened and enraged.

The old brain also includes a structure called the limbic system, which has been implicated in emotions, motivation, and learning. This system is fully developed only in mammals. It is this system, and particularly one component of it called the amygdala, that is most ravaged by rabies. Electrical stimulation of the amygdala in humans (in preparation for surgery) produces intense emotional responses of fear (a strong desire to run away in terror) or rage (a strong desire to strike out at someone in the immediate environment).[6] Removing the amygdala entirely (in animals) produces very tame and hypersexual animals who also show reduced fear.

The picture that appears to be emerging is that the septum (which is involved in sexual pleasure) and the amygdala operate in opposite ways on the hypothalamus. The septum normally exerts a restraining influence on the hypothalamus; hence when it is damaged, rage results. The amygdala exerts an excitatory influence; hence, when it is damaged, docility and hypersexuality results.[7]

Processing emotions is not restricted to these older, more primitive brain structures. Recent work strongly implicates the two hemispheres of the cerebral cortex (our two brains) in the processing of emotions. It seems that the two hemispheres process different kinds of emotions and emotional reactions, working together in a "push-pull" type of relationship to help keep us in balance.[8] The right brain seems to be specialized for processing negative emotions (such as sadness, fear, disgust, and anger) and initiating withdrawal reactions. The left brain, in contrast, appears to be specialized for processing positive emotions (such as happiness, pleasant surprise, and amusement) and initiating approach reactions.

For example, some researchers showed film clips designed to elicit amusement or disgust to volunteers while monitoring their EEGs.[9] The left brain was found to respond more strongly than the right brain to the positive clips, while the right brain was extremely more active than the left in response to the negative clips.

Similar results have been observed using a slightly different methodology. In chapter 5, we saw that information could be presented to the right or left halves of the brain by having people fixate on a central point and then flashing a picture or word on either the right or the left side of that point. In patients with split brains, the information sent to one hemisphere never gets to the other. In people with normal brains, the information gets to the other hemisphere by traveling over the corpus callosum. But this takes time, meaning that the hemisphere that gets the information first has a definite time advantage in producing a response. Using this technique, researchers have been able to tease apart the recognition capacities of the two hemispheres for emotional stimuli.

One group of researchers presented pairs of cartoon drawings of different emotional expressions to a group of normal volunteers.[10] The first member of the pair was flashed for 85 milliseconds to either the right or the left brain; then the second member was presented for 1 second. The volunteers were required to indicate whether the second slide showed (a) the same cartoon character or a different one (face recognition), and (b) the same emotion or a different one (emotion recognition). The results showed that the right brain excelled at both tasks, especially when the face displayed a negative emotion. Results like these have been reported so often that some researchers believe the right brain contains a "lexicon" of facial emotions, much like the verbal lexicon of the left brain.[11]

These differential responses on the part of the left and right hemispheres can be observed even among newborns. Tastes that produce facial signs of disgust in newborns are accompanied by more activity in the right brain than tastes that produce positive facial expressions.[12] Similarly, when watching videotapes of an actress displaying laughter and distress, the left brains of ten-month-old infants responded more strongly (showed higher activity) during the laughter displays than during the distress displays.[13]

In fact, interpreting other people's facial expressions turns out to be remarkably easy for us. Ten–week–old infants have been shown to require only 1 *second* to figure out and respond to their mothers' facial displays.[14] When Mom displayed a happy face, the baby matched her expression by smiling back. When Mom displayed anger, the baby turned away, became fussy, and cried. When Mom displayed sadness, the most common response among the babies was a "self-soothing response" that included looking down and "mouthing" (e.g., lip and tongue sucking and moving the lips in and out).

This suggests that we are born with the ability to interpret emotional facial expressions in particular ways, a conclusion that is supported by cross-cultural studies. In a series of studies, photographs of Americans displaying emotions such as fear, anger, and happiness were shown to natives of more than a dozen countries, including Kenya, Japan, and Sweden, and to a preliterate tribe in New Guinea.[15] The participants' task was to identify the emotion in each photograph. The emotional expressions displayed by the Americans were readily interpreted by all participants regardless of culture, with nearly universal agreement occurring for displays of happiness, fear, and disgust. Conversely, American college students were asked to label the emotions portrayed by New Guineans in response to hypothetical situations, such as "You hear that your son is dead," or "Your friend has come and you are happy." Despite the enormous cultural differences between the groups, the Americans had little difficulty identifying the emotions portrayed. Certain emotional expressions seem to be universally understood.

These results would come as no surprise to Charles Darwin, originator of evolutionary theory. In 1872, Darwin published a companion volume to his 1871 book *The Descent of Man;* the 1872 book was entitled *The Expression of the Emotions in Man and Animals.*[16] Darwin was intrigued by the rich diversity of emotional displays among animals. Dogs snarl to threaten, and certain birds lower their tail feathers to achieve the same end. Mating displays broadcast "come hither" desires. Darwin believed the capacity to interpret emotional expressions played an important role in the survival of species. Put simply, if you can't tell the difference between a grin and a grimace, you could find yourself in deep trouble.

Interestingly, the two sexes have been found to respond differently to emotional facial expressions.[17] Females were found to be more sensitive overall to emotional expressions in pictures of *male* faces than to identical emotional expressions in female faces. Males were found to be even less sensitive than females to feminine expressions of sadness. It seems that when females are expressing sadness, no one is interested.

While the "division of labor" between the two hemispheres allows efficient processing of emotions, it also leaves us vulnerable to rather severe emotional imbalances if one hemisphere is damaged. Damage to the left anterior (front) side of the brain produces *catastrophic depression syndrome,* including deep apathy, a severe loss of interest and pleasure in objects and people, difficulty initiating voluntary action, and a tendency to react with deep sadness and depression to life stresses.[18] Injury on the right side of the brain, in contrast, is more likely to produce mania—feelings of exhilaration and an ability to inhibit one's actions.[19]

Damage to the right hemisphere also has catastrophic results for recognizing emotions. Studies of stroke and accident victims indicate that right-brain injuries produce severe deficiencies in the ability to remember emotional material, comprehend emotional tone of voice, appreciate humorous stimuli, and process emotional aspects of stories.[20]

The results of the following study illustrate this exceptionally well: Brain damaged patients and normal volunteers were asked to tell a story about three-picture sets.[21] One set depicted a neutral scene about frying an egg. The second set showed a visual/spatial sequence of activities involved in moving a box down off a high shelf by piling books on a chair and standing on them. The third picture set was the crucial one: It depicted a story about a girl whose dog is hit by a car. This is an emotional event and there was a good deal of emotion expressed by the cartoon characters.

Compared to normal volunteers, brain-damaged patients told stories that left out some of the important elements depicted in the pictures. But patients whose right brain was damaged showed a bigger deficit in producing emotional content in their stories than those with damage on the left side. They didn't mention, for example, crying on the part of the little girl or the witnesses in the cartoon. It was as though the emotional content of the story wasn't even there.

If you can't perceive, feel, or respond to emotional events, this could put you at a pretty distinct disadvantage socially. In fact, patients who've suffered right brain injuries do suffer socially. Brain-injured kids typically have great difficulty identifying emotional facial expressions, and make more errors, confusing positive and negative emotional tones of vignettes.[22] Following their accidents, they also display significantly less appropriate social behavior. This isn't surprising. As Darwin pointed out, if you can't read the emotions around you, how can you act appropriately?

Naturally occurring hemispheric asymmetries also seem to play a role in personality development. At any given moment, there is a certain amount of neural activity in our brains, even when we're not responding to any stimulation. Some people naturally show more activity in one hemisphere than the other, and these asymmetries seem to correspond to differences in temperament. Among psychiatric patients, those who have naturally higher activity in their right brains than in their left brains also show strong withdrawal-related emotional reactions to stimuli, more negative emotions, and a tendency to panic.[23] Depressed patients tend to have less activity in their left frontal lobes than their right frontal lobes, even when they are not currently suffering from an episode of depression.[24] This asymmetry seems to predispose them to depressive reactions to events. It is as though the asymmetry predisposes them to feel negative emotions more strongly.

Even benign emotional tendencies such as shyness seem to be associated with brain asymmetries.[25] Shyness (or behavioral inhibition, as it is technically known) is defined as a tendency to withdraw or freeze in unfamiliar situations. For example, shy two-and-one-half-year-olds refuse to play with unfamiliar toys, approach strangers, play with unfamiliar same-sex peers, or climb in toy tunnels, preferring instead to stand near their mothers. When the brain activity levels of shy kids were monitored, the results showed significant brain activation asymmetry, with more activity occurring on the right side of the brain than the left. In contrast, kids who were rated as uninhibited by their parents and by the experimenters showed the opposite asymmetry—more activity on the left than the right. Average kids showed a balanced level of activity between the two brain hemispheres.

When these asymmetries were more closely analyzed, it became apparent that the difference is really a matter of how active the left brain is. This means that shyness is a matter of not wanting to approach an unfamiliar object or person (left brain) rather than wanting to avoid or withdraw from it (right brain). If the results of brain activity analyses like these are correct, then shy kids don't really want to run away from new or unfamiliar things—they just don't want to approach them.

Given the close relationship between our individual physiological makeups and our emotional experiences, should we now conclude that our emotions are determined by physiology, pure and simple? As usual, real answers are never that simple. Just because we have more right brain activity than left doesn't mean we are doomed to a life of extreme shyness and depression. As one researcher put it: "This pattern [of brain activity asymmetry] is a marker of *vulnerability* to emotion and behavior which is associated with deficits in the approach system. Such vulnerability will become expressed as psychopathology only in response to relatively extreme life stresses."[26] In other words, it takes two to tango, and the dancers in this case are our internal physiology and our environment. In a kind and safe environment, differences in shyness might not even be noticed. In a destructive one, shyness might develop into full-blown depression and extreme withdrawal. For this reason, the power of the environment to shape our emotional responses should not be underestimated, particularly during the childhood years.

Developing organisms need nurturance, and the best way to ensure delivery of that nurturance is to form a mutual emotional attachment with an adult. Put another way, kids need to love parents who love them back. Freud believed this dependency on a parent's nurturing capacity formed the basis of a child's attachment to its parents (particularly mothers). He believed kids become attached to objects that provide them physical sustenance. The first such object is usually the mother, and so that is where the strongest bond is formed.

There is good reason to dispute this conjecture. In the 1950s, an experimental psychologist named Harry Harlow explored the mother-infant bond among a primate species very close to ours—rhesus monkeys.[27] He placed individual infant monkeys in cages with two kinds of artificial mothers. One "mother" had a body made of wire mesh, and was equipped with a nipple that dispensed nourishing milk. In contrast, the second "mother" had a soft, cuddly body with fuzzy, terry-cloth "skin." This "mother," however, was not equipped to deliver milk. If you were a monkey, which mother would you become attached to, the one that gave you vital nourishment or the one that gave you emotional "contact comfort"?

The answer in countless studies using this methodology was unequivocal: the cuddly mother won hands down. Although the monkeys nursed from the nourishing mother, they immediately returned to the cuddly mother and spent most of their time clinging to her. When they were placed in an unfamiliar room, they clung to the cuddly mother for comfort. The same was true when strange objects, such as noisy mechanical toys, were placed in their rooms—they headed straight for the cuddly mom to reassure themselves. It seems that where emotional attachments are concerned, the benefits derived from "contact comfort" outweigh the benefits derived from food.

If infants derive such emotional satisfaction from physical contact with a cuddly caretaker, what happens if they are reared without such contact? Harlow investigated this question as well.[28] He isolated infant rhesus monkeys in empty steel chambers for periods ranging from three months to one year. Then they were reintroduced into monkey "society."

The three-month isolation period had little effect on the monkeys' subsequent behavior, but isolation for periods longer than three-months was devastating. The monkeys were observed to huddle in corners, clasping themselves and rocking back and forth. When they were reintroduced to other monkeys, they cowered in fear. When faced with normal displays of aggression from their siblings, they withdrew, cowered, and bit themselves. When the motherless monkeys became mothers themselves, they rejected, ignored, or abused their infants.

Were these monkeys doomed to spend their lives in fear and

withdrawal, abusing their own offspring? Surprisingly, the answer is no. The ill effects of isolation were reversible under certain conditions.[29] When previously isolated monkeys were paired with normally reared, younger monkeys, they initially withdrew in fear from their roommates and huddled in corners. But over a period of a few weeks, as the roommates continued to pursue them and cling to them, the isolated monkeys began to cling back and eventually to play. After six months, they appeared to have recovered completely.

Interestingly, previously isolated female monkeys who were observed to abuse and reject their firstborns usually behaved in a normal, caring manner toward their subsequent offspring.[30] It seems that the younger, clinging firstborns had cured their abusive mothers in much the same way that the younger, clinging monkeys cured their antisocial roommates—but with great risk and suffering for themselves.

Perhaps you're wondering just how much we can generalize from monkeys to humans. There certainly is a good deal of similarity between the behavior of human kids and monkey kids. Frightened kids run to their parents just as rhesus monkeys do. Kids derive a good deal of emotional satisfaction from cuddling their parents and cuddling stuffed animals just as rhesus monkeys do. But the similarities run deeper than this.

Studies on infants in orphanages underscore the importance of contact comfort. Orphanages that separate infants into individual cubicles (to prevent the spread of disease) and limit physical contact to include only feeding and diapering also report high infant mortality rates.[31] Like Harlow's monkeys, infants who manage to survive appear relatively normal during the first three to four months of life. After that, however, they begin to show serious impairments in intellectual, emotional, and social development. Typically they either become extremely demanding of attention or withdraw from people entirely. Long-term detrimental effects have also been reported, including delinquency and heightened aggression.

Fortunately, just as in Harlow's studies, the ill effects of growing up without a family seem to be reversible. The key is transferring the kids to environments that are more emotionally nurturant. A paper published in 1966 on the long-term effects of orphanage environments makes this point clear. One group of children from an overcrowded orphanage were transferred to a home for mentally retarded adults where each was "adopted" by one adult to whom they became especially attached.[32] The results were quite dramatic. The children improved markedly on a number of behavioral and emotional measures and their intelligence test scores rose. As adults, they were indistinguishable from the rest of the population. In contrast, the children who remained in the orphanage lagged behind the rest of the population their whole lives on a variety of measures, including the intellectual, educational, and occupational levels achieved.

It seems pretty clear that emotional attachment depends more on obtaining emotional sustenance from an adult caregiver than nutritional sustenance. This brings us to another question: Does emotional attachment between kids and their parents depend on the *amount* of time they spend in contact with each other? This question is usually brought up in the context of working mothers, but I'd like to approach it from a slightly different perspective: Are kids attached to their working *dads?*

Psychologists define a secure attachment as one in which the child shows some distress over a parent's brief departure (such as leaving them with a new babysitter for a while) and a good deal of enthusiasm upon the parent's return. Children who panic when the parent departs, show indifference or ambivalence upon the parent's return, or ignore the parent entirely are said to have "insecure attachments." Using this definition, one group of researchers found that the majority (55 percent) of twelve- to twenty-one-month-old infants were more attached to their mothers, 25 percent showed more attachment to their fathers, and 20 percent were equally attached to both.[33]

Why the stronger attachment to the mother? Maybe the question should be why the infants were attached to their fathers at all. Studies done around the same time (the 1970s) showed that while at-home mothers spent a good deal of time interacting with their infants, working fathers spent disappearingly small amounts of time with them, sometimes as little as one minute a day during the first three months of life.[34] Despite such limited interaction, these kids still showed pretty strong attachments to their fathers. In fact, by the second year of life, boys prefer to interact with their fathers, and begin to show stronger attachments to them.[35] Even very young kids seem to know who their fathers are and develop pretty strong attachments, regardless of how much time he spends with them. But as the stronger attachment to the mothers in these studies show, more interaction results in an even stronger bond.

Along the same lines, numerous studies have compared emotional attachments to the mother formed by kids who spend their days in day care with those of kids who spend all day at home with their mothers. With the possible exception of infant day care,[36] no differences between the groups have been found on this factor, despite herculean efforts to find them.[37] It is remarkable how youngsters zero in on their parents and develop strong attachments to them, sometimes even despite abusive and dysfunctional behavior on the part of the parents.

Which brings us to another important question: Do *all* abused kids grow up to become child abusers themselves? An analysis of more than fifty studies dating back to 1963 of parents who were physically or sexually abused or were extremely neglected as children addressed this question.[38] On average, only about 30 percent of abused children went on to become abusers themselves as parents. The incidence of child abuse among parents who were *not* abused as children is 5 percent. This means that if you were abused as a child, you are six times more likely to become an abusive parent than someone who was not abused during childhood, but it is not inevitable.

Why do some abused kids go on to become abusers themselves while others don't? Several "protective factors" that act to break the cycle of abuse were identified in this exhaustive analysis. Some of these factors make intuitive sense. For example, parents who didn't repeat the cycle tended to have more extensive support from family and friends, including warm and supportive spouses. As children, they also were more likely to have had a relationship with an adult who did not abuse them, and who helped to soothe the hurts inflicted on them.

Interestingly, one counterintuitive factor was also found. Survivors of child abuse who didn't abuse their own children tended to be *more* openly angry about the abuse they received as children. This seems counterintuitive because you might assume that the more angry you are, the more likely you are to take that leftover anger out on your kids. In fact, what seems to happen is that by becoming angry at their abusive parents and rejecting them, these abused kids are also rejecting their parents' way of raising them. In effect, they are saying, "What you did to me was wrong and I reject you and your way of treating kids." Those who don't feel angry over their ill-treatment are more likely to accept and hence identify with their abusive parents. By accepting them and identifying with them, they put themselves at risk for incorporating their parents' abusive behavior into their own approaches to parenting. The old "It was good for me so it's good enough for my kids" attitude. This, of course, repeats the cycle. In fact, numerous studies have shown that children who receive severe physical punishment at home are more aggressive than other children.[39] This is true even when other factors are equated between the families, such as socioeconomic status, degree of marital violence, and the child's temperament.[40]

Our social environments continue to impact on our emotional states even when we are grown and our personalities are pretty well developed, as the results of the following study make especially clear.[41] Four groups of volunteers were shown a movie of circumcision rites among Australian aborigines. Aborigine males are circumcised when they reach adolescence as part of a rite of passage to adulthood. Needless to say, this is not a painless experience for the boys, and it is not a pleasant thing to watch. The movie was therefore expected to produce some pretty strong emotional responses from the viewers.

Although all volunteers saw the identical movie, the sound tracks that accompanied the movie differed among the four groups. The sound track played to the first group of volunteers (Trauma sound track) emphasized the gore and the pain suffered by the boys. The sound track for the second group (Denial sound track) ignored or downplayed the gore and suffering, stating, for example, that the boys were young and strong and would soon recover from any ill effects of the procedure. The third group heard an intellectually oriented sound track (Intellectual sound track) that talked about the anthropological significance of the rite and its effects on the culture. The fourth group (No sound track) watched the movie being shown in silence—no sound track accompanied it. Importantly, each participant's GSR (drop in the electrical conductance of the skin) was measured while he or she watched the movie. Like heart rate, GSR increases under stress, thereby providing an objective measure of emotional repsonses.

The GSRs of the group that saw the movie without any sound track provided a baseline measure of how distressing the movie was on its own, without any other information to "muddy the waters." These viewers showed pretty large responses, indicating that they were experiencing a good deal of distress. The Trauma sound track group showed even larger responses to the movie. Having the gore and pain emphasized verbally made the viewing of this movie even more stressful. But—and this is a very important point—the Intellectual sound track group showed very little distress while watching the movie. Their skin conductance levels changed very little, indicating that the sound track that legitimized the pain and gore significantly reduced the viewer's emotional responses to what they were seeing. The Denial sound track also blunted the viewers' emotional reactions, but not as much as the Intellectual sound track did.

These results show quite clearly that what we're told can sometimes override what our eyes are plainly telling us—especially if it legitimizes what we see. They might also explain the huge disparity sometimes seen between a jury's emotional reaction to a videotape of a crime and non-juror's reactions. In 1992 a man named Rodney King was severely beaten by Los Angeles police during an arrest. A witness videotaped the entire incident, and the tape was shown during the subsequent trial of the arresting officers. The jurors essentially watched the videotape with an "intellectual sound track," that is, with experts explaining and justifying each blow the police delivered. The rest of the country just saw the videotape on the evening news. Like the groups in the study described above, very different emotional reactions were observed: The jury acquitted the police, and Los Angeles erupted in violent riots.

In fact, determining how to interpret emotionally tinged stimulation is really a very difficult task. Exploring this on a lighter note, consider a typical "girl meets boy" scenario. The girl knows she is smitten with the boy because just being with him causes her heart to pound, her palms to sweat, and her stomach to flutter as though it were filled with butterflies. Now consider a typical "girl meets dinosaur" scenario. The girl knows she is terrified of the dinosaur because . . . well, her heart is pounding, her palms are sweating, and her stomach flutters as though it were filled with butterflies. In fact, similarities like these led one playwright to conclude that one could mistake falling in love for a severe case of indigestion.

As far-fetched as this might seem, it is not far from the truth. There is an odd but interesting literature on interpersonal attraction whose results can be summarized as "Adrenaline makes the heart grow fonder." What they all seem to show is that we often misinterpret physiological arousal as interpersonal attraction. If our hearts beat rapidly, our palms sweat, and we feel flushed in the presence of another person, we think it must be love—even if these physiological reactions are induced by something else in the environment. (Unfortunately, most of these studies use male participants only.)

For example, young men in one study were asked to meet a female experimenter individually on a bridge where they would be interviewed and asked to write a brief story.[42] Half of the men met the experimenter on a safe, solid wooden structure, 10 feet wide, which spanned a small stream. The other half, however, met her on a rickety structure, only 5 feet wide and 450 feet long, that tilted, swayed, and wobbled 230 feet in the air above rocks and rapids. When the participant had written his story, the experimenter gave him her phone number. The experimenter received substantially more callbacks from the men she had interviewed on the rickety bridge, suggesting that these men had misinterpreted the physiological arousal they felt on the bridge (i.e., fear) as romantic or sexual interest in the experimenter.

In some related work, young men who anticipated receiving strong and painful electric shocks reported feeling more interested in dating and kissing an attractive female confederate than men who anticipated receiving only mild shocks.[43] (Of course, no one received any shocks at all.) Similar results were observed among men asked to run in place for 120 seconds. These men gave higher romantic attractiveness ratings to women on a videotape than men who were asked to run in place for only 15 seconds.[44] In each case, the men misinterpreted their pounding hearts and sweaty palms as romantic arousal. (Maybe we should all arrange for our first dates to take place in amusement parks or hot air balloons!)

Taken together, this body of research indicates that whether we experience an emotional response or not—and which emotion we experience—depends on three factors: our own particular neural design, an external event, and how we interpret things. What we experience emotionally depends as much on how we label internal and external events as on the events themselves.

One final area of research that I would like to touch on addresses an issue of great concern today, and that is inappropriate, unbridled aggression. Billions of dollars are being spent in the United States alone in an effort to contain and redirect the growing propensity to engage in violent aggression. Inappropriate aggression has been the subject of decades of research by scientific psychologists, and entire books have been devoted to it. I can't begin to do justice to the enormity of this literature. Instead, I will highlight some of the findings that address the question "Why do we aggress?"

The simplest answer to this question is that our brains are designed for it. There are two pathways that mediate aggression in the brain. This doesn't mean, however, that aggressive behavior is inevitable. Electrically stimulating either aggression pathway anywhere from the brain stem to the old brain produces an aggressive response, but the intensity that is required to produce the response increases the higher up the path the stimulation occurs. One interpretation of this phenomenon is that lower brain structures, such as the hypothalamus, don't initiate aggressive behavior, but instead feed their information to the cerebral cortex, the seat of rational thought. The cortex organizes all the information at its disposal into a meaningful whole and initiates the appropriate emotional and behavioral responses.

For example, if an aggressive pathway is stimulated in dominant rhesus male monkeys, they will aggress against subordinate males in the immediate environment—but not against females who are also present.[45] If the same pathways are stimulated in the subordinate males, they will cower and behave submissively. Clearly, their basic aggressive responses are modified by what they've learned about their places in the social hierarchy.

Like other primates, we also modify our aggressive behavior based on a number of different factors. For example, frustration is known to increase the likelihood of aggressive behavior. But having the right environmental cues matters as well. For example, the level of shock participants in one study chose to administer to another person depended on two things: the level of frustration they experienced while trying to solve a series of puzzles and the type of movie they saw.[46] The more frustrated the participants were, the greater the level of shock they chose to administer. But frustrated participants who watched a violent boxing movie delivered more shock than frustrated participants who watched a nonviolent track movie. (The shock generator was not hooked up, so no shocks were in fact administered. But the volunteers didn't find that out until the debriefing that followed completion of the experiment.)

Similar results were found when participants were frustrated in rooms containing either a gun or a badminton racket.[47] When they were later allowed to deliver "shocks" to a confederate, those who were frustrated in the presence of the gun delivered more shock than those who were frustrated in the presence of the badminton racket. Environmental cues that are associated with aggression seem to elicit more aggression from us when we are frustrated.

Another factor that influences whether or not we behave aggressively is whether we have reason to believe the victim will retaliate. Generally speaking, fear of retaliation inhibits aggressive behavior. But there are two caveats. First, fear of retaliation doesn't work for "crimes of passion," that is, when the aggressor is extremely angry with the victim.[48] When in the grip of intense anger, many of us will aggress even if we know we will suffer for it later. Second, and more interesting, threats of retaliation work only when the aggressor is *sure* that the intended victim will retaliate.[49]

This has clear implications for law enforcement. As law enforcement officials often point out, if a crime is not solved within a few days of its being reported, the probability of its ever being solved plummets. In large urban areas where crime is rampant and police departments are understaffed, literally hundreds of crimes are unsolved in any given year. According to some analysts, the reduced probability of being caught has played a major role in increasing crime rates, a belief reflected in the following excerpt from a *Time* magazine interview with a convicted murderer who has been in prison since 1962:

> Q. Then what will stop violent crime?
> A. Only one thing: the certainty of apprehension. If a criminal fears that he is going to get caught, he will think twice before he robs or steals. And it won't matter if the sentence is one year or 100 years.[50]

Another factor that seems to be instrumental in reducing aggressive behavior is watching someone handle anger nonaggressively. One technique that has been used successfully with aggressive children involves having them generate alternatives to aggressive behavior.[51] Aggressive children typically live in family environments where aggression is the response of choice to any problem. They literally have never seen anyone handle a frustrating or provoking situation in any other way. The key is getting them to understand that they can choose how to behave. To do this, they are asked to imagine a particular situation (e.g., someone calls them a name on the playground), and then to generate as many possible responses as they can think of. The first is invariably an aggressive response (e.g., "I'd slap him upside the head"). That response is accepted as one alternative, and the child is asked to think of what else he can do (e.g., "Yep, that's one thing you could do. What else could you do?"). This is continued with a variety of imagined scenarios, and then in actual situations. Eventually, the "Provoked-Act" cycle is broken, replaced by a "Stop–Think of alternatives–Choose–Act" cycle instead. The child becomes empowered by realizing he has a choice about how to respond to provocation.

The difficulty, of course, is that while one is busy demonstrating nonviolent ways to handle anger, the media are busy bombarding us with glorification of violence. Does watching violent TV programs increase aggressive behavior? A series of studies were conducted to investigate this issue, tracking people from several countries from age eight in 1960 to age thirty.[52] People who watched the most TV violence as children were found to have a higher incidence of criminal convictions as adults, rely more on physical punishment when disciplining their own children, and display more aggression than average.

The complicating factor is: How do we know which way the causal arrow points? The results reported could also be interpreted to mean that insensitive people who are prone to aggression like to watch TV violence. Other studies, however, suggest that watching violence really does cause insensitivity. For example, GSR responses (skin stress responses) of a group of eight- to ten-year-old children were monitored while they watched either a violent excerpt from a TV police show or an exciting but nonviolent volleyball game.[53] Overall arousal to the violent TV show and the nonviolent volleyball game was found to be nearly identical, indicating that both shows were clearly exciting to the viewers. Then the children were asked to monitor another group of children over closed-circuit TV while the experimenter went to make a phone call. Unbeknownst to the children, they were shown a videotaped sequence in which a group of pre-schoolers engaged in a series of aggressive actions beginning with an exchange of derogatory comments and escalating into physical aggression and property damage. The group that saw the violent TV show responded significantly less strongly (had smaller GSR responses) to the display of violence among the preschoolers than the kids who saw the volleyball game. They just weren't as shook up by it.

Using this same technique, other studies have shown that viewing TV violence makes kids slower to seek adult help when witnessing real-life violence and more willing to witness a much higher level of physical violence before seeking help.[54] In fact, after viewing a violent movie, many kids in these studies didn't bother to seek help at all.

Similar results have been found with adults (college students). After watching violent film clips, male undergraduates showed reduced physiological responses when witnessing real-life violence (e.g., film clips of the 1968 Democratic convention in Chicago)[55] and when retaliating against someone who has angered them.[56] Not only did they show less distress while retaliating, they also retaliated with higher levels of aggression.

If watching violence tends to make us more violent, how does all the sex on TV affect us? A good deal of research seems to indicate that watching *violent* erotica makes men more violent against women. For example, male participants in one study were given the opportunity to deliver shocks (again, no real shocks were delivered) to a male or female confederate, supposedly as punishment for errors committed on a learning task.[57] Before doing this, they watched a short videotape. Some saw a nonviolent erotic film, some saw a violent rape, and some saw a film containing neither sex or violence. The men who saw the erotic film delivered no greater shocks to the confederates than those who saw the bland film. But the men who saw the film of the violent rape delivered significantly stronger shocks *to the female confederate*. The rape film seemed to have elicited more aggression against women specifically.

Similarly, after watching two violent rape films, a group of men gave higher acceptability ratings for violence against women and exhibited stronger beliefs that women secretly liked to be raped ("rape myth") than men who had watched two neutral films.[58] Women showed the opposite reaction. After watching the rape films, women showed lower acceptance of violence against women and more disbelief in the rape myth. The bottom line on pornography and aggression seems to be that erotica alone has little affect on male aggression, but mixing violence with erotica unleashes aggression *aimed specifically at females*.

In numerous studies on sexual aggression, 40 percent of men surveyed agreed with the statement "I might force a woman to commit sexual acts against her will if I thought I could get away with it." When the words "force a woman to commit sexual acts" were changed to "rape a woman," 18 percent still agreed with the statement.[59] Why this willingness to aggress against the physically weaker sex? Perhaps the answer lies in the sexual behavior of our brethren primates.

In the wild, great apes mate infrequently, and sexual aggression occurs rarely. When male orangutans, gorillas, or chimpanzees are housed with females *who cannot escape,* however, sexual aggression appears. For example, orangutans in the wild mate approximately three times a month. But when researchers at the Yerkes Regional Primate Center of Emory University housed male orangutans with females who could not escape, mating occurred every day, with the majority involving forcing copulation on the females. The aggression stopped immediately and mating resumed the frequency observed in the wild when the females were given a way to escape. This was done by making a door in the female's enclosure that was too small for the male to fit through. Interestingly, even if the female came into the male's compartment, he did not aggress against her. *As long as he was aware that she could get away, he did not aggress.* The researchers also noticed that the females struggled and resisted when they knew they could get away; when they knew they couldn't get away, on the other hand, their attempts were halfhearted, and they gave up quickly.

Can we generalize from the great apes to humans? The researchers concluded: "These data support the interpretation that sexual aggression to some degree is an inherent characteristic of the behavioral repertoires of our closest biological affiliates and that conditions that render the females vulnerable to such aggression lead to its increased occurrence." Which conditions are those? ". . . the probability of a human female encountering sexual aggression is directly related to conditions—social, cultural, and environmental—that *permit the male's dominance over the female to assume the predominant role in the regulation of sexual interactions* and thereby reduce the female's prerogatives for refusing sexual overtures" (italics mine). They also point out that ". . . such aggression is likely to be expressed under a variety of conditions unless society and individuals take specific measures to preclude it."[60]

So let's take stock of what these studies tell us: Like murder and thieving, sexual aggression is in the nature of the species. The greater the dominance of males over females, the greater the likelihood of sexual harassment and rape. Situations that strongly hinder a female's ability to say no by giving the male a good deal of power over her (e.g., male boss and female worker; angry working husband and dependent wife; frustrated, aggressive male and lone female) will be exactly those situations in which sexual harassment and rape are most likely to occur.

The antidote is to ensure that it is realistically possible for females to say no. This means empowering women so that they are not in positions of dependency—an argument the United States strongly advanced at the 1994 Cairo conference on world population growth. And just as the U.S. delegates pointed out at that conference, the surest way to empower women is to increase their earning power.

Economic and political issues aside, one nagging question still remains: If inappropriate aggression causes so many of the world's evils, then *why* do we aggress inappropriately? The simplest answer is, well, because it makes us feel good. When we become angry or frustrated, we suffer a number of changes in our physiology. The most destructive is an increase in blood pressure. Expressing that anger or frustration through retaliation has been found to reduce blood pressure more quickly than ignoring an attack or making a friendly response.[61] In fact, holding anger in when provoked is associated with a higher incidence of chronic high blood pressure and blocked arteries than an expressive "anger-out" response style.[62]

But the relationship between aggression and cardiac events doesn't end there: If you feel frightened or guilty after you aggress, your blood pressure doesn't return to normal. It just hangs up there in the stratosphere.[63] Furthermore, a good deal of research indicates that, like the subordinate monkeys whose aggression pathways were stimulated, we are most likely to feel frightened or guilty when we aggress against a high-status person. The results of one study illustrate this point clearly: Individual men and women were abused and harrassed by a male experimenter and later given the opportunity to give him electric shocks.[64] Sometimes the experimenter presented himself as a faculty member (high status) and sometimes he presented himself as a lowly student (low status). Angering the volunteers caused their blood pressure to rise significantly. But when the angered volunteers believed the experimenter was a lowly student, they experienced a quick return to baseline blood pressure levels after shocking him. In contrast, when they believed he was a professor, their blood pressure remained high. Other studies have shown that when given a choice whether to aggress or not aggress against someone who has provoked us, most of us will aggress only if the provocateur is of lower status than ourselves.[65] In fact, many of us will even choose to aggress against an innocent third party in order to reduce our frustration rather than retaliate against a person whose status is higher than our own.

Well, you can see the quandary we are in. Being provoked and frustrated raises our blood pressure and makes us feel very uncomfortable. If we keep that anger in, we will do ourselves physical damage. If we express it, we feel relief. It is immensely reinforcing, therefore, to behave aggressively. In fact, a good deal of research shows that provoked individuals who behave aggressively are *more* likely to respond with aggression in future encounters—no doubt because it provides such immediate relief.[66] But if the ones who deserve our retaliation are high-status individuals, many of us just go right on feeling physically uncomfortable even if we do aggress. So what do we do? We find scapegoats. Aggressing against those smaller or less powerful than ourselves relieves our physical discomfort. In fact, some people become quite *addicted* to this rush of relief. They're called bullies, tyrants, muggers, rapists, child abusers, wife beaters, and sexual predators.

7

Two Extremely Simple but Extremely Powerful Adaptive Mechanisms

As I pointed out in previous chapters, brain tissue has a very curious property, and that is the ability to *learn*. In fact, our brains automatically detect two fundamental aspects of its experiences and those are (1) the associations that naturally occur among stimuli and (2) the relationship between behavior and its consequences. Of the two, the capacity to automatically detect associations among events is more fundamental. This capacity can be observed among creatures as primitive as a sea slug or as complex as a human being. Through a process of stimulus substitution, called *classical conditioning,* brain tissue can generalize among stimuli, discriminate among stimuli, and extinguish learned associations. These properties can be observed even in nerve tissue in petri dishes (in vitro).

Classical conditioning is an extremely powerful mechanism that influences who we are and how we react to situations, particularly emotionally charged ones. If you have ever found yourself feeling nauseous at the sight of a certain food, such as oysters, after a single bad experience, you've been classically conditioned. If you have ever found yourself feeling nostalgic upon hearing a song that was playing the first time you fell in love, you've been classically conditioned. Psychological research has even implicated classical conditioning in two seemingly un-related phenomena: drug addiction and phobias. But before I go into that, let's answer a more basic question: What is classical conditioning?

The best way to explain classical conditioning is via an example: The time is 1970, the height of the Vietnam War. A healthy young man (call him George) has just received a summons from his draft board to report for a qualifying physical. Like many young men of the time, George isn't a conscientious objector to all war (he'd have served gladly in World War II), he just doesn't believe in the Vietnam War and the "domino effect" of communism in Indochina. Being a cynic, George also doesn't believe in battling bureaucracies. As his mother told him, you can't fight city hall.

With these thoughts in mind, George concocts a plan. He borrows a sphygmomanometer (the contraption used to measure blood pressure) from a friend who is a nurse. He locks himself in his garage and spends the rest of the afternoon doing something mysterious. When George reports for his physical, the medical attendant is alarmed to find that George's blood pressure is dangerously high. He is rejected by the draft board and told to see a doctor to obtain medication for controlling his blood pressure. When George leaves, his blood pressure mysteriously returns to normal.

How did George manipulate his blood pressure? He used classical conditioning to teach his body to respond quite violently to sphygmomanometers. Here's how: George knew that one of the effects of electric shock is to raise blood pressure temporarily. (Most· fear- or pain-inducing stimuli have that effect.) Armed with this information, an electric battery, and a sphygmomanometer, George set up a conditioning session that allowed his body to learn an association between sphygmomanometer cuffs and painful electric shock. He did this by shocking himself everytime he pumped up the cuff. He repeated this procedure numerous times: pump-shock, pump-shock, pump-shock, etc. Soon, just pumping up the cuff was enough to send George's blood pressure soaring. The pumping itself became a frightening stimulus to George's emotional system. When the medical attendant at the draft board wrapped the sphygmomanometer cuff around George's arm in order to take his blood pressure,

George's blood pressure soared. His body anticipated a painful shock.

Let's analyze what George did a little more closely. George continually paired a neutral stimulus (cuff pumping) with another stimulus (shock) that naturally evokes a certain response (rise in blood pressure). Eventually, the neutral stimulus came to *substitute* for the "unlearned" one in producing the blood pressure response. For reasons that I won't go into, psychologists refer to this type of learning as classical conditioning.

George's scenario might sound familiar to you. It probably reminded you of Pavlov's dogs. With good reason. It is the same phenomenon. The actual research interest of Ivan Pavlov, the Russian physiologist, was the digestive system. When animals (including humans) take food into their mouths, they salivate. Salivation is the first step in digestion and, once begun, it is almost impossible to stop. It is a reflex, like jerking your leg when the doctor whacks your knee with a mallet.

In 1927, Pavlov noticed something very interesting among his experimental animals.[1] When his lab assistant rang the bell that signaled feeding time, the animals began to salivate. He found this very intriguing because it meant that his animals had, in his words, *"learned* a reflex": The bell substituted for food in eliciting the salivation reflex!

Pavlov discovered some other interesting properties of this mechanism. The first is *stimulus generalization.* Let's use George as an example. Suppose I were to take a scarf and tie it around George's arm. You might be surprised to find out that George's blood pressure would rise. The scarf-tying event is highly similar to the cuff-pumping event, and George's blood pressure response *generalizes* from the original stimulus to one that is highly similar to it. The more similar the new stimulus is to the one used in the conditioning trials, the more likely it is that generalization will occur.[2]

Now suppose we redo the conditioning trials with two cuffs, a red one and a black one. Shocks are delivered only when the red cuff is applied and never when the black cuff is applied. Soon, George's blood pressure would rise only when he saw that the red cuff was applied; very little if any effect would be observed when he saw he was getting the black one. This is called *discrimination;* George's body has learned to discriminate between the dangerous, shock-producing event (red cuff) and the safe, no-shock event (black cuff). Remember that George isn't "trying" to learn anything. Instead, his brain is automatically recording an association between some pretty striking environmental events. It is responding to environmental contingencies whether George is aware of it or not.

Finally, we might ask whether George must now go through life having his blood pressure sky-rocket every time someone tries to take it with a sphygmomanometer. The answer is yes— conditioned responses can last a lifetime—unless the response is extinguished. This means that George must repeatedly put on the cuff and pump it up without delivering any shock. It may take thousands of *extinction* trials; it is very difficult to get the brain to "forget" a learned reflex. In fact, "extinguished" responses are often just "masked" or "suppressed" responses; they can reappear years later if the right conditions are present. This is called *spontaneous recovery.*

Given this framework, let's now return to the issue of drug addiction. Consider the following puzzling facts:

- When drug addicts overdose, typically they have *not* taken more than their usual dose. In one study, 70 percent of heroin addicts receiving emergency treatment for overdoses had *not* taken more than their customary dose, but they had shot up *in unfamiliar surroundings.*[3]
- When addicts do shoot up repeatedly in familiar surroundings, they require higher and higher doses in order to achieve the same "high." This is called *drug tolerance.* The same is true of alcoholics.
- When addicts don't get their usual "fix," they typically go through withdrawal symptoms. These symptoms are usually much worse if the addict undergoes them *in the environment where he or she normally shoots up.*

These facts have one thing in common: In each case, the environment seems to be modulating the drug's effect on the addict.

How? One answer is classical conditioning.[4] According to the *opponent process theory of drug dependency,* the brain learns to compensate for the upcoming stress of drug intake *when there are environmental cues that are reliably associated with the stress.* It does this by producing a response that is the *opposite* of the drug's effect.

A variety of drugs have been used in testing this theory, but the studies I'll be reporting here used morphine. For this reason, I will refer to the effects of morphine rather than heroin in explaining how the opponent process works: Morphine causes heart rate and pain sensitivity to drop—you feel relaxed and released from pain. This is the unconditioned stimulus-response system. But there are a lot of environmental cues that surround the shooting up event, such as needles, tourniquets, Bunsen burners, and the room or neighborhood where the event occurs. What happens if the addict shoots up using the same dosage in the same environment over and over again? The first time, the brain hasn't yet learned anything, and the addict gets the full impact of the drug. As the environmental cues continue to be paired with the drug, however, the brain begins to compensate for the drug's effect. As soon as the needles and tourniquets are brought out, the addict's brain "knows" that very soon something is going to happen that causes a dramatic drop in heart rate and pain sensitivity, just as George's brain came to "know" that the sphygmomanometer cuff meant that painful shock was coming. In this case, however, the brain attempts to compensate for the upcoming dramatic changes by producing a response that negates those changes, that is, by *increasing* the body's heart rate and pain sensitivity. This is the learned part of the physiology of drug addiction. When the morphine is injected, its effects are canceled out because it will lower heart rate and pain sensitivity levels that are *already elevated.* As a result, the addict doesn't get as high, and he or she increases the drug dose. The brain learns to compensate for that dose, and in time the addict doesn't get as high with the new higher dose. So he or she increases the dose again. This is called *drug tolerance.* An addict can take a much larger dose of a drug than the average person and still feel normal. An alcoholic can drink a lot more than the average person and not seem drunk. They have become tolerant to their respective drugs.

But what happens if these drug-tolerant addicts change environments, shooting up with their customary high dose in a new place with unfamiliar equipment? Since the old environmental cues aren't there, the learned compensatory response won't occur. Heart rate and pain sensitivity stay at their normal levels. Hence when they take their usual dose, they overdose—they get the full impact of the high drug dose without the body's compensating response. And that's how they can overdose on their usual dosage.

What happens if addicts return to their old environment, but don't shoot up? The old environmental cues evoke the learned compensatory response (increased heart rate, increased pain sensitivity), but now the drug isn't taken to bring things back to normal. In other words, they'll feel intense physiological withdrawal symptoms. Withdrawal symptoms, or cravings, are just the body's learned compensatory responses, and without the drug's "normalizing" effect, they are very unpleasant. That's why addicts need to shoot up—to bring their bodies back to equilibrium.

Support for this theory comes from two sources: The first source is clinical case studies of human addicts. In severe addiction cases, addicts are frequently sent to detoxification programs, usually in hospital settings. After a period of weeks or months "in the tank," they are sent back home where they struggle to "stay clean." Does this work? The relapse rate after release from detoxification programs has been estimated at 90 percent in the first year, a rate that mystifies and frustrates doctors and addicts alike.[5] Julia Phillips, the Hollywood producer who made the movie *The Sting,* tells of her attempt to kick her cocaine habit by going to the famous Mayo Clinic.[6] Upon returning home, she managed to stay clean for only one week. As you can imagine, these rapid relapses take a great emotional toll on addicts who are struggling to overcome their addictions, leading to feelings of hopelessness and disgust with themselves.

Perhaps this statistic is a bit less puzzling now that you can see it within the framework of opponent process theory: When the addicts change environments by going into the hospital, it is much easier for them to "kick the habit" since the old environmental cues are not there to help trigger withdrawal symptoms. When they return home, however, all those cues are reinstated, and the cravings begin again in earnest. This leads to relapse. Here is a typical case:

The patient was a twenty-eight-year-old man with a ten-year history of narcotic addiction. He was married and the father of two children. He reported that while addicted, he was arrested and incarcerated for six months. He reported experiencing severe withdrawal during the first four or five days in custody, but later he began to feel well. He gained weight, felt like a new man, and decided that he was finished with drugs. He thought about his children and looked forward to returning to his job. On the way home after release from prison, he began thinking of drugs and feeling nauseated. As the subway approached his stop, he began sweating, tearing from his eyes, and gagging. This was an area where he had frequently experienced narcotic withdrawal symptoms while trying to acquire drugs. As he got off the subway, he vomited onto the tracks. He soon bought drugs, and was relieved. The following day he again relieved his withdrawal symptoms by injecting heroin. The cycle repeated itself over the next few days and soon he became readdicted.[7]

In a more controlled study, former addicts were found to display physiological signs of narcotic withdrawal months or even years after kicking their habit when they were asked to perform the "cooking up" ritual while their vital signs were monitored.[8] Large changes in GSR (skin stress conductance) and heart rate have also been observed in former heroin addicts while they watched a videotape of heroin preparation.[9] These former addicts also reported intense cravings and anxiety while watching the film. Withdrawal symptoms and cravings like these have also been reported among former alcoholics when they were asked to enter a mock barroom complete with a lingering odor of bourbon.[10]

If it's easier to overcome an addiction in a new environment (such as a hospital), what if addicts never returned to their old, drug-linked environment? Would they stay clean? Some data on Vietnam vets suggests they very well might.

In September of 1971, fourteen thousand soldiers were brought home from Vietnam. Twenty percent (or twenty-eight hundred) had become addicted to drugs while serving there. Congress was aware of this, and significant social problems, including a high incidence of drug-related crimes committed by the vets, were expected when they came home. In fact, the relapse rate for Vietnam vets turned out to be only seven percent.[11] The veterans left their drug-associated environments behind them, making it easier to kick their addiction habits. In comparison, Vietnam vets and other men of comparable age and socioeconomic status who developed addictions *at home* and then tried to kick their habits evidenced a 70 percent incidence of relapse.[12]

The difficulty with clinical case studies is that so many factors are free to vary, one is never really sure which factors in fact produce the phenomenon under study. One can't rule out the possibility, for example, that the low relapse rate among vets was simply due to their having left a life-threatening situation for the safety of home. In situations like this, it becomes particularly important to take the issue into the laboratory for more controlled study. This is what a number of researchers have done, and the results of such studies continually show that the impact of simply changing environments on drug addiction can't be dismissed.

For example, rats made tolerant to morphine by giving them gradually increasing doses of morphine were then given an extremely large dose of morphine either in the same environment where they received their tolerance training or in a different environment.[13] Only a few of the drug-tolerant rats died when they received the shot in the old environment. When the shot was administered in a new environment, however, twice as many drug-tolerant rats died. These results are consistent with the opponent process theory. When the overdose was administered in the old environment, the familiar environmental cues triggered the body's compensating responses, so the effect of the drug was ameliorated. In the new environment those cues were absent, so the body's compensating responses were not triggered, and the rats got the full impact of the overdose.

In another study, one group of rats received increasingly larger shots of morphine whenever an audiovisual cue (flashing lights and a musical tone) was present. Another group received the same schedule of increasingly larger doses, but *never* received a shot when the cue was present.[14] In effect, the audiovisual cue was a "safe" time for the second group of rats, since it meant no shot was going to be delivered then. After both groups had achieved the same level of drug tolerance, they received a shot of morphine while the audiovisual cue was present. Notice that the shot should have been expected by the first group because they always got their injections when the cue was present. But the shot should have come as a surprise to the second because the cue had always meant "safe time" for them.

As predicted by opponent process theory, the group that was expecting the shot remained drug tolerant; they showed a normal degree of sensitivity to pain. The second group, however, for whom the shot was a surprise, showed a high degree of insensitivity to pain. (Pain sensitivity is usually tested by seeing how long it takes them to jerk their paws or tails away from a heat source.)

These studies strongly suggest that drug tolerance is not just a matter of the body's "numbing out" to repeated exposure to the drug. If that were the case, all rats that received drug tolerance training should have shown the same amount of tolerance since they all received the same amount of exposure to the drug. This didn't happen; instead, it mattered a good deal whether the environment remained the same or not when the new dose was administered.

Withdrawal symptoms have also been induced among drug-dependent rats by placing them in their tolerance-training environment without their expected shot.[15] Their brains tried madly to compensate for an injection that never came. That left the rats with hypersensitivity to pain and racing hearts. In contrast, another group, who had not learned to associate that environment with drugs, didn't show these effects when placed there.

Interestingly, another study showed that morphine-addicted rats who overcame their addiction habit were far more likely to become readdicted if the morphine was reintroduced in their old, drug-associated environments as opposed to new environments.[16] The rats in these studies were not injected with morphine; instead, the morphine was placed in their water source for sixty days, and then withdrawn for thirty days. Following the withdrawal period, the rats who were returned to their old drug-associated environment showed a decided preference for morphine-tainted water, unlike the rats who were moved to a different environment.

These results have been replicated in numerous laboratories using a variety of drugs including alcohol, barbiturates, and Adrenalin. There seems to be a learned component to drug addiction and alcoholism—and probably cigarette addiction as well—that makes it easy for us to become tolerant of drugs and hard for us to give them up. But the final vote is by no means in. Furthermore, even the authors of the theory admit that overdoses are often the result of just plain taking too much of the stuff, or are due to failed health on the part of the addict. *One should not assume that overdose or tolerance will not occur as long as the environmental cues are manipulated properly.*

As mentioned in the beginning of this chapter, classical conditioning has also been implicated in the development of phobias. A phobia is an intense irrational fear of a harmless object or situation. Why do people develop phobias?

In 1909, Sigmund Freud published what was to become one of his most famous cases, that of a five-year-old boy named Hans, who suffered from a phobia of horses.[17] Little Hans was so terrified of horses that he refused to leave the house for fear of encountering one (which, in 1909, was pretty hard to avoid). He particularly feared white horses with black mouths and blinkers.

The entire case was handled through correspondence between Freud and the boy's father. The father would observe the boy, ask questions requested by Freud in his last letter, and relay the information to Freud by mail. Freud noticed that little Hans often described his father in the same terms he used to describe horses. Both his father and horses were "proud" and "very white"; once, he had even asked his father not to "trot away." Hans's father also had a black beard around his mouth and wore glasses. From these similarities, Freud decided there was some connection between little Hans's fear of horses and his relationship with his father. He also noted that Hans was terribly fond of crawling into bed with his mother when his father was away.

Well, you can see where this is leading. Freud concluded that little Hans's phobia stemmed from an unconscious conflict, namely, that he was sexually attracted to his mother and jealous of his father—his rival for his mother's affections. What to do? After all, he couldn't go around hating his father, who was so much bigger and stronger than he. His father might notice and suspect Hans's desire for his mother. He would surely be punished severely for that. According to Freud, little Hans resolved his conflict by displacing his discomfort and fear onto horses. After all, they're big and strong like papa, and white ones with blinkers even look a lot like him. Hans eventually overcame his phobia. Perhaps his parents' divorce following Freud's analysis had something to do with it.

John B. Watson, the father of behaviorism, was disenchanted with Freud's analysis of phobias. Watson was a professor of psychology at Johns Hopkins University (and a former student of John Dewey's) who believed that Pavlovian classical conditioning was the stuff of which phobias were made. To prove his point, he conducted an "experiment" (if you can call it that), in 1920, with his graduate student, Rosalie Rayner, using an eleven-month-old child called Albert B. as their subject. Albert was chosen because he was a healthy, unemotional child, and because his mother was a wet nurse in a Baltimore hospital near Johns Hopkins, which made him readily available. The point of the "experiment" was the formation of a phobia in "Little Albert" (note that dig at Freud's "Little Hans") using classical conditioning. Watson was unconcerned about the ethics of what he was doing, rationalizing that "Fears would arise anyway as soon as the child left the sheltered environment of the nursery for the rough and tumble of the home."[18]

The chosen hapless object of Little Albert's phobia was a white rat. Albert liked the rat, and would play with it often. Watson and Rayner's procedure consisted of showing Albert the rat, and then suddenly whacking a metal bar with a hammer behind his back. The whacking produced a piercingly loud sound from the metal bar and a piercingly loud shriek from Albert, accompanied by crying and fear. After two such pairings, Albert hesitated to reach out to the rat; after five more pairings, showing him the rat alone made him cry. Watson and Rayner had proved their point: Phobias can be induced using classical conditioning. Moreover, the phobic fear generalized. Albert cried when they showed him a white rabbit, a white dog, a Santa Claus beard, and a white seal coat.

This "experiment" captured the imagination of the scientific community at the time—despite its shaky ethics and even shakier experimental methodology—because it showed that mental phenomena such as phobias could be produced, controlled, and explained through a simple physical process called classical conditioning.

This analysis also suggested a way of treating phobias. If a phobia is a conditioned response, then the way to get rid of it is through the process of extinction. The feared object must be faced repeatedly—without the frightening stimulus—until the fear response no longer occurs. This procedure is a bit too draconian for intense phobias, so a modified extinction procedure is used called *systematic desensitization*. This involves having the patient list a number of situations involving the feared object or event ranging in order from least to most frightening. For example, one case involves a woman who had difficulty achieving orgasm during sex with her husband.[19] She'd been in Freudian psychoanalysis for years and sex was still no fun. When asked if she achieved orgasm during masturbation, she replied that she did. Further questioning revealed that she could experience orgasm just fine—as long as she was alone. As she put it, she couldn't achieve orgasm during sex with her husband because her husband was there. The thought of someone actually seeing her in the throes of orgasm unnerved her. The therapist had her rank a number of masturbation situations in terms of their anxiety-provoking status. The least anxiety-provoking involved her masturbating while her husband was across town at work. Imagining her husband on the way home while she was masturbating caused moderate anxiety, and imagining him in the room sent her right over the edge. Using systematic desensitization, the therapist had her imagine each situation in turn, over a number of weeks. When she'd get a good image of it, she was given a series of relaxation exercises to do until she felt quite calm and relaxed with the image. When she could imagine having an orgasm with her husband present and not feel anxious, she was well on her way to recovery, and eventually was cured.

Too bad Watson didn't think to try this technique with little Albert. Following the "experiment," Albert was removed from the hospital by his mother and never seen again. He received no extinction trials, no therapy for his newly acquired phobia. Incidentally, it is interesting to note that Johns Hopkins found it acceptable for Watson to condition a phobia in an innocent eleven-month-old child, but he lost his faculty position for conducting experiments on the physiological responses of human beings in the act of sexual intercourse. Maybe it had something to do with the fact that he himself acted as a subject along with (you guessed it) Rosalie Rayner. He subsequently married Rayner and made his fortune in advertising.

As pointed out in the beginning of this chapter, we have the capacity to automatically learn associations not just between stimuli but between our behavior and its consequences. This type of learning, called operant conditioning, is the type made famous by B. F. Skinner.[20] It is also the type of learning that permeates nearly all of our social interactions. Our child-rearing systems, our justice system, our economic theories—indeed, almost all of our social institutions—are based upon the belief that behavior can be shaped by its consequences. When a parent rewards a child for doing well in school, the parent implicitly assumes that the reward will increase the frequency of doing well in school. When workers strike, they assume their employers will give in to their demands in order to stop the strike, and be more willing to negotiate next time to avoid a strike. When a judge sentences a defendant to a year in prison, he assumes that punishment will decrease the frequency of law-breaking behavior on the part of the defendant.

As these examples demonstrate, there are three ways in which the environment can shape our behavior. Behaviors can be increased by rewarding them; this is called positive reinforcement. Behaviors can also be increased if they terminate an unpleasant situation; this is called negative reinforcement. The workers use actual or threats of strike to *increase* the probability that the employers will give in to them. When employers give in to workers' demands in order to end or prevent a strike, ending or preventing the strike is enormously reinforcing. Unlike negative reinforcement, punishment is a stimulus that *decreases* a behavior. When the judge punishes the defendant, he does so with the hope of decreasing the probability that the defendant will break the law again.

To make the distinction between negative reinforcement and punishment a little clearer, imagine you've just been given an unusual alarm clock as a present. As you're examining it, the alarm goes off. It is an incredibly loud and obnoxious noise. There are dozens of unlabelled buttons on the front of the clock, and you begin frantically pushing them as quickly as you can, hoping one of them will terminate the grating noise. None of them have the slightest effect. Just as you're about to give up and throw the thing out of the window, you notice a small bar on the back, and you press it. Blessed silence ensues. The termination of the noxious stimulus is tremendously reinforcing. The next time the alarm goes off, you'll go right for the bar on the back, not even bothering with the buttons on the front of the clock. The bar-pressing behavior was strongly reinforced, and that is the behavior that becomes part of your behavioral repertoire for dealing with this alarm clock when it rings. That is what is meant by negative reinforcement—the termination of a noxious stimulus by a response strengthens that response. In contrast, punishment is a noxious stimulus that is used to eliminate, not strengthen, a behavior.

While these principles of operant conditioning seem quite mundane, it might surprise you to discover that they play very large roles in two very different phenomena: gambling and biofeedback.

In the fiscal year ending June 1980, Nevada's gambling commission reported that the taxable income for the state's casinos was $2.3 billion; more than $1 billion was collected by the forty-five major casinos on the "strip" in Las Vegas.[21] Recent estimates indicate that more than 61 percent of us participate in some form of gambling each year, from casino gambling to bingo. More than seventy-four million people attend horse races, and twenty-one million attend dog races. State lotteries are enormously popular and lucrative. Clearly, we as a species love to gamble. The question is why. Why would someone risk their hard-earned money on a risky outcome? And why do some people become compulsive gamblers—risking far more than they can afford to lose?

The psychopathology of compulsive gambling is quite complex, but it grows out of the fundamental propensity of brain tissue to respond to the principles of operant conditioning. Even pigeons, for example, become compulsive gamblers under the right circumstances.[22] For example, two female pigeons were placed in an environment where they earned all their food by pecking either of two small disks. One of the disks delivered food on a fixed schedule; after thirty pecks, a grain hopper appeared, allowing them to eat for four seconds. This disk was a sure thing—thirty pecks, four seconds of food. Guaranteed. The other disk, however, was a gamble. If the pigeon chose this disk, she would either receive food after ten pecks five times in a row *or* she would receive a time-out during which no food was delivered. The time-outs varied randomly from one minute to thirty minutes. So she could win big by getting a chance to eat five times or she could end up waiting anywhere from one minute to half an hour before getting a chance to eat again.

Surprisingly, these birds chose the gamble. Bird 1 was more of a gambler than bird 2. No matter how long the time out was, this bird continued to choose the gamble more than 90 percent of the time. Bird 2 was more cautious, but even she chose to gamble more than 70 percent of the time.

The most striking thing was the impact gambling had on the number of times the birds actually got to eat. If the birds had consistently chosen the sure thing, their winnings (opportunities to eat) would have been 100 percent. But because they chose the gamble so often, they lost a lot of eating opportunities. Bird 1, the more adventurous of the two, lost the most; she received only about 15 percent of the eating opportunities she'd have gotten if she consistently chose the sure thing. Bird 1, the more conservative of the two, received only about 55 percent.

Not surprisingly, both birds lost weight during this experiment; in fact, the adventurous one lost 15 percent of her initial weight by the end of the experiment. Translate these eating opportunities into dollars, and you have a pretty good model of compulsive gambling and its consequences.

Why did the birds continue to choose to gamble? It's hard to believe it's because they had abusive childhoods or lousy morals. I might believe it was because they were just plain bored and the gamble livened things up a bit. But a better answer lies in the fundamental impact of reinforcement schedules on the behavior of organisms.

If you want to keep people (e.g., children, employees, students) performing, reward them intermittently. Countless studies have shown that behavior that is rewarded only intermittently continues quite strongly after the rewards stop. But if a behavior is rewarded every time it occurs, it stops shortly after the rewards stop coming. Intermittent reinforcement builds more durable behavior.[23]

It also matters a good deal when the intermittent reward is delivered. Behavior is most persistent when rewards are delivered randomly, that is, when one doesn't know how many times the behavior must be done in order to get a reward. It could be two times, it could be twenty. Under these conditions, humans and other animals work the hardest, and keep on working even when no more rewards are distributed.[24] It's as though they just can't believe the reward isn't just around the corner.

Now think of the gambler's fallacy: You decide to have a bit of a flutter at the roulette wheel in a reputable gambling house. Half of the numbers are red and half are black. You decide to bet on red. Black wins. You bet on red again. Black wins again. This happens ten times in a row. Do you give up or switch to black? Probably not. You probably think something like "Given that black has come up so many times in a row, red is bound to come up soon. It's the law of averages. So, if I stick with red, I'll win soon." So you keep betting on red, feeling certain it's bound to come up in the next few turns.

Gotcha! If the wheel is fair, the probability of black winning again in the next turn is exactly the same as it was for each of the previous turns: 50 percent. It doesn't matter what happened before or what will happen later. On every turn, the probability is the same—assuming the wheel is fair, that is, assuming it truly replicates a random process. But, like the pigeons, the longer the run of unreinforced (nonwinning) trials, the more convinced we are that we're going to win very soon.

It probably seems logical that voluntary behavior, like work, can be shaped by its consequences. But involuntary behavior (such as heart rate, blood pressure, EEG brain waves) can be shaped by their consequences, too. In fact, this is the principle upon which biofeedback is based. The basic biofeedback procedure is to hook a person up to an apparatus that measures some involuntary response and signals changes in that response in some way. Then the person is reinforced every time the response changes in a desired direction. Here are some examples:

When people become bored or drowsy, a certain pattern appears in their brain waves called theta rhythm. It becomes very pronounced during boring tasks. Students in one study were told to try to maintain the louder of two tones broadcast by the machine while their EEGs were measured.[25] Neither the experimenters nor the students knew how the students were to accomplish this. The students were simply told to "try" to keep the louder tone playing.

For half of the trials, the louder of the tones was broadcast whenever theta rhythm increased; for the other half, the louder of the tones was broadcast whenever theta rhythm decreased. The results were quite striking. When the students were reinforced (by hearing the louder tone) for increasing theta, the frequency of theta response increased. When they were reinforced for decreasing theta, the frequency decreased.

This technique has been used quite successfully to assist patients suffering from migraines or high blood pressure. In migraine cases, it is crucial to reduce blood flow to the brain because this reduces the pain and visual impairments that constitute migraine headaches. To do this, patients are told to try to increase blood flow to their hands (to get their hands to "warm up"). Electrodes or thermal detection devices are attached to their hands and fingers, and a tone is played whenever hand temperature reaches some desired level. The patients simply "try" to keep the tone playing. In most cases, they are successful, meaning that blood flow to the hands increases, reducing the painful "pressure" in their brains. The same technique is used to help people with high blood pressure. A sphygmomanometer cuff is wrapped around the patient's arm and a certain tone is played whenever blood pressure drops to some desired level. Once again, most patients can successfully lower their blood pressure simply by "trying" to keep the tone playing.

The principles of reinforcement are so fundamental that even species lower on the phylogenetic scale can learn to regulate involuntary behavior. Rats, for example, have been shown to raise or lower their heart rates using biofeedback.[26] Electrodes were surgically implanted in the brain "pleasure centers" of a group of rats, and their muscles were injected with curare, a drug that temporarily paralyzes the muscular system. This prevented them from moving their muscles in order to change their heart rates. The rats were also put on ventilators to assist their breathing.

For half of the trials, the rats received electrical stimulation of their "pleasure centers" whenever their heart rates increased; for the other half of the trials, they received a pleasure zap whenever their heart rates decreased. Like the college students who learned to control their theta rhythms, these rats learned to control their heart rates—without changing their breathing or contracting their muscles—simply by "trying" to keep the pleasure coming (as it were).

CHAPTER 8

Language:
The Uniquely
Human Capacity

Why do humans rule the earth? Lions, horses, elephants, and bears are much bigger and stronger than we are. In a match of strength, the strongest human would have quite a time battling a lioness intent on protecting her cubs. We are smaller, weaker, and (during the first few years of life) remarkably helpless creatures. Yet we have clearly "won" the evolutionary competition for control of the planet—much to the detriment of certain aspects of it! Why?

Jurassic Park made it grimly apparent that greater size and strength are not sufficient to win the battle of the species.[1] Rather, the key lies in two crucial elements—greater intelligence and greater cooperation among the members of a species. The huge tyrannosaurus rex was less of a problem for the protagonists than were the smaller—but social and intelligent—raptors. Social creatures like the raptors who communicate and cooperate with one another are formidable foes. The largest and most ferocious lion or bear has no hope of standing up to the wolf pack—predators that communicate and cooperate with one another in the hunt. And nothing can stand up to human beings—highly intelligent creatures who communicate and cooperate with one another in remarkably complex ways.

How did we gain this evolutionary advantage? Our brains do not differ much from those of other species. Subcortical structures—particularly those that process emotions—are nearly identical across species. But there is one very special difference between our "new brains" (the cortex) and the cortex of other species. Of all species on earth, only human brains are specialized for *language*. As Descartes put it: "Now, all men, the most stupid and foolish, those even who are deprived of the organ of speech, make use of signs, whereas the brutes never do anything of the kind; which may be taken for the true distinction between man and brute."[2] Like us, other animals experience emotions, compete with each other, show altruism, engage in sex and reproduction, hunt socially, learn, and even communicate with each other. But *none* on earth except humans use language. Language is the uniquely human capacity. For this reason, scientific psychology has devoted decades of research to exploring how we learn and use language.

One of the startling conclusions of this work is that language is a *biological* capacity, that is, that humans can acquire language not because we are more intelligent but because our brains are specially designed for it. This conclusion was first presented by Noam Chomsky, a noted MIT linguist, in a now famous attack on Skinner's behaviorism.[3] Chomsky posited the existence of a Language Acquisition Device, or "mental organ," that facilitates acquisition of one's first language.[4] From this perspective, humans do not learn language in the way that we learn, say, tennis or geography. Instead, *language emerges* at its own pace as long as certain environmental conditions are present. This is analogous to birds learning to fly. Mother birds don't teach their offspring to fly. As long as conditions are right, flying ability *emerges* as the infants' bodies develop.

There is a good deal of evidence supporting this biological view of language learning. So much, in fact, that it is easy to get overwhelmed by it. For this reason, I will present the most compelling evidence in a systematic way. (For a more complete treatment see Steven Pinker's book *The Language Instinct*.)

Our brains are specially designed for language. The most unequivocal evidence is that the human brain contains special structures devoted specifically to language. There is a very special place in the left frontal lobe of the cortex called Broca's area. This place is special because it is involved in speech production.

In 1861, a doctor named Paul Broca reported a case of a patient who could understand speech perfectly well but who suffered an enormous amount of difficulty in speaking.[5] The patient's speech was slow and halting, words were badly formed or nearly incomprehensible, and his sentences were ungrammatical. An autopsy after the patient's death revealed severe damage to a certain part of the patient's left frontal lobe, the place we now call Broca's area. Since that time, other cases of "Broca's aphasia," as this syndrome is called, have been reported following stroke, tumor, and gunshot wound damage to this area.

Also located in the left brain (in the left temporal lobe) is Wernicke's area. In 1874, Karl Wernicke reported that damage to this area of the brain resulted in an inability to comprehend—not produce—speech.[6] People with damage here can speak perfectly well, but their speech tends to be meaningless, and they have difficulty understanding what is said to them. For example, Wernicke asked one of his patients the following question: "Who's minding the store?" The response he got was: "I don't know. Yes, the bick, uh yes, I would say that the mick daysis nosis or chipickters." Unlike patients suffering from Broca's aphasia, this patient produced speech sounds just fine, they just didn't mean anything. Certain types of damage to this area also produces "word deafness," a syndrome in which patients can no longer comprehend spoken language although their ability to hear and identify other types of sounds is not affected.

People who suffer from dyslexia—an inability to read and comprehend symbols—also have disturbances in Wernicke's area.[7] This conclusion is based on autopsies of dyslexics. In one case, a dyslexic man died in a car accident. The structural abnormalities discovered in his brain during the autopsy were striking. The cortical cells in the left hemisphere were scrambled and whirled. There were primitive, larger cells in that area that don't usually appear there. And both temporal lobes were equal in size—in most people, the left side is slightly larger than the right.

Some particularly intriguing evidence of left-brain language specialization comes from research on Japanese aphasics. In Japanese, there are two writing systems called kana and kanji. The kana system is more like English in that it is sound based; a given symbol (such as the written symbol "a" in English) represents a certain sound (such as "ah" or "ay"). A kana symbol represents the sound of an entire syllable, and these syllables are put together into larger structures to form words and sentences. In kanji, however, written symbols look more like pictographs, and each symbol represents an idea or object rather than a sound. Kana, therefore, is the more "verbal" of the two systems, while kanji is more pictorial. Importantly, Japanese who suffer damage to their left brain show impaired processing of kana only, not of kanji.[8]

The left-brain advantage for language is not restricted to spoken language. Any communicative system that relies on combining symbolic units into complex structures appears to be handled by the left brain. American Sign Language (ASL), for example, is a complex, well-defined grammatical language used by the deaf to communicate with one another. Despite the fact that it does not involve hearing or speaking, the same language areas that control spoken language in hearing people appear to control ASL communication.[9] Damage to these areas (e.g., Broca's and Wernicke's areas) produces aphasias in deaf people in that they are no longer capable of producing or understanding ASL hand signs.

Language acquisition has a biological clock. Like fertility, language acquisition appears to have a biological clock: *If humans do not acquire a natural language by the time they reach puberty, they never will.* The case of Genie is a striking example.[10] Genie was locked in a room by her abusive father and deprived of normal human contact from the age of twenty months until the age of thirteen; by then she had reached puberty. When she was rescued, attempts were made to socialize her, including teaching her language. Although she learned to speak some words, grammar remained beyond her reach, and she never became fluent in her native tongue. This probably was not due to mental deficiency; according to her mother, she had begun to speak single words before her monstrous father locked her up. Other cases have been reported of abandoned children who were raised by animals in the wild, with similar results: Unless humans are exposed to language prior to puberty, language never emerges.[11]

You might be tempted to suggest that the abuse or extreme

social deprivation suffered by these children had more to do with their failure to learn language than did puberty. But the same results have been observed with deaf learners of American Sign Language: The younger one is when learning ASL, the easier it is to learn, and those who attempt to learn it as their first language after puberty never really master it.[12] Clearly, the capacity to comprehend and master the *abstract structure of language* (e.g., grammar, syntax, etc.) diminishes with puberty.

In a similar vein, humans who learn to speak a *second* language after puberty rarely become fluent. One pair of researchers investigated the English language skills of Chinese and Korean immigrants to the United States.[13] Those who arrived after puberty never became completely fluent in English, regardless of how long they had lived in this country. Interestingly, there was a significant drop-off in fluency if immigration occurred after the age of seven, with further reductions for each age from seven up until puberty. After puberty, it didn't matter how old the immigrant was upon arrival or how long they lived here, they never became fluent. Given these results, it is rather astonishing that American children are not introduced to foreign languages until high school—when it becomes not only excruciatingly difficult to learn a second language but impossible to speak it without an accent.

Acquiring language depends on having the right genes. Dysphasia is a syndrome which is characterized by an inability to learn the grammatical structure of language despite having normal intelligence and memory capacities. It is also a syndrome that tends to run in families, suggesting a genetic origin. One researcher recently traced the syndrome through three generations of a single family, implicating a single dominant gene in its transmission.[14] For example, the rule for forming the past tense for English verbs is to add "-ed" to the verb stem. The past tense of "fix" is "fixed," the past tense of "wag" is "wagged," and so on. There are, however, numerous exceptions to this rule, such as "run" becoming "ran" and "sing" becoming "sang" in the past tense. When learning English, one must learn the rule plus the exceptions to the rule. The interesting thing about dysphasics is that they can memorize the exceptions, but they can't learn the rule. For example, when asked to form the past tense for a nonsense word, they're stumped. Yet this is an amazingly simple task for most people. Try it: "Here is a man who likes to rick. Yesterday, he did the same thing. Yesterday, he____." Did you say "ricked"? So do most four-year-olds.[15] In fact, the formation of the past tense seems to come naturally to children—despite the fact that, in the overwhelming majority of cases, no one ever teaches them the rule (i.e., add "-ed" to the stem of the verb). But dysphasics, regardless of how smart they are, can't seem to learn this simple grammatical rule.

In contrast, another rare genetic disorder, called Williams syndrome, severely impairs intelligence.[16] People suffering from this disorder have IQ's on the order of fifty. But they can learn language just fine. In fact, they acquire the rules of grammar so well that they often overgeneralize them, saying "runned" instead of "ran." Because their intellectual and memory capacities are impaired, they have difficulty remembering the irregular forms of these verbs, but they acquire the rule for forming the past tense of regular verbs effortlessly. This pattern is the mirror image of the pattern observed among dysphasics.

These two disparate patterns show quite clearly that learning a first language is not merely a matter of memorizing words and "figuring out" or learning the rules of language in the way we figure out or learn the rules for playing chess. If this were the case, you would predict that people with Williams syndrome would have trouble learning language due to their deficient memory and intellectual capacities, but dysphasics, who have normal intelligence and memory capacities, would learn it easily. Language learning indeed depends on general memory processes, but those alone are insufficient. We need some innate sensitivity to grammar and syntax, or else certain aspects of language will remain forever beyond our reach. In fact, the interplay of general memory processes and innate sensitivity to the structure of language is apparent during normal language learning.

If you listen to average two- or three-year-old children speaking, you'll probably notice that they use the correct past-tense versions of common verbs, such as "I ran" and "You ate." If you listen to these same children at age four or five, you'll hear them using incorrect forms of these same verbs, saying such things as "I ranned" or "You ated"—forms any child is unlikely to have ever heard spoken.

What's happening is this:[17] Like dysphasics, very young children memorize the particular sounds (i.e., words) that communicate just what they want to communicate. As they mature, however, their genetic "programs" for acquiring grammatical aspects of language emerge, and they become capable of acquiring the grammatical rules of the language in their community. Once these rules are acquired, they tend to be overgeneralized, that is, applied to instances where they are inappropriate. The past tense of "run" is "ran"; by overgeneralization of the "-ed" rule, however, "run" becomes "runned" or even "ranned." This is what dysphasics—who seem to lack these genetic programs—can't do.

Are these rules explicitly understood by the child? Probably not. Most adults can't even tell you how the past tense is formed in English, but they know how to do it implicitly. Are these rules learned through instruction? Probably not. Most parents don't explicitly tell children, "If you want to express a verb in past tense, add '-ed' to the stem of the verb, unless it is irregular." In fact, there is ample evidence that trying to intervene won't have much effect, as the following exchange shows:

CHILD: My teacher holded the baby rabbits and we patted them.

MOTHER: Did you say the teacher held the baby rabbits?

CHILD: Yes.

MOTHER: What did you say she did?

CHILD: She holded the baby rabbits and we patted them.

MOTHER: Did you say she held them tightly?

CHILD: No, she holded them loosely.[18]

As this excerpt shows, there is no sense in trying to intervene during certain stages of the language-learning process.

Newborns show special sensitivity for speech sounds. Infants who are only a few days old show acute sensitivity to speech sounds. In fact, it has been shown that they can discriminate their own language from other languages. In one set of studies, newborn infants of monolingual families were played tapes of someone recounting a story in their family's language (e.g., French, English, Russian) or a different language.[19] The tape began with the story being told in one language and then at some point switched to another language. When the tape switched from one language to another, the infants responded to the change, indicating that they could detect the difference. Interestingly, they responded more strongly when the tape switched to their native tongue (e.g., from Russian to French for French babies) than when it switched from one foreign tongue to another (e.g., from Russian to Italian for French babies).

Why the preference for the native tongue? There is some evidence that from about the sixth month of pregnancy, fetuses respond to voices around them.[20] They can't, of course, make out the words (try making out what someone says to you while you're under water), but they seem to respond to the timbre, prosody, and other "melodic" aspects of human speech. These aspects differ among languages. Even if you don't speak French or German, you can clearly recognize that they are different languages because they sound so very different to the ear (or perhaps we should say to the brain). Infants who are a few days old have in fact been hearing the prosodic elements of their native tongues for two or three months, and seem to prefer these familiar elements to unfamiliar ones.

Although these results are startling, we should reflect on the fact that most animals respond to prosodic elements of human speech, too. Unlike other animals, however, human infants are capable of detecting and producing the tiny differences in speech sounds that are the building blocks of spoken language.

Humans speak by moving the tongue, lips, and larynx while expelling air up from the lungs and out through the mouth. Some of the noises we make while doing this are meaningful sounds in our language (such as the hissing sound for "s" and the humming sound for "m") while others are not. Linguists call these small meaningful sounds phonemes; they are the smallest components of speech. Each language has about forty such sounds out of which words are composed, but the set of forty differs among languages.[21] For example, two important sounds in English are the "l" sound and the "r" sound, as in "lead" and "read." These sounds are not distinguished in Japanese; instead the "l" and "r" sounds fall within the same phoneme. Japanese adults cannot even hear the difference between these two phonemes, unlike American adults who can distinguish between them easily. For example, some researchers asked American and Japanese adults to listen to a tape of a voice saying "la-la-la" repeatedly.[22] At some point, the voice switched to saying "ra-ra-ra" repeatedly. The American adults had no difficulty indicating when the switch occurred. The Japanese adults, however, could not reliably tell when the switch occurred. They couldn't *hear* the difference between "la" and "ra." This is not surprising since this distinction does not occur in the Japanese language, and hence is rarely (if ever) heard in the Japanese-language community.

Very different results were observed, however, among two-month-old American and Japanese infants. Using the same tapes, the researchers did the following. They rigged a pacifier so that whenever an infant sucked on it, a tape player was activated that broadcasted the "la-ra" tape. When the "la-la" sound began playing in response to their sucking, the babies were delighted, and kept sucking on the pacifier to keep the "la-la" sound playing. After a while, they began to lose interest, and sucking frequency declined to about half its initial rate. At this point, the experimenters switched the tape so that the voice now said "ra-ra-ra" repeatedly. Surprisingly, the Japanese infants began sucking again with vigor, indicating that they *could* hear the difference between the old, boring "la" sound and the new, interesting "ra" sound.

The results of these and numerous other studies indicate that human infants can distinguish among the various phonemes that occur in *any* natural language; with time, and greater brain specialization, we lose the ability to distinguish sounds that carry no information in our native language. That is partly why it is so difficult to learn a second language as an adult. You might not be able to even *hear* some of the speech sounds that carry crucial information in the language you want to learn, much less pronounce them properly. Your brain has become too specialized for your native language.

Human infants babble. Between the ages of seven and ten months, human infants begin to do something else unique to the species: They begin to babble speech sounds. This type of babbling is called reduplicative babbling because they will repeat a single syllable over and over, such as "babababa" or "dadada." This might drive their parents nuts, but it is absolutely crucial to language development. Babbling babies are doing very important work: They are practicing the sounds they will need to use to speak a language.

Regardless of the language they hear spoken around them, all infants go through the same babbling sequence. For example, dentals such as "d" and "t" appear in infant babbling before nasals such as "m" and "n." This frustrates English-speaking mothers because no matter how much time they spend with their infants relative to the infants' fathers, the little darlings still say "dada" before they say "mama." Even deaf babies' babble shows this babbling sequence. They don't babble as much, and their babbling is delayed relative to hearing children's (beginning around eleven months rather than seven), but they do babble, and their babbling sequence is the same as that of hearing babies.[23]

The propensity of human infants to babble doesn't seem to be due to a mere maturing of the vocal apparatus. Deaf infants whose parents communicate using American Sign Language begin to babble *manually* at the same age that hearing children begin to babble vocally—between seven and ten months.[24] Their babbling consists of sign language syllables that are the fundamental components of ASL. At this stage of life, humans as a species begin to search for a communicative means that exploits the language capacity of our specially designed brains.

Once phonemes appear in their babbling, babies move on to the next important stage. They begin to focus on those phonemes that are most relevant to the language they hear being spoken or signed around them. For example, more labials, such as "b," occur in French words than in English, and there are more in English than in Japanese or Swedish. If you listen to French babies babbling, they will babble labials more often than American babies, who in turn will babble more labials than Japanese or Swedish babies.[25] While babbling, infants "practice" the speech sounds that occur most often in the speech they hear around them. Babbling is very important work, and no one has to teach infants how to do it or what to focus on. When the time comes, that part of the language development process will just kick in on its own.

To make it through the babbling stage effectively, infants need to establish a feedback loop between producing a babble and hearing the babble, or making a sign and seeing the sign. They need to witness their own babbling in some way or they don't do it. In fact, delayed vocal babbling or the cessation of vocal babbling is often an indication that there is something wrong with an infant's hearing. If your baby suddenly stops babbling—without moving on to speaking words—you ought to have his or her hearing checked. Often, a minor ear infection is the culprit. This is crucially important because if the feedback loop is disrupted, permanent speech and hearing impairments will result.

Kids acquire language remarkably fast. The average one-year-old has a vocabulary of ten words. In a mere four years, this tiny vocabulary expands to over ten *thousand* words. It doesn't take a rocket scientist to figure out that to expand a ten-word vocabulary to a ten-thousand-word vocabulary in four years requires learning, on average, about six or seven new words *every day*. This is an astonishing rate.

The time course for the rest of language learning is also remarkably fast. By around two-and-one-half years of age, toddlers progress from the one-word stage to generating two-word sentences. What comes next? Not a three-word stage: From two-word sentences, they begin to generate entire sentences.[26] Sometime during the third year, speech undergoes an explosion in complexity. By the time children reach the age of four, they speak and understand language better than the most powerful computers around today. And they accomplish all of this without anyone ever giving them formal instruction in the rules of their language. Furthermore, the same pattern of language development occurs the world over, regardless of child-rearing approaches and regardless of the language community—including sign language in the deaf![27]

Kids commit remarkably few errors while learning language. The language rules that every human child instinctively knows are vastly underdetermined by the information they get from the environment. If you find this a bit hard to believe, consider that of the millions of errors kids could make while learning a language, they commit only a few. And those few are sensible. For example, there are 3,628,800 ways to rearrange the words in any ten-word sentence, but only a few of these arrangements (and in some cases only *one* arrangement) will be both grammatically correct and meaningful.[28] The fact that four-year-old kids effortlessly distinguish the right arrangement(s) from the over 3.6 million wrong arrangements seems like pretty persuasive evidence that they possess an innate sense of linguistic structure. Trying to learn to do this by imitation or rote trial and error would take much too long—maybe on the order of several lifetimes. Instead, all that human kids seem to need are their specially designed brains and exposure to adult speech.

As another example, consider the rule for turning a statement into a question. How would you turn the following sentence into a question? The man is tall. Easy. Move the verb "is" to the front of the sentence: Is the man tall? How about the next sentence: The angry man is tall. That's easy, too: Is the angry man tall? How about the next one: The angry man who is pounding on the door is tall. Piece of cake. Is the angry man who is pounding on the door tall? But wait a minute. Why didn't you say, "Is the angry man who pounding on the door is tall?" Why did you move the second "is" to the front and not the first "is"? Why didn't you move both of them? You can't tell me, can you? Neither could a four-year-old, but kids *never* make mistakes like this while they're learning their language. Kids can turn sentences into questions just fine without anyone ever telling them how to do it.

More evidence comes from the way negative statements develop in children's language. All English-speaking kids generally go through the same four stages.[29] The first involves using an old familiar form to serve a new function, as in using the familiar words "all gone" to mean "no" in the statement "All gone milk." The second stage involves placing the negation term outside of the sentence as in "No take ball." In the third stage, the negation is placed after the subject of the sentence as in

"Daddy no go." Finally, the negation is incorporated into the auxiliary verb in accordance with the rules of English, as in "I don't want some supper."

The important point is that they don't just try to stick the negative terms any old place. Their progression toward the correct usage is systematic and sensitive to roles played by other words in the sentence. Their early attempts treat the sentence as a whole unit that cannot be disturbed, e.g., "No [take ball]"; later attempts break the sentence up into its syntactic constituents. They place the negative after the subject of the sentence, *not* just after the first word or in some other randomly selected place. Language unfolds in very systematic ways, and it is very resistant to intervention during these early stages. You can't hurry it and you can't correct something until its time in the sequence has come, as this excerpt shows:[30]

CHILD: Nobody don't like me.
MOTHER: No, say "Nobody likes me."
CHILD: Nobody don't like me.
MOTHER: No, say "Nobody likes me."
CHILD: Nobody don't like me.
            [Seven more repetitions of this.]
MOTHER: No, now listen carefully: "Nobody likes me."
CHILD: Oh! Nobody don't likes me.

Kids receive remarkably little instruction in language. As the excerpt above shows, you can't intervene until the language development process allows you to. But more important, if your kid came home from school saying, "Nobody don't like me," I'd consider you to be a pretty insensitive parent if you tried to correct his grammar rather than exploring why he thought no one liked him. Fortunately, this is rarely the case. Generally speaking, parents respond to the truth content of children's speech and not to its grammaticality. In fact, one study reported virtually no correlation between the grammaticality of children's speech and parental approval or disapproval of their utterances.[31] Despite this, kids learn to speak pretty well by the time they reach school age. Again, language development seems to have its own schedule, evolving in its own good time and in its own stages—as long as the child's brain receives quality samples of speech or sign language during that development. No one needs to teach us what verbs and nouns are, or how to utter a well-formed sentence. We implicitly know this. Grammar school just teaches us names for things we implicitly know, and polishes our speech to make it more acceptable to the community.

Kids show innate sensitivity to syntax. To speak and understand a first language, children must learn how to put words together to form meaningful sentences. This is not a simple task. In many languages, such as English, meaning changes dramatically depending on word order. "Paul saw Mary" means something very different from "Mary saw Paul," and "Mary Paul saw" is just plain meaningless. But in other languages, inflection is used instead of word order to convey who is doing what to whom. Latin, for example, is a heavily inflected language in that word endings, rather than word order, conveys who's doing what to whom. "Paulus vidit Miriam" means "Paul saw Mary"—but then so does "Miriam vidit Paulus" and "Miriam Paulus vidit."[32] The word endings "-us" and "-am" indicate who saw whom, not the order in which the words appear. Despite these differences, human infants acquire the rules that govern the structure of sentences with incredible speed.

A study of two-year-olds watching cartoon videos makes this point clear.[33] The video showed a cartoon rabbit pushing a duck up and down while both animals made circles with one arm. While they watched, the researcher said to one group, "Look, the rabbit and the duck are gorping!"; another group was told, "Look, the rabbit is gorping the duck!" Then they were shown two new videos. In one, the rabbit and duck both made circles with their arms—but no pushing occurred. In the other, the rabbit pushed the duck—but no circling occurred. The researchers said, "Where's the gorping now? Find the gorping!" The kids who heard the intransitive form, "The rabbit and duck are gorping," pointed to the video in which the animals circled their arms. The kids who heard the transitive form, "The rabbit is gorping the duck," pointed to the one in which the rabbit pushed the duck. Even these extremely young humans were sensitive to the syntax of the sentences they heard, mapping the transitive statement onto the transitive event and the intransitive statement onto the intransitive event. Notice that this doesn't mean they could tell you what "transitive syntactic form" or "intransitive syntactic form" means. In fact (alas!), most college grads can't either. Nonetheless, whether we studied grammar in school or not, we are extremely sensitive to syntactic form. We "instinctively" know that syntax carries meaning about actions and events in the world.

Language processing is modularized. Once we've mastered the fundamentals of our native tongue, we can begin doing what language is supposed to allow us to do: Communicate with other humans. Here again, our brains seem to be specially designed to allow language processing to take place without interruption. In fact, some language functions are so important that they are "modularized," that is, they operate as uninterruptible units that are *isolated from our other knowledge.*

Consider the first time you heard a foreign language being spoken. It probably seemed like an unbroken stream of sound coming your way. You probably couldn't even figure out where one word ended and another began. That is what speech is like. Put your hand anywhere on your throat and say the following sentence aloud: "Mary had a little lamb." Could you feel the breaks between the words? If you're like most people, the answer is emphatically no. You just felt a constant vibration that ended when you stopped speaking. Where were the words?

The first step in understanding spoken sentences is breaking up the speech stream into words and recovering their meaning. Having a decent-sized vocabulary matters because recovering one word helps to recover others that are related to it. You probably noticed this when trying to communicate in a foreign language. If you could make out one word that the other person way saying, it helped you make sense out of the rest of the gibberish that was coming at you. That is probably why infant speech begins with mastering single words.

This phenomenon is easy to demonstrate in the laboratory. People have been shown to decide more quickly whether or not a word is an English word if the word is accompanied or preceded by another English word to which it is related.[34] For example, people require only a little more than half a second to decide that "BREAD" is an English word when it appears with or after the word "BUTTER," but they require a full second when it appears with or after an unrelated word such as "DOCTOR" or a nonword such as "MARB." The first word "primes," or facilitates access to, the second word when the words are related to each other, a result that has been replicated numerous times using various materials and languages. This facilitation enhances our ability to process speech quickly and efficiently.

More surprising is the fact that we appear to momentarily activate *all* possible meanings for words we hear or see. For example, consider the following sentence: "The man was not surprised when he found several spiders, roaches, and other bugs in the corner of his room." Notice that the word "bugs" has more than one meaning. It could mean insect, listening device used in espionage, or errors in a computer program. But notice that only one meaning (insect) is appropriate in this context. Suppose I were to flash "ant" on a computer screen immediately after the word "bugs" is played to you over earphones. Do you think "bugs" would prime "ant" in the way that "butter" primes "bread?" Seems reasonable, especially since the context also is consistent with the "insect" interpretation of "bugs." Suppose instead I were to flash "spy" on the screen immediately after "bugs" is played over the earphones. Now what would you predict? The most reasonable prediction seems to be that only "ant" would be primed by "bugs" because "spy" is inconsistent with the story context.

In fact, hearing "bugs," primes *both* "spy" and "ant," relative to an unrelated word such as "sew"; people respond equally fast to "spy" and "ant" and much more slowly to "sew" in this context.[35] Even more interestingly, if tested a mere second *after* hearing the priming word, "spy" no longer benefits from the priming. Then, people respond much more quickly to "ant" than they do to either "spy" or "sew." This result has been replicated numerous times with hundreds of words and sentences: *When reading or hearing language, we briefly activate all meanings of each word that comes our way.* Recovering word meaning is an *automatic, insulated process:* Once the process is started, it can't be interrupted, and the module pays absolutely no attention to what came before or after. After the module has finished activating *all* meanings for a word, the context *selects* among these meanings. This happens so fast that we are not even aware of it.

Only when the context doesn't provide enough information to select among the various meanings do we become aware of the ambiguity that most of our words carry: "Flying planes can be dangerous" is ambiguous because neither the syntactic nor the semantic context helps us settle on a single interpretation. The sentence could mean that piloting an airplane is a dangerous business, or it could mean that planes roaring overhead can be dangerous to people on the ground. The thing to notice is that nearly every sentence we hear is ambiguous in this way because nearly every word in English has more than one meaning. Yet our brain settles these ambiguities so rapidly we're not even aware of it, relying on syntactic, semantic, and pragmatic cues.

In fact, syntax is so important to the disambiguation process that your brain processes it tenaciously when speech comes its way, refusing to be interrupted. For example, consider the following two sentences:

1. As a direct result of their new invention's *influence the company was given an award.*
2. The retiring chairman whose methods still greatly *influence the company was given an award.*

Notice that the second half of the sentences are identical, but they are parsed very differently. The first clause in sentence 1 ends with the word "influence"; all of the words up to that point belong to the same substructure. The first clause in sentence 2, however, ends with the word "company." So if we were to break these sentences up into two major subparts, we would break them up like this:

1. As a direct result of their new invention's *influence /* / *the company was given an award.*
2. The retiring chairman whose methods still greatly *influence the company //* *was given an award.*

One group of researchers recorded sentences like these by splicing the unique sentence parts onto the common (italicized) fragments.[36] This ensured that the resulting taped sentences were acoustically identical—no rising or falling inflection indicated where the clausal breaks were. When volunteers listened to these sentences, a loud click occurred somewhere in the middle. In the above sentences, the click occurred in the middle of the word "was." The volunteers' task was to indicate where the click occurred.

Surprisingly, the volunteers didn't perceive the click to occur where it actually occurred. Instead, they perceived it occurring at the sentences' major constituent boundary. Those who heard sentence 1 thought the click occurred just after the word "influence." In contrast, those who heard sentence 2 thought the click occurred after the word "company." Their perception of the click was "transported" to the end of the clause boundary.

Perhaps this makes all that grammar you learned in grade school and high school seem less arbitrary. The syntactic constituents of sentences aren't just arbitrary rules made up by linguists. Your brain actively breaks up sentences into their important syntactic constituents, and it cannot be interrupted when it's in the middle of one. Whatever is happening out there just has to wait until a syntactic break comes along before your brain will consciously register it.

Innate and acquired knowledge interact fluidly. We've talked so far about processing speech by relying on our lexicon and syntactic cues. But we're not out of the woods yet. Understanding a conversation depends on much more than just syntax and semantics. We also need pragmatics—knowledge of the world and knowledge of people's communicative intentions. There are two curious things about the role pragmatic knowledge plays in language comprehension. The first is that it interacts so smoothly with innate knowledge of syntax and grammar as to make it nearly opaque to conscious introspection. For example, consider the following two sentences:[37]

Tom got the picnic supplies out of the car.
The beer was warm.

Did you have trouble understanding the vignette? Probably not. Were you aware of any ambiguity? Again, probably not. But imagine for a minute that you are, say, a computer that knows only word meanings and syntax. The second sentence refers to "the beer." What beer? The first sentence does not contain the word "beer," yet the second sentence refers to it as though it were already mentioned. And what has "warm" got to do with anything? What is the relationship between "warm beer" and the information given in the first sentence?

Unless you know a good deal about people, picnics, cars, and proclivities for outdoor activities during warm weather, these two sentences are non sequiturs; they seem to have nothing to do with each other. But if you know that beer is often part of the supplies people take on picnics, and that picnics usually take place during warm weather, and that things put in cars typically get warm when the outside temperature is warm, including picnic supplies, then these two sentences make perfect sense. In fact, you've engaged in an enormous amount of tacit inferencing in order to understand these two simple sentences.

To communicate, three processes must operate in parallel: The meaning of words must be recovered, the syntactic structure of the speech signal must be deciphered, and world knowledge must be activated concerning the intentions of the speaker. Put them all together, and you can end up having conversations like this:

Speaker 1: The cat is on the mat.
Speaker 2: I'm on the phone.
Speaker 1 (*indignantly*): I always have to do it!

What could this bizarre conversation mean? Suppose the cat in question belongs to you and a roommate. The cat always sits on the mat in front of the door when it wants to go out. You notice this, but don't want to get up from watching TV, so you utter the first sentence. Your roommate responds with the second. You, feeling put upon and exploited because you *always* end up having to let the cat out, hurl the last retort with some annoyance.

That's a long way to go to understand this conversation. You not only have to understand English, you must know something about the situation and the speakers' shared history in order to make sense out of these three simple sentences. How do we get from sentence meaning (e.g., the literal meaning of "The cat is on the mat") to speaker meaning (e.g., the intended meaning of "Please let the cat out")?

This should give you some idea why you can't talk to your computer. There are currently no computers that do a decent job of parsing normal, idiomatic speech. It is far too complicated a task. When researchers first began the task of developing natural-language-processing computer systems approximately thirty years ago, they believed it would be relatively simple. Projections were made about marketing such systems in a few years. That was before they came to appreciate the complexity that underlies the processing of spoken and written speech: All you need are (a) a very large computing system, (b) a good-sized vocabulary, (c) a decent grasp of grammar and syntax, (d) knowledge about the world, that is, knowledge about things that people are likely to be referring to when they speak, and (e) knowledge of people's intentions. Moreover, you've got to be able to manipulate each of these components so fluidly and effortlessly that most of it takes place in the "background," out of one's awareness. If that's what you need to have done, the easiest thing to do is hire a human to do it. Thirty years of computer design has not yet matched five million years of evolution.

The point to appreciate is that understanding any bit of conversation is a lot like deciphering a riddle or solving a mystery. A good deal of reasoning happens spontaneously and so rapidly that the listener isn't even aware of it. And that reasoning typically depends on knowing something about the topic under consideration (e.g., picnics).

The second curious thing about pragmatic knowledge is that we seem to acquire it without much instruction. In fact, when we communicate, we unconsciously adhere to a tacit contract between hearer and speaker, which philosopher H. P. Grice called the *cooperative principle*.[38] This principle states that *speakers should endeavor to be informative, truthful, relevant, and clear.* No one ever taught you this principle, yet you obey it instinctively. Why? Because if you unwittingly violate this contract, you will either fail to communicate, insult the hearer, or communicate something very different than you intended.

To illustrate the first component of the contract—being informative—suppose you are an employer who is reviewing the credentials of an applicant for a very high level engineering job. You've asked the candidates to have people who know them well send you letters of recommendation. You tear open a letter of recommendation from the candidate's major professor, a person who knows the candidate very well. The letter says, "Mr. Jones's command of English is excellent, and his class attendance has been regular." End of letter. What do you conclude? Does this professor think very highly of the candidate? Probably not. The recommendation is not at all informative about the candidate's performance in school. The information given is not even relevant to a job in engineering. Something's amiss. The cooperative principle has been violated, and the message communicated is very different from the one written.

Next, consider a review written by a hypothetical theater critic about a voice recital by famous soprano Jane Doe: "Ms. Doe produced a series of sounds that corresponded closely to the score of 'Home Sweet Home.' " Did the critic think much of Ms. Doe's performance? Probably not. There is a very simple word for what Ms. Doe was supposed to do during her recital: sing. The critic chose a very unclear and convoluted way of describing Ms. Doe's performance, thereby violating the clarity component of the cooperative principle. By so doing, he communicated something very different than the literal interpretation of his statement.

Particularly surprising is that even very young children obey this principle.[39] For example, preschoolers, first-graders, and third-graders were asked to pick the "silly" answer to a series of question-answer pairs like the following:

"Jane and Mary were talking about what they wanted to be when they grow up. Jane said she wanted to be an astronaut. What do you want to be, Mary?"

Answer 1: I want to be a teacher

Answer 2: I want to be a grown-up.

The "silly" answers violated one or more aspect of the cooperative principle. (This one violates the informative component.) Second- and third-graders had little difficulty with this task; in fact, 83 percent of the second-graders and *all* of the third-graders performed above chance. The preschoolers, however, found this to be a rather difficult task; only 19 percent of them performed above chance. Sometime between preschool and first grade, we acquire a good deal of sensitivity toward what is expected of us in conversation, without anyone explicitly teaching us.

This might explain why children's humor is often lost on adults. You probably have found yourself in the position of listening to a child tell you a joke that he or she thinks is outrageously funny and not even realizing what the punch line was. One theory of humor has it that violation of expectations, like those embodied by the cooperative principle, underlies humor. According to this theory, the body of a joke sets up expectations.[40] If the punch line is expected, it isn't funny. If it isn't expected but still makes sense, then it is funny. If it's unexpected but doesn't make sense, then it's just puzzling. For example:

"Two guys walk into a bar. They order beers." Expected, and ho hum, not really very amusing.

"Two guys walk into a bar. Luckily, the third guy ducked." Unexpected, and amusing—at least to some of us.

"Two guys walk into a bar. They lived happily ever after." Maybe a four-year-old would get this one. It just seems strange to me. . . .

The appearance of language shaped human evolution. The work described so far demonstrates the enormity of the tasks involved in acquiring and processing language. This should give us some appreciation of why special-purpose brain structures evolved to subserve this function. This has nothing to do with level of intelligence. It isn't the case that we can acquire language because we happen to be smarter or because we have bigger brains. If anything, it seems that the reverse is true—we evolved the capacity to acquire language, and that capacity boosted both brain expansion and overall intellectual capacity. This should also make you suspect that the capacity to acquire and use language had greater evolutionary significance than just making talk radio possible.

To understand why language matters so much, let's take a giant step back in evolution: It will probably surprise (and maybe offend) you to learn that at a molecular level, humans and chimpanzees are only 1 percent different.[41] In fact, chimpanzees are closer to us than they are to gorillas. Humans and chimpanzees diverged quite late in the evolutionary process, having a common ancestor as recently as five million years ago.

Now, if you've ever been to the zoo and observed the other primates for a while, it might seem unbelievable to you that our closest cousins on earth are chimpanzees. While we are closely related to them genetically, we don't seem a whole lot like them. The other primates seem more similar to one another than they do to us with regard to intelligence and behavior. In fact, there seems to be a "missing link" between us and them, something in between we of the giant brain and chattering speech and they of the swinging arms and hoots and calls.

Millions of years ago, there were several "missing links," if you will, between us and chimpanzees, creatures that were "midway" between modern humans and apes. *But none of them survived.* Their lifelines overlapped a good deal—some for hundreds of thousands of years as is shown in Figure 1 on the next page. Neanderthals, for example, coexisted with *archaic Homo sapiens* and *Homo sapiens sapiens.* Yet only creatures from the last of these species are still around today. They are us.

The earliest humanlike species identified so far is *Australopithecus ramidus.*[42] These creatures emerged around four-and-one-half million years ago. They had brains and bodies *about the size of chimpanzees,* but humanlike faces, and they walked upright on their two hind legs like modern humans. By two million years ago, there were several species of australopithecines around, and only one species of Homo, *Homo habilis.* Shortly after Homo arrived on the scene, the australopithecines became extinct, and shortly after our own species, *Homo sapiens sapiens,*

Millions of
years ago

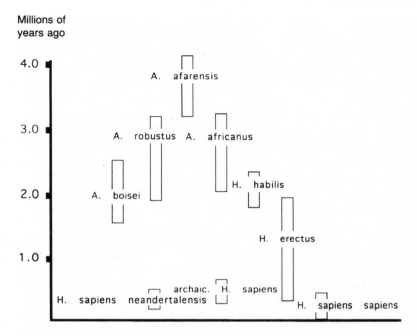

Figure 1. The precursors of modern humans (*Homo sapiens sapiens*). The earliest known species, *Australopethicus ramidus*, is not shown. This species was discovered very recently (1994), and its time line is not certain.

appeared, every other form of Homo disappeared. What happened?

For one thing, the various species differed in brain size. *H. habilis*'s brain was about 50 percent bigger than the australopithecine brain. Successive species of Homo sported even larger brains: By the time *H. sapiens sapiens* appeared, brain size had tripled relative to *A. afarensis*. Relatively speaking, that's a lot more brain than one would think necessary for creatures the size of *H. sapiens sapiens*. In fact, if you look at the ratio of brain size to body size for all species, the average modern human brain is three times as large as would be expected for a primate of average human build.

But it wasn't just the size of *H. habilis*'s brain that hearkened something new and powerful on the planet. Something else mysteriously appeared. *H. habilis's* brain sported a groove in the left frontal lobe of the cerebral cortex that resembles Broca's area. We saw that Broca's area is responsible for the productive and syntactic aspects of language. Damage to this area disrupts our ability to speak or to sign, that is, to communicate using sign language. The fact that *H. habilis* had evolved something like Broca's area suggests that the rudiments of language may have emerged with them, around two million years ago. This suggests that *language was the driving evolutionary force behind the tripling of brain size during this period of hominid evolution.*[43]

Other evidence supports the central role of language in the evolution of *Homo.* The right and left cerebral hemispheres in both humans and monkeys are specialized for certain functions, with communication and certain symbolic functions housed in the left hemisphere.[44] The left hemisphere areas that are involved in primate calls are thought to have expanded during this period of evolution, driving the development of a brain specialized for language. This suggests that the brain specialization necessary for language had already emerged *prior* to the evolutionary split between humans and apes. For whatever reasons, this special-ization evolved more rapidly in humans, producing an evolu-tionary advantage that promoted the species.[45]

A rival theory places evolutionary advantage not on language per se, but on the recursive quality of thought that underlies language.[46] Recursion means that small units can be used to generate larger units by using rules that refer to themselves and one another. For example, a rule for generating a noun phrase might be "Generate an article, an adjective, a noun, and a relative clause." A rule for generating a relative clause might be "Gen-erate a relative pronoun, a verb, and a noun phrase." Notice that the two rules specify how to create larger units (noun phrases and relative clauses) from smaller units (nouns, articles, adjectives, pronouns) and that they refer to each other in their instructions. Using these two rules, one can generate a noun phrase of infinite length. Using the noun–phrase rule, one might generate "the mystery thief," which consists of an article (the) followed by an adjective (mystery) followed by a noun (thief). The noun–phrase rule says to now use the relative-clause rule. Using this rule, one might generate "who stole the blue car," which has a relative pronoun (who), a verb (stole), and then a noun phrase (the blue car = article adjective noun). But notice that the noun phrase says to use the relative-clause rule again. Continuing in this fashion, we could end up with a phrase like this: "The mystery thief who stole the blue car that had a diplomatic license plate that belonged to the old diplomat who met with the young president who visited the rich sheik . . ."

Even if the rules seemed difficult to understand, you probably had no difficulty understanding this phrase. Because recursion is part of our genetic language capacity, we can effortlessly generate and understand sentences of enormous complexity, even though we are not consciously aware of how we do it.

Because the rules refer to each other, this phrase also has a hierarchical structure, as follows:

The mystery thief

|

who stole the blue car

|

that had a diplomatic license plate

|

that belonged to . . .

And so on. "License plate" refers to the car, which in turn refers to the thief who stole it. The recursive quality of human language allows smaller units (like nouns and verbs) to be combined in hierarchies like this.

According to this rival theory, *Homo* evolved a "generative assembling device," or GAD, that was responsible for constructing complexes from small vocabularies of primitive units. The evolutionary significance of this recursive capacity was immense: Around thirty-five thousand years ago—during the dawn of *H. sapiens sapiens*—there was an evolutionary explosion. Cave drawings appeared, as did cosmetics, jewelry, and tool manufacture. This last evolutionary occurrence is of particular importance. Other species modify objects to use as tools (e.g., elephants modify tree branches to use as fly swatters), but *only humans manufacture them according to plan.* What does that mean? *Humans use tools to make tools,* generating objects of greater complexity by combining a small number of more primitive units in a variety of ways. Do you begin to see the recursive quality of thought emerging here?

If *H. habilis* possessed this ability, why didn't this creature make drawings and manufacture tools? The answer, according to this theory, was that habilis relied on a *gestural* form of communication. What distinguished *H. sapiens sapiens* from other species of hominids was a switch from a gestural means of communication to a vocal one.[47] This is easier said than done (pun intended).

In order to produce the wide variety of sounds that make up human language, the larynx must be positioned low in the neck. If it is too high, there is not enough space in the throat to modify the airflow, so the array of sounds that the animal can make is limited. The larynx of australopithecines was located very high in the throat, similar to that of apes. The larynx began its descent somewhere around the time *H. habilis,* but it did not arrive at its modern low destination until *H. sapiens* appeared. (Incidentally, modern human infants are born with larynxes in the high "ape" position, which allows them to swallow and breathe at the same time. Around eighteen months of age, the larynx begins a dramatic descent to a lower, adult position. We can no longer swallow and breathe at the same time, but we can now make the speech sounds required for language.)

Switching to a vocal means of communication freed the hands so that the GAD could be applied to functions other than language, such as depiction (e.g., cave drawings) and tool manufacture. It also increased the evolutionary advantage of early humans because both manufacturing and communicating (both in the cave and during the hunt!) could operate cooperatively. Cooperative action led to greater output, greater complexity of objects created, and hence a greater need for communication. Thus, according to this theory, the feedback loop between manufacturing and language complexity spurred the evolutionary explosion that occurred during the dawn of *H. sapiens sapiens.*

Other theories have been proposed to account for the evolutionary explosion and the extinction of other species. Regardless of which theory is correct, however, they all appeal to two crucial factors. The first is that *language played a crucial role in the evolution of apes into humans.*[48] The rudimentary specialization of communicative and symbolic functions that can be seen in the brains of modern-day apes underwent evolutionary selection to produce a creature specialized for symbolic, vocal communication. The second is that these *evolutionary forces favored greater cooperation within species.* In a very real sense, we didn't get where we are by having a bigger or better dominance hierarchy, but by having greater cooperation and communication among members of our own species relative to members of other species. Because we had a well-developed capacity for abstract, recursive language, we could also plan, make complex tools, and manipulate the environment.

By contrast, other animals, including apes, have intensely intricate within-species dominance hierarchies but less advanced communication or cooperation among members. Our early ancestors probably evidenced this reliance on dominance as well. *A. afarensis* males were twice as large as females, a characteristic that is common among species whose males compete with one another for females. By the time *H. erectus* showed up, this ratio had greatly diminished, becoming more like the ratio between modern female and male humans. This suggests that *H. erectus* had developed a social pattern of cooperation, which undoubtedly gave it an enormous competitive advantage.[49] If you've ever tried to teach the concept of a "pass" to elementary school hockey, football, or basketball teams, you know what I mean. All the kids huddle around the ball like metal filings around a magnet, trying to muscle each other out of the way. The first coach who can get his or her team to assume positions and pass the ball according to plan wins every time.

Does the lack of an abstract, recursive language mean that other animals don't communicate with each other? Of course not. But they do not communicate via language, and their communicative ideas are not as rich as ours. Bee dances tell where the honey is, but they are not recursive. Apes can be taught the basics of American Sign Language, but they sign at most two-word sentences. As one researcher put it, "Nature provides no intermediate language, nothing between the lowly call system [of other animals] and the towering human language."[50]

If this reconstructed evolutionary history of the impact of language on the ascendancy of humans seems a bit strained, a compelling example from recorded history makes this point even more forcibly.[51]

During archaeological excavations in the Middle East, archaeologists frequently turned up tiny clay objects, including cones, spheres, disks, animal figurines, and tiny models of human-made items. Their presence constituted a bit of a mystery for the scientists. They thought the disks might be lids for tiny jars and the spheres might be marbles, but they were clueless as to what the other objects might be. The mystery was finally solved when scientists began to understand that the objects were not functional but were instead abstract representations. They were in fact precursors of *writing*.

Around 8000 B.C., people in Mesopotamia began a transition from the hunter-gatherer lifestyle to farming. Villages sprang up, and the population grew. To accommodate the large crops of cultivated grain, the villagers built large communal silos. And therein lay a very serious problem: They needed some way of keeping track of the amount of grain individual farmers had stored in the communal silos. The answer: They used small clay tokens to stand for, or *represent,* specified amounts of different kinds of grain and other stored products. For example, the Sumerians used clay spheres to stand for bushels of grain, and egg-shaped tokens to stand for jars of oil. The farmer was given a token for each filled bushel or jar he brought to the silo. To get the stuff back, the farmer brought the tokens and was given a bushelful of grain for each sphere and a jar of oil for each egg-shaped token.

This might seem pretty elementary to you, but think of this in an evolutionary context: Perhaps for the first time in the considerable lifetime of the planet (millions of years), objects were used to represent other objects. Funny little bits of clay came to *symbolically represent* very important food resources in this budding human economy. This was a unique evolutionary phenomenon—unique to humans. No other species on earth does this.

But there was a problem with this system: If you brought a lot of stuff to the silo over time, you had to keep track of an awful lot of tokens. So someone came up with the idea of baking the tokens inside a clay envelope, pressing the tokens onto the front of the envelope before baking so the farmer could tell how many there were inside. Somewhere along the way, someone figured out that if the clay envelope bore impressions of the tokens inside, you didn't need the tokens. A stylus or other writing utensil could be used to make marks on a clay tablet representing the bushels and jars left in the silo. An oval could *represent* the egg-shaped tokens which in turn *represented* the cylindrical jars. A circle could *represent* the spheres which in turn *represented* the round bushels. The tablets were less cumbersome to store and more easily manufactured than the tokens. Writing with a stylus was quicker than choosing and pressing tokens onto an envelope. Notice that this constituted another huge leap in symbolic, representational thinking—from physical tokens to pure written symbols. Again, we are the only species that does this.

The next big leap is truly one of genius. Around 3100 B.C., some budding CPA figured out that rather than making, for example, thirty-three marks to represent thirty-three bushels of grain, it would be a lot simpler to make a symbol that represented "ten" and another that represented "one." Then all you had to do was make three "ten" marks, three "one" marks, and then make the impression for bushel or jar. Anyone who knew the system would then know that thirty-three bushels of grain or thirty-three jars of oil had been stored in the silo. "Ten" and "one" were the first two numbers to be assigned abstract, symbolic representations.

Eventually the Sumerian system was adopted by the Babylonians and expanded to handle more abstract quantities. The system eventually spread to Greece, where it evolved into the mathematical systems proposed by the likes of Pythagoras, Euclid, and Archimedes. These eventually led to algebra, calculus, tensor analysis, and other modern forms of mathematics used today. And these, of course, led to the development of modern technology.

Our capacity to represent numbers abstractly piggybacked on

our startling and unique capacity for language. Because we evolved the capacity for communicating in symbols, we now have talk radio, space shuttles, television, penicillin, turbine engines, books, music, and theater. In a very real sense, we owe our ascension to the top of the phylogenetic scale to this evolved capacity for symbolic thought—a capacity that is afforded by our capacity for language.

CHAPTER 9

Why We Think
the Way We Do

As one philosopher of science put it, thinking is the capacity that "permits our hypotheses to die in our stead."[1] If you have a very simple and kind environment, you don't have to be very smart in order to survive long enough to reproduce. But if your environment is hostile (e.g., hungry saber-tooths) and you're a bit on the small side, you will enjoy a great survival advantage if you can think. Thinking allows you to plan your actions and consider their consequences before you execute them. It allows you to manipulate the environment in the world of ideas before attempting to manipulate the environment itself. It allows you, in short, to save your muscles some wear and tear, outwit your larger opponents, and mold your environment into a more hospitable place.

I am going to focus almost exclusively on human cognition, but I don't want to leave you with the impression that only humans think. We tend to conceptualize thinking as talking to ourselves, and since animals can't speak, we assume they can't think either. But if that were the case, we'd have to conclude that deaf-mute humans can't think either, and, as Helen Keller's autobiography shows, that is clearly false. Thinking is one of the things brains do. All of that neural activity constitutes thoughts—whether verbal, imagistic, or sensory—and anything with a brain thinks. The species differ, however, in terms of the sophistication of their thinking apparatus, and hence the richness of their thoughts. You'll never teach your dogs about calculus, economic policy, grand opera, or existentialism no matter how many dog yummies you use in the process. Their neural architecture is just not sophisticated enough to entertain such abstract thoughts.

Given all of that, we might ask just how well we illustrious humans think. Decades of research by scientific psychologists indicate that the answer to that question depends on the nature of the thinking task. Human thinking is a composite of three factors: innate knowledge, basic categorization processes, and formal reasoning. As we saw in previous chapters, we are born knowing quite a bit about certain aspects of our environment. We acquire subsequent knowledge primarily through *categorization processes,* a fundamental neural process that allows us to group patterns of events in the world. *Formal reasoning* is reasoning that depends on abstract formalisms, such as algebra, geometry, and logic. We have the ability to invent or learn these formalisms *because we have the ability to learn language.* If our reasoning differs from that of other animals at all, it is because of this capacity for formal thought afforded by our capacity for language.

The most fundamental distinction our evolved reasoning system makes is the one between creatures and objects. Because they act of their own volition, creatures can harm or nurture us when we are helpless infants. Because objects cannot act of their own volition, they are less of a threat and less of a help to us. Not surprisingly, then, sensitivity to this distinction appears very early in life. Three-month-old infants become very upset when a person stands very still in front of them, but are indifferent when an unmoving object of the same size is placed in front of them.[2] Seven-month-old infants look where their mothers' attention is directed, even if they have to turn around to do it.[3] Changing the orientation of an object doesn't have the same effect. They seem to appreciate that a creature's focus of attention carries potentially useful (or at least interesting) information.

Infants as young as three months also respond to changes in their mothers' facial expressions, especially expressions that signal safety or danger.[4] In contrast, these same expressions don't mean much (or are upsetting) when they come from a video-taped image of their mothers.[5] A videotape is not a living creature, no matter how similar its images are in physical appearance to the real thing.

Our innate knowledge about living things is shaped around a sensitivity to fundamental biological distinctions and fundamental social concepts. The first fundamental biological distinction that emerges concerns the distinction between natural kinds and artifacts. Natural kinds are classes of things that occur naturally in the world, independently of human activities—animals, plants, and minerals. They cohere in nature as groups of entities that are governed by common sets of laws. Artifacts, on the other hand, are classes of things that are made by humans or other agents to serve particular functions, such as toasters, chairs, and dams.

By three years of age (the youngest tested so far), humans distinguish between natural kinds and artifacts, and use this distinction to guide the inferences they make.[6] Some researchers showed a group of three-year-olds picture triads and told them something about the triads that they didn't already know. One example consisted of a large bird with outstretched wings, a similarly sized bat with outstretched wings, and a flamingo standing on one foot with wings closed. The bat and the bird with outstretched wings looked more similar to each other than did the bird and the flamingo. Then they told the children things such as "See this *bird* [pointing to flamingo]? It feeds its babies mashed up worms. See this *bat* [pointing to bat]. It feeds its babies milk. See this *bird* [pointing to bird with outstretched wings]? Do you think it feeds its babies mashed up worms or milk?" The majority of three-year-olds answered, "Worms." Effects like these have been replicated countless times with a variety of materials. Even three-year-olds know that their inferences should be constrained by the biological category referred to by certain nouns (e.g., bird and bat) and not by simple perceptual similarities.

We also seem to appreciate very early the constraints that govern membership in basic biological categories. For example, even four-year-olds know that you can't turn a cactus into a porcupine, a porcupine into a cactus, or a pincushion into a cactus.[7] They believe artifacts are artifacts, plants are plants, and creatures are creatures. Period. But they think it might be possible to change things into other things as long as they stayed within the same ontological category. They believe, for example, that a raccoon can be turned into a skunk by dyeing its fur black, putting a white stripe down its back, and sewing a bag of smelly stuff inside it. They also believe structural changes can turn a cactus into a tree, and a chair into a table. At this age, kids seem to think that things can change *within* their fundamental category, but they cannot change from one fundamental category to another. In other words, creatures can become other creatures, but they can't become plants or objects. Plants can become other plants, but they can't become objects or creatures. And objects can become other objects, but not creatures or plants.

Sensitivity to ontological category also constrains the types of inferences very young children make about the internal structures of things. For example, if you tell a four-year-old that humans have something inside of them called a spleen, they will infer that other mammals (e.g., dogs, cats) and birds do, too. But they won't think it likely that plants or objects (e.g., dolls and stuffed animals) do.[8]

Innate or early emerging knowledge like this continues to shape the nature of our reasoning about living beings and objects well into adulthood.[9] For example, a group of adults were told that a chemical waste accident had transformed the appearance of a birdlike creature into that of an insectlike creature. Before the accident, the creature had wings, built nests, and laid eggs. After the accident, it grew a shell and two more legs, and lived on flower nectar. They were then asked to rate the new creature on three dimensions: its category membership (Is it more likely to be a bird or an insect?), its similarity (Is it more similar to a bird or an insect?), and its typicality (Is it more typical of a bird or an insect?). The ratings indicated that adults believed the accidental but permanent changes in appearance made the creature seem more similar to and typical of an insect, but that the creature was still a bird nonetheless. In contrast, when adults were told that an umbrella-like object was designed to be used as a lampshade, they decided that the object was a lampshade even though it was more similar to and more typical of an umbrella.

Along with biological distinctions, distinctions among social concepts also emerge very early in life. By the end of the second year of life, children distinguish between moral rules and social regulations.[10] For example, tell a group of average three-year-olds that their day-care center has a rule requiring them to pick up their toys. Then ask them if it's possible another day-care center might have a different rule saying children don't have to pick up their toys. The overwhelming majority will say yes. Now tell them their day-care center has a rule against hitting other children, and ask them if it's possible another day-care center might have a different rule saying children could hit each other. The overwhelming majority will say no. Children as young as two-and-one-half years of age distinguish between social conventions (You must pick up your toys) and moral rules (You must not hit anyone). They consider social conventions to be rules formed by authorities to coordinate social interactions, which makes them alterable by other authorities. In contrast, they believe moral rules are obligatory, not determined by personal inclination, nonchangeable on an arbitrary basis, and applicable across situations and societal contexts. This appears to universally true, having been observed in other cultures, including non-Western ones.[11]

The early emergence of sensitivity to social and moral rules suggests an innate predisposition for detecting and reasoning about such rules. This is apparent in reasoning tasks that pit logical reasoning against social reasoning. Children as young as three years old have little difficulty reasoning about permissions, but fail miserably on identical reasoning tasks that don't have a permission context.[12] For example, three-year-olds in one study were shown a group of rubber mice playing in a dollhouse and an identical group playing outside in the backyard of the house. They were told that some of the mice squeaked when you squeezed them and some didn't. Some of the children were then told by Minnie Mouse that "All squeaky mice are in the house," and were required to indicate which mice had to be squeezed to find out if she was right or wrong. They said the mice that were inside the house had to be squeezed. Other children were told by the "queen" mouse (the same Minnie Mouse stuffed animal) that "All squeaky mice must stay in the house." They were then asked which mice had to be squeezed to find out whether anyone was breaking the rule. These children said the mice that were outside the house had to be squeezed. In both cases, the correct answer is "outside." (Finding a squeaky mouse outside disproves the rule "All squeaky mice are in the house.") Even at this young age, children have little difficulty reasoning well about social rules.

If you had trouble figuring out that the outside mice had to be tested in the first scenario, you're not alone. Even adults show the permission effect. For example, suppose I were to tell you that "If I go to Phoenix, then I travel by car." I then show you four cards that have a travel destination on one side, and a means of transportation on the other: Phoenix, Tucson, Car, Airplane. Your job is to indicate all and only those cards that must be turned over to test whether or not the rule I told you is true. Did you choose Phoenix and Car? Most people do.[13] The correct answer is Phoenix and Airplane. It's not necessary to turn over the Car card because the rule says nothing about my not being allowed to drive other places. I could have driven to work or to Miami or anywhere else. But if Phoenix appears on the other side of the Airplane card, the rule is disproved. It is therefore necessary to turn the Airplane card over.

Contrast that scenario with the following: You are a bartender, and there are four customers in your bar who are represented by the following information: Drinking Beer, Drinking Coke, 21 years old, 16 years old. Indicate which customers need to have their id's or their drinks checked to ensure that the following rule is being obeyed: "If a customer is drinking beer, then the customer must be at least twenty-one years of age." Did you say the customer who is drinking beer and the customer who is sixteen years old? Most people do.[14] In fact, this reasoning problem is so easy for most of us that it doesn't even seem like a problem. Yet it is identical in logical form to the former problem. Both rules are of the form "If p, then q," and both sets of items are of the form "p," "not p,", "q," and "not q." In both cases, the p item (Phoenix, drinking beer) and the not-q item (Airplane, 16 years old) must be checked to test the rule.

Results like these have been reported countless times in hundreds of studies. When a task requires people to reason about informal social contracts such as permissions, promises, obligations, threats, or warnings, people perform remarkably well. But when we are required to reason about nonsocial rules—even those we're familiar with—we don't perform very well.

We are also endowed at birth or shortly thereafter with a good deal of knowledge about objects and their behavior. By three months of age, human infants appreciate that objects are solid, rigid, and permanent entities that travel in continuous paths and can causally influence one another only by making direct contact

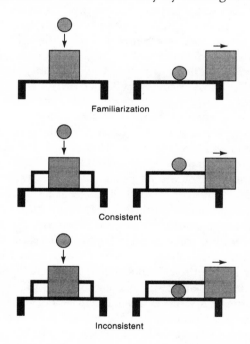

Figure 1: Infants watch as a ball is dropped behind a screen, and the screen is lowered to reveal it lying on the table. This is repeated until they get bored. Then the ball is dropped, but this time, when the screen is lowered, the ball appears either in its old resting place on the table (as though it went right through the platform) or in a new place on top of the platform. Which is more surprising? The impossible event: Infants as young as three months spend more time looking at the impossible than the possible event. (After Spelke, 1991, figure 5.1)

(that is, no action at a distance).[15] For example, infants in this age group were allowed to watch a rotating screen until they got bored and looked away. Then a block that they'd played with recently was put in the screen's path. The infants regained interest when the screen reached the block and stopped. But they were not nearly as interested in this event as they were in another in which the screen appeared to rotate right through the block! (There was a hidden trapdoor that the block dropped into, allowing the screen to pass through.) The infants spent more time examining the impossible event, and their emotional reactions showed surprise. In Figure 1, similarly, a ball was dropped so that it fell behind a screen. Sometimes when the screen was raised, the ball appeared to have fallen onto a solid table. Other times, it appeared under the table, as though it had somehow fallen right through the table. Infants as young as two-and-one-half months spent more time looking at the impossible event.

Results like these indicate that infants expect solid objects to be permanent and impenetrable. Appreciation of object permanence is apparent from the fact that the infant's view of the block is completely occluded once the screen reaches a sixty-degree orientation. If they thought the block ceased to exist once it was out of view, then they wouldn't be surprised that the rotating screen continued to travel through the space it formerly occupied. The same holds for object impenetrability. If they believed solid objects were penetrable, they wouldn't be surprised to see two solid objects (the screen and the block, or the ball and the table) pass through each other.

Similar results have been observed by rolling a ball so that it disappeared behind a screen and then lifting the screen to reveal the ball either resting against a vertical partition or resting on the other side of the partition—as though it had traveled right through the partition or jumped over it. Infants spent more time looking at the impossible event in which the ball seemed to have passed through or jumped over the partition. They also spent more time looking at an event in which a large ball appeared to have fallen through a very small hole in a table than an event in which a small ball appeared to have fallen through a very large hole. They seemed to appreciate that solid objects travel in continuous paths (can't jump over a partition) and are rigid (can't compress to fit through an opening smaller than itself).

Infants also seem to grasp the concept of physical causality in that they respond quite differently to causal and noncausal events. For example, in a series of studies, groups of six-month-old infants were shown videotapes of various events involving blocks.[16] One videotape showed a block banging into another block and sending it flying. A second videotape showed one block coming to rest next to another block, and then after a pause, the latter taking off, seemingly of its own accord. In still another, one block changed color after coming into contact with another block. Infants were allowed to watch a given videotape until they became bored and looked away. Then the tape was played backward. The infants spent more time looking at the reversal of the causal event where one block sends another flying by banging into it. They seemed to find the reversal of the causal relation more interesting and novel than the reversal of the noncausal events.

By at least six months, then (and perhaps younger), we seem to be sensitive to the notion of causation. This is particularly interesting because, as philosopher David Hume pointed out in the eighteenth century, one can't directly perceive causation.[17] What is available to our senses are the sensory aspects (e.g., visual, auditory) of two things occurring in close succession in the same physical location. For example, we see the swinging hammer make physical contact with the crystal vase, and then see the vase explode into glinting shards. But where is the "causing"? What allows us to perceive the difference between "The hammer hit the vase, *and then* the vase shattered" and "The hammer hit the vase, *therefore* the vase shattered"? Philosopher Immanuel Kant argued that the mind supplied the "therefore"; the concept of causation was an innate property of the mind.[18] If we didn't have the concept of causation innately, we'd never be able to learn it because we'd never be able to see it. It seems that perhaps Kant was right. Even very young infants who have had very little exposure to the world distinguish between causal and noncausal events.

Taken together these results seem to indicate that by the tender age of six months (and possibly earlier), we appreciate the constraints of a Newtonian world. Or do we?

The impressive performance of infants on these physical reasoning tasks breaks down when the tasks require an appreciation of gravity and inertia.[19] For example, if a ball is dropped behind a screen, and the screen is lifted to reveal the ball hovering in midair above a table, very young infants don't find this any more surprising than if the ball is revealed to have fallen onto the table. Somewhere between six and nine months of age, they begin to look longer at the hovering ball, suggesting a budding appreciation of the effects of gravity. Prior to this, their reactions seem to suggest that solid objects can defy gravity by hovering over the table, but they cannot defy the impenetrability and rigidity constraints by passing through the table. As long as the dropped ball appears on the table or over the table, everything is fine. But the ball can't drop *through* the table.

An even more dramatic demonstration corroborates this conclusion. While on vacation at the Grand Canyon, psychologist Eleanor Gibson saw an infant crawl dangerously close to the edge before he was snatched up by his mother. Gibson wondered if the child really hadn't realized the danger he faced. To test this, she constructed a safe canyon. It consisted of a small rectangular pool that had a checkboard pattern painted on the bottom and sides. One side of the pool was very deep (several feet) and one side was shallow (a few inches). The checkerboard pattern made it easy to see this. A heavy sheet of glass was placed over the pool and a board was positioned across the middle, dividing the deep end from the shallow end. Infants were placed individually on the board. The mother stood either at the deep end or at the shallow end and called to the infant to crawl to her. Infants of all ages happily crawled to their mothers when she stood at the shallow end. But when she stood at the deep end, only infants younger than six months of age would crawl to her. Those older than six months hesitated, patted the glass to see if it was sturdy, and still often refused to come.[20] Gravity, it seems, doesn't play a big role in our cognition until about six months of age.

Like gravity, appreciation of inertia seems slow to emerge during infanthood. Until about nine months of age, infants don't find it surprising when a ball rolled with great force seems to stop suddenly of its own accord. They also don't seem to mind if a ball appears to change direction on its own while it is rolling.

So let's take stock: By three months of age, human infants seem to appreciate that objects are solid, permanent, and rigid entities that travel on continuous paths and can causally influence one another only through direct contact. In contrast, appreciation of gravity and inertia does not begin to appear until infants are six to nine months of age. Now, the most intriguing thing about this pattern of results is that the physical knowledge that emerges first in infancy constitutes a core group of concepts that direct our reasoning even as adults. In contrast, the knowledge that emerges later remains foreign to our world view, and is difficult to learn and understand. Let me prove it to you:

In studies of "naive physics," intelligent twentieth-century adults who had not studied physics were asked about the behavior of physical objects.[21] Rarely did they make mistakes regarding continuity, solidity, rigidity, or direct causation. These things seem perceptually obvious to them. Errors frequently occurred, however, on judgments concerning inertia and gravity as depicted by Figures 2 and 3. Look at Figure 2. When the ball comes shooting out of the spiral, which direction will it travel? Did you choose path (a)? So did the majority (51 percent) of volunteers in these studies. And so did nearly every ancient and medieval scholar. For centuries, it was believed that setting an object in motion impressed in the object a force, or impetus, that served to keep it in motion. When released, it continued to trace the same trajectory until the force dissipated. Newton showed us otherwise. When the ball leaves the spiral, it will obey the law of inertia, retaining the same direction it was traveling the second it emerges from the spiral until some other force acts upon it, as in option (b).

Now consider Figure 3. Which trajectory will the bomb travel when it leaves the plane? Did you choose (c) or (d)? So did a plurality of the people in these studies (47 percent). The correct answer is (a). Why? Because inertia causes the bomb to continue traveling in the same direction it was traveling upon release (forward) while gravity pulls it down. The combination is a graceful arc, as in (a).

In contrast, adult reasoners exhibit sophisticated reasoning about causal events.[22] They take into consideration whether

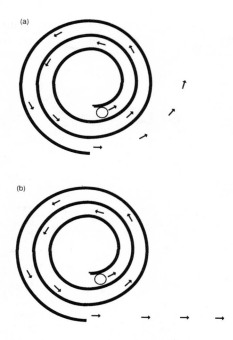

Figure 2: When the ball comes shooting out of the spiral, which path will it follow? See text for the correct answer, and for the answer most people give. (After McCloskey, 1983, figure 13.2)

more than one cause could have produced an effect under consideration, and whether intervening circumstances could prevent an effect from occurring even though a viable cause is present. As a simple example, most reasoners believe knowing that the streets are wet is insufficient evidence to conclude that it rained recently. Their refusal to draw this conclusion is based on their consideration that other factors could cause the streets to be wet, such as a street cleaner, or someone washing their car, or a burst water main. In contrast, if told about a planet whose surface becomes sticky when a natural process known as "thardronning" occurs, and are then asked whether observing a sticky surface on that planet is sufficient to conclude that it thardronned, reasoners agree that it is indeed likely that thardronning occurred. Reasoners temper their conclusions of simple

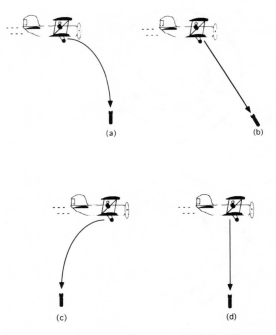

Figure 3: When the bomb is dropped, which path will it follow? See text for the correct answer, and for the answer most people give. (After McCloskey, 1983, figure 13.4)

causal arguments based on their untutored but sophisticated theories of causal structures.

Our innate knowledge shapes not only our own physical reasoning as individuals, it also shaped the history of Western technology. The invention of modern technology was an unlikely—if not miraculous—event. Although *Homo sapiens sapiens* appeared on the scene about thirty-five thousand years ago, it was not until the sixteenth century A.D. that we as a species began to appreciate and understand the true physical laws of inertia and gravity, and it took the genius of Galileo and Newton to explicate them. In fact, we owe nearly all of modern technology to the genius of just a handful of gifted people who were able to break free of the innate reasoning constraints nature provided us.

Prior to Galileo, Western societies maintained a view of the world that was shaped partly by Aristotle (384–322 B.C.) and partly by biblical scripture. The concept of inertia did not play a major role in either. Aristotle believed that in order to keep an object in motion, a continual force needed to be applied.[23] Without it, the object would eventually slow down to a halt, a belief that was accepted for centuries.

Now, here is a conundrum. The ancients knew that the planets moved through the heavens. If objects required a force to maintain their motion, why didn't the planets come to a grinding halt? That is where God comes in: Aristotle believed in a "Prime Mover," an eternal and ultimate source of all causation and all movement. The planets were kept in motion by this Prime Mover, and that satisfied the mystery of planetary movement. (Later, the concept of angels served this same purpose.) Aristotle also held some odd beliefs about gravity. He wrote, for example, that the speed with which objects fall depends on their weight, and this was accepted as fact for centuries.

In 1598, the Italian scientist Galileo Galilei undertook a meticulous series of experiments using balls of various sizes and weights and inclined planes.[24] He observed that contrary to Aristotle's teachings, a constant push was not needed to keep an object moving *as long as friction was removed*. He also showed that as long as the balls were heavy enough not to be influenced by air resistance, they rolled down the planes at the same rate regardless of weight, gaining speed at a constant rate under the constant pull of gravity.

Putting these ideas together, he concluded that gravitational force was all that was needed to explain planetary motion—no angel or Prime Mover was needed. Then he made a very bad move. He wrote a book based on his researches in which he argued that the Earth was not the center of the universe, but a planet revolving around the sun. His conclusions were found to be at variance with biblical doctrine (particularly the bit about the Earth not being the center of the universe), and *he was placed under house arrest for the rest of his life*. Although forbidden to conduct any further work in science, he managed to write his last treatise on motion and mechanics, which became the foundation of the modern field of kinematics.

But some ideas just won't die. The torch was taken up by Sir

Isaac Newton, who in 1687 published the *Principia Mathematica,* which codified Galileo's findings concerning falling bodies into three laws of motion.[25] From these laws, he deduced that the inertial mass of a body is identical to its gravitational mass. This meant that the gravitational force exerted by an object is proportional to its inertia. Period. It doesn't depend on the matter it's made of. This delivered the last blow to the idea that heavenly objects operated under different laws than those lowly ones on Earth. (Incidentally, Newton had a good deal of difficulty publishing the *Principia*—perhaps the greatest scientific book ever written—because his enemy, scientist Robert Hooke, violently opposed it and the Royal Society refused to become involved in the controversy. Fortunately for posterity's sake, Newton's friend, astronomer Edmond Halley, inherited a fortune when his father was murdered by unknown assailants, which provided him enough money to publish the book at his own expense.[26]

Why did it take so long for us as a species to learn about these very basic physical laws? It is hard to escape the conclusion that we find it difficult to learn what we are not born already knowing. Gravity and inertia are not part of the arsenal of innate concepts nature gives us, and perceiving them—not to mention learning them—is rough going. If this is the case, then how do we ever learn these things?

When we can't relie on innate knowledge, we fall back on a fundamental characteristic of our brain tissue, and that is its capacity to learn associations among events. We noted this capacity repeatedly in earlier chapters, and it strongly shapes the quality of our reasoning processes. Because brain tissue can learn which events tend to occur together, we are capable of dividing up the world into categories. Things that tend to occur together get grouped together in the mind. In fact, much of our cognition can be simulated rather well using computer systems called *connection machines* that do nothing but form categories by strengthening the links between events that occur together frequently.[27] As simple as this process sounds, it leads to remarkably powerful learning.

To give you an example, consider the dot configurations in Figure 4. The two top pictures represent the "prototype" for two categories. The bottom pictures were generated by ran-

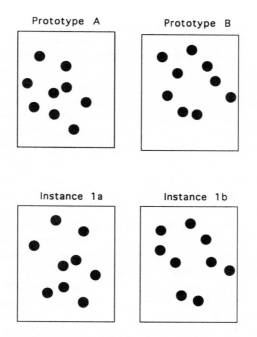

Figure 4: The top two dot configurations were used to generate a series of other pictures by randomly displacing the dots vertically, horizontally, or diagonally. These materials were then used to study categorization learning. (After Posner and Keele, 1968)

domly displacing one or more of the dots vertically, horizontally, or diagonally. Series of pictures like those on the bottom were shown one at a time to individual volunteers, and the volunteers were required to learn to categorize them all correctly.[28] They were given feedback as to whether their categorization decisions were right or wrong during the learning phase. The next day, they were shown more pictures from these categories, and asked to categorize these new pictures. Unbeknownst to the volunteers, two of the new pictures were the prototypes. Even though the volunteers had never seen the prototypes before, they classified these pictures as accurately (and as quickly) as the old pictures they saw before. In contrast, they found it harder to classify the other new pictures, and required more time to do it.

These results show that while learning the categories, the volunteers' neural classification processes had abstracted the prototypes from the pictures they were shown—whether the volunteers were aware of it or not. Their brains automatically registered the locations of the dots in each picture, and the tendency of some dots to cluster together frequently in certain configurations was also noted. As a result, the volunteers ended up representing the categories in terms of the "average," "best," or most prototypical representations—even though they had never been shown these representations during the learning phase. These results were later simulated using a computer program that simply noted the correlations among the locations of the dots.[29]

This same process allows us to acquire knowledge about natural kinds and artifacts in real life. Much of our acquired (as opposed to innate) knowledge about natural kinds is represented as *prototypes*.[30] The most prototypical member of a category is usually the one that shares the most features with other members of the category. Another way to say this is that *categories are formed by detecting correlations among features,* and membership in the category is graded in terms of how many features a member shares with other members. For example, when Americans were asked to describe what a bird is, they typically described a bird as a creature that is *small, has wings, build nests in trees, and flies.* These features are highly correlated with each other, and they form the core of our understanding of the category "bird." They were then asked to describe a number of different species of birds, such as robin, canary, ostrich, and penguin. Robins were described as *small* creatures that *have wings, fly, make nests in trees,* show up in spring, and have red breasts. Ostriches were described as large creatures that have *wings but don't fly,* live in Africa, and stick their heads in the sand when frightened. Notice that the description of "robin" has more features in common with the description of "bird" than the description of ostrich does. Not surprisingly, when these (or any other Americans) were then asked to rate these bird species in terms of how typical they are of the category bird, they consistently gave higher ratings to species like robin than to species like ostrich. Typical category members (like robin) are also categorized faster on speeded tests where the decision maker must decide as quickly as possible whether each item on a list is a member of a particular category (e.g., Is a robin a bird? Is an ostrich a bird? Is a plum a bird?).

This process of detecting correlations among features and forming categories based on them is extremely powerful. In fact, it's too powerful. And that's why we need innate knowledge: Without it, every coincidence would be dutifully noted by our correlation detectors and a category formed. We'd end up believing some pretty crazy things, such as that model airplanes are birds, or that when you wash your car, it rains. In fact, we do end up believing some pretty crazy—and superstitious things—for that reason. But fortunately our innate knowledge often disciplines our wanton categorization system, drawing our attention to the correlations that matter and away from those that don't.

This point can be easily appreciated by considering a related phenomenon, the Garcia effect:[31] A group of rats were given saccharine-sweetened water to drink. While they drank, bright lights were flashed and a clicking noise sounded. Then half of the rats were given a strong electric shock and the other half were exposed to a dose of X-rays strong enough to make them feel nauseous. Notice that all of the rats were exposed to the same stimuli while drinking—flashing lights, clicking noises, and sweet taste. Now here is the interesting part: The rats who were shocked developed a strong aversion to drinking water when the flashing lights and noise were present, but they had no problem with drinking sweetened water. The rats who were made nauseous by X-rays developed a strong aversion to drinking sweetened water, but had no problem with drinking while the lights and noise were present.

This is a clear example of how innate knowledge disciplines the categorization process. Rats are pretty primitive creatures, yet their innate knowledge of causation helped organize their experiences pretty intelligently. This knowledge said, in effect, that bright flashing lights belong to the "can cause shock" category, but not to the "can cause nausea" category. The reverse is true of funny-tasting water. Just like kids, they are conservative about which inferences are worth making and which are probably spurious.

But our innate knowledge is sometimes wrong, as we saw in the case of physical reasoning. How then do we overcome incorrect biases in our reasoning system? There are two ways we do this. The first is by restructuring our categories. The second is by constructing abstract representations of the world and manipulating them, as we do when we construct equations to represent the stress factors affecting a bridge. Each of these allow us to break free of constraints on our reasoning. The surprising thing is that of the two, the former—restructuring—appears to be most involved in expertise development and creative genius.

There's been a good deal of investigation of the processes involved in becoming an expert, particularly in the domain of physics. The bottom line seems to be this: Mastering a new domain requires reorganizing your knowledge base around new concepts introduced by the domain. In other words, you must come to *recategorize* your old and new knowledge. If you don't, then your new domain-specific knowledge will remain forever isolated from the rest of your knowledge base, leaving your naive theories untouched.

Richard Feynman, the late great physicist and Nobel laureate, noted just this type of knowledge isolation among physics graduate students. He reported: "After a lot of investigation, I finally figured out that the students had memorized everything, but they didn't know what anything meant. When they heard 'light that is reflected from a medium with an index,' they didn't know that it meant a material *such as water*. They didn't know that the 'direction of the light' is the direction in which you *see* something when you're looking at it, and so on. Everything was entirely memorized, yet nothing had been translated into meaningful words."[32] Using our vocabulary, these students hadn't *recategorized* "water" as an instance of the category "media with an index." Their new physics concepts remained isolated from the other concepts. Without the necessary recategorization, their new concepts remained meaningless. It's a little like having a file in your filing cabinet for "123 Main Street" and another for

"Jane's house" and never realizing that the two refer to the same house.

In another instance, Feynman describes how the students knew that "Two bodies are considered equivalent if equal torques will produce equal acceleration." But they didn't know this had anything to do with the fact that it is very hard to push a door open if you put weights on the far outside edge as opposed to at the hinges. These students knew all about physics and they knew all about the physical world. They just didn't know how the two related to each other. They had memorized their physics textbooks, but they hadn't recategorized their old knowledge in terms of the new.

The importance of this categorization process is evident in another classic set of studies. In these studies, advanced physics graduate students and undergraduate physics majors were asked to sort a selection of elementary physics problems and to solve them.[33] The graduate students were found to sort the problems based on the underlying physics principle that governed the behavior of the physical events described in the problem, putting, for example, all problems that were instances of Newton's second law in one pile, all problems that were instances of conservation of momentum in another, and so on. In contrast, the undergraduates tended to sort the problems in terms of *similarity in surface features,* putting, for example, all problems with inclined planes in one pile, all problems with springs in another, and so on. The novices relied on their naive categories when sorting the problems, while the experts had recategorized their knowledge bases to accommodate the formal theories they'd learned.

The same pattern emerged when it came time to try and solve the problems. The experts went about it systematically, accessing relevant knowledge, carefully constructing a "picture" or representation of the problem, complete with arrows describing unseen physical forces, such as inertia, and finally writing a set of equations to solve the problem. Their behavior clearly indicated that their knowledge was categorized around core physical principles, including their knowledge about solution procedures.

The novices, on the other hand, displayed very different problem-solving strategies. They tended to use the objects mentioned in the problems as cues to search memory. For example, "inclined plane" was used to retrieve every equation they could remember that contained coefficients of friction. They then immediately began plugging numbers into the retrieved equations in a sort of blind-search attempt to solve the problem. Clearly, their knowledge bases were categorized in terms of naive categories about objects and their attributes.

It is important to remember that the novices "knew" what they needed to know in order to solve these elementary problems. Like the graduate students, they too knew all about Newton's second law and all of the other laws needed to solve the problems. They had done very well in their physics classes, and could recite these laws by heart. But that knowledge had not yet been used to recategorize their experiences. Opening a door was still opening a door, not an example of torque. Their physics knowledge was isolated from their everyday knowledge. Once new, formal knowledge is used to recategorize the rest of your knowledge, you quite literally see the world differently.

How do you make this transition? One very powerful mechanism for integrating new knowledge with old knowledge is *analogical reasoning*. Reasoning analogically basically means working out how "this is like that." For example, if the concept of an atom was first introduced to you as "An atom is like the solar system," you were invited to reason analogically.[34] Your task was to work out a set of correspondences, or mappings, so that the atom's nucleus corresponded to the sun and its electrons corresponded to the planets. Then you were free to understand that electrons revolve around the nucleus in the way that the planets revolve around the sun. The mechanism that produced this system could then be explained to you in terms of relative masses (i.e., the nucleus is more massive than the electrons, just as the sun is more massive than the planets) and gravitational force (i.e., the gravitational force exerted by a body is proportional to its mass). The analogy helped to ground all of that talk of "masses" and "gravity" and what-not in something concrete and understandable.

Analogical reasoning is a very powerful reasoning tool and

an excellent instructional device. But, as we've seen before, sometimes powerful tools can be too powerful. For example, consider the solar system–atom analogy above. What is to prevent you from inferring that the nucleus of an atom is hot, just like the sun? Really, the answer is nothing: It's a perfectly reasonable inference. Reasoning analogically without constraints and guidance can end up producing some very odd inferences. That is why one example is worth two hours of lecturing on a subject, but the example had better invite the listeners to make all and *only* the right inferences.

While category restructuring and analogical reasoning seem useful as pedagogical tools, the question still remains how great minds such as Galileo, Newton, Curie, and Einstein made their startling discoveries. As a clue, consider the fact that Einstein is said to have developed his theory of relativity by imagining himself riding on a light beam as though it were a streetcar. As this anecdote illustrates, what we normally think of as creativity and insight are really just our old friends pattern recognition and categorization in disguise.

With that in mind, try to solve this problem: A patient has an inoperable tumor in the middle of his abdomen. The tumor can be destroyed with X-rays, but the intensity needed to destroy the tumor would also destroy the healthy tissue surrounding it and hence kill the patient. How can the tumor be destroyed using X-rays without killing the patient?

Unlike the kinds of problems we've considered so far, this problem is more like the ones many of us face in real life. The most difficult problems we face in life are *moral dilemmas,* that is, problems that have conflicting constraints, such as abortion, waging war, and the balancing of individual rights against the rights of society. There is no simple answer, no simple set of equations that will do the trick. We must be creative in our solutions, relying on our knowledge, experience, and intuition to show us the way.

People often fail to see solutions that are readily available because of what is termed "problem stellung": The problem statement suggests unnecessary constraints that limit or preclude genuine possible solutions.[35] In order to overcome these imaginary constraints, the problem solver must restructure the problem so that the new problem description suggests possible means. This is a matter of developing the *problem* rather than developing a *solution*. As we saw earlier, this is exactly the difference between expert and novice problem solvers. Experts spend more time thinking about and refining their understanding of the problem than novices do. Novices like to jump right in, trying solutions willy-nilly.

Try to solve the problem in Figure 5. Here the person just cut a piece of string in half with a scissors and attached the two pieces to the ceiling. Now he must tie the two strings together, but he cannot reach the second string while holding onto the first string. The ladder is gone. What can he do?

Give up? Did you consider tying the scissors to one of the strings like a weight on a pendulum and setting it swinging? Then you can run over to the other string, grab it, wait for the scissors to come swinging your way and grab them. Voilà, both strings are now in hand!

If this solution didn't occur to you, why didn't it? Probably

Figure 5: What a quandary! The little man wants to tie the strings together, and he knows they're long enough to do that. But, he can't reach the second string while holding onto the first. What can he do? (After Maier, 1930)

because it didn't occur to you to *use the scissors as a pendulum weight*. Scissors are for cutting, not for swinging things about. Their normal function hinders your seeing other uses for them.

Now here is the important part: *Problem restructuring like this is the heart and soul of creative insight.* Here's an example:

When mathematician Karl Friedrich Gauss was in grammar school, his teacher asked the class to add all the numbers from one to ten.[36] Rather than plodding through the addition like his classmates, Gauss produced an immediate answer by restructuring the problem. Imagine the numbers one through ten lined up on a balance beam as in Figure 6. Notice that $1 + 10 = 11$, $2 + 9 = 11$, and so on. That's because the numbers increase by one going to the right and decrease by one going to the left.

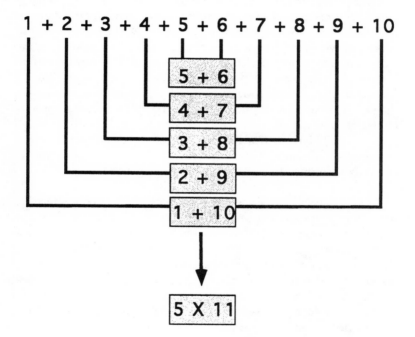

Figure 6: The solution young mathematician Karl Friedrich Gauss created to solve a problem put to him in grammar school Gauss imagined the numbers 1–10 lined up on a balance beam, and realized that the problem reduced to 5 × 11. (After Wertheimer, 1945/1982, Figure 73)

Pairing the numbers this way yields five sums equal to eleven, or 5 × 11. That's easy. The answer is 55. Moreover, the solution procedure generalizes to series of any length [1 + 2 + . . . + N = N/2(1 + N]. This simple restructuring produced a very powerful yet simple solution strategy, and uncovered an intriguing truth about arithmetical series.

Notice that Gauss's restructuring turned the problem into one with a known or readily apparent solution. In fact, that's one way we can characterize insight—making something familiar out of the unusual. Does this sound familiar? Does this sound like pattern recognition? *The heart and soul of creative insight is pattern recognition, that is, fiddling around with the problem representation until we recognize a familiar pattern with a known solution.*

Perhaps you're thinking, "Well, that might be true for science and mathematics and other stuffy fields like that, but what about *really* creative fields, like music and art." Well, consider these words of Mozart: "Those ideas that please me I retain in memory, and am accustomed, as I have been told, to hum them to myself. If I continue in this way, it soon occurs to me how I may turn this or that morsel to good account, so as to make a dish of it, that is to say agreeably to the rules of counterpoint, to the peculiarities of various instruments, etc. All this fires my soul. . . ."[37] Here, Mozart clearly describes restructuring, turning about, and considering from other angles until a pattern that "fits" is recognized.

I'd like you now to consider the following story: There is a fortress on an island which a general would like to conquer. He has a very large army, powerful enough to conquer the fortress. But the only way to get to the fortress requires traveling over very narrow, rickety bridges that radiate out from the island to the surrounding land. This presents two problems. First, it would take too long for the entire army to get to the fortress, and the defenders of the fortress can easily kill the small, steady streams of soldiers approaching them. Second, any given bridge would not be able to support the weight of any entire army marching over it for a long period of time. What to do?

The general has an insight. He divides his army into smaller units, and sends the smaller units down the many bridges to converge upon the fortress at the same time. The bridges do not collapse, and enough soldiers are there at once to conquer the fortress. The general and his army are victorious.

Did this story remind you of anything? No, I don't mean Desert Storm, I mean something from this chapter. Did it remind you of the X-ray problem? Can you now solve that problem? If so, you are in a very small minority. Typically, only 30 percent of people shown the fortress problem spontaneously see the connection between it and the X-ray problem, and even fewer use the fortress solution to solve the X-ray problem.[38] Congratulations!

In case you're scratching your head in confusion, let me demonstrate that the solution to the fortress problem can be used to solve the X-ray problem because the two are analogous to each other: They have the same abstract problem structure. In both cases, there is a target that must be destroyed, but it is surrounded by fragile stuff that must not be destroyed. The force required to destroy the target would also destroy the fragile stuff, and there lies the problem. The solution is to have many smaller or weaker forces *converge* on the target so that they sum to a force strong enough to achieve the goal. Reasoning analogically requires recognizing that two (or more) problems have the same *pattern* of constraints and goals. In other words, *they are both instances of the same solution-defined problem category*. In fact, requiring students to compare algebra word problems analogically improves their ability to both classify and solve the problems correctly.[39]

Now that you see the similarity, can you use the fortress convergence solution to solve the problem? Typically, once a hint is given to use the fortress problem solution, 50 percent of problem solvers can solve the X-ray problem using the convergence solution strategy. The solution is to surround the patient with X-ray machines, each delivering an intensity too weak to damage healthy tissue, but converging on the tumor to destroy it with their combined strength.

Analogical problem solving is difficult because the patterns to be recognized are *not* skin deep. It requires seeing the abstract similarities between two problems, that is, the similarities in their constraints and goals. It also requires understanding the solution's *functional role,* in this case, that weak forces are combined by convergence to produce a strong force. Unless a solution's functional role is grasped, transfer of the learned solution won't work. For example, knowing that the general won by sending smaller armies over the bridges won't help you solve the X-ray problem unless you understand why breaking the army into smaller units mattered. You can't send small armies to kill a tumor. Rather, you must understand the functional role played by the smaller armies; they allow weaker forces to *converge* on a target to form one large force. But once the deeper patterns of goals and constraints are recognized to be identical, the solution becomes apparent: We have an "Aha!" experience of insight.

So let's take stock: Most of our cognition consists of primitive yet extremely powerful and fast pattern recognition and classification processes. These processes enable us to have creative insights. But before we get too puffed up about this, I must point out that other species show creative insight as well. One of the most famous examples took place in the Canary Islands during World War I.[40] A soon-to-be famous Prussian psychologist named Wolfgang Köhler was trapped on the island of Tenerife, where he bided his time by observing and testing the problem-solving capacities of a colony of chimpanzees. The smartest of the chimps was named Sultan. One of the tasks Sultan was given required him to retrieve some bananas that were outside his cage. He readily used a long pole that was made available to him to pull the bananas toward him. Then he was given two poles, each of which was too short to reach the bananas but which could be fitted together to make one pole long enough to reach them. Sultan spent a long frustrating time trying to reach the bananas with one pole and then the other, culminating in his stomping off in frustration and sulking. His keeper later observed him playing with the poles, during which he managed, quite by accident, to put the two together. Sultan immediately recognized the enormity of his discovery and took off for the edge of his cage, where he used the newly elongated pole to fetch the much desired bananas.

Other experiments required the chimps to retrieve a banana hanging from the ceiling by gathering and stacking boxes scattered about their cages. Once again, the chimps (especially Sultan) evidenced creative insights and novel solutions. The most creative involved Sultan pulling Herr Köhler himself over to stand beneath the banana while Sultan clambered up on his shoulders to reach the coveted prize.

Creative insights have been observed in other species as well, including invertebrates, fish, amphibians, birds, and other mammals.[41] Elephants have been observed to fashion flyswatters out of tree branches with their trunks, and blue jays have been seen to use newspaper to rake food pellets into their cages.[42]

If the capacity for creative insight is present in so many other species, why is our problem solving so much more advanced? Well, you know what I'm going to say: Because our capacity for language enables us to represent and manipulate *symbols* like the spoken word and algebraic expressions.

Nowhere is the blending of symbolic language capacities, classification processes, and innate knowledge more pronounced than in our capacity to learn mathematics. It might surprise you to discover that even here, we seem to be pretty well equipped at birth to handle the world. Using the looking-time technique, we've discovered that newborns can discriminate small numerosities; by six months of age, infants can recognize numerical equivalence across modalities.[43] For example, they prefer to look at a picture of two objects if they hear two knocks, and at three objects if they hear three knocks. This is even more convincing evidence that infants can detect and respond to the abstract characteristic of *same number*.

If that's not enough to impress you, here is something that surely will: Infants as young as five months have been found capable of *adding and subtracting* small numbers.[44] Infants were allowed to watch as a Mickey Mouse doll was placed in a case. A screen then came up to cover Mickey, and then the infant watched as the experimenter placed another Mickey behind the screen. (One Mickey plus another Mickey.) In another case, two Mickey dolls were placed in the case, the screen was raised, and the infant watched as the experimenter reached in and removed one Mickey. (Two Mickey's minus one Mickey.) In both cases, dropping the screen revealed one, two, or three Mickey dolls in the case. The infants were found to look longer at the surprising, incorrect result than they did at the ho-hum predictable result. They knew what the correct answer was to these simple addition and subtraction problems.

I should point out here that humans are not the only creatures who are sensitive to the characteristics of abstract number.[45] Rats can be trained to press a lever a prescribed number of times (up to about twenty-four) before pressing a second lever to get a reward of food. The same is true of pigeons trained to peck lighted keys for reward. Rats can also be trained to turn down the third, fourth, or fifth tunnel in a maze, regardless of varying distances between the tunnel entrances. Canaries can be trained to select an object based on its ordinal position (first, second, third, etc.) in an array, regardless of the distances among the objects. And raccoons can be taught to select collections of objects based on their numerosity. The concept of number seems to be a very primitive, very basic concept that is part of many cognitive architectures, not just ours.

If even raccoons understand something about number, then why is math such a tough subject for students? There are probably as many explanations as there are researchers and educators, but I will offer my explanation for your consideration: Math is hard because it requires us to learn an "unnatural" language system that does not jibe well with natural languages. Let me explain.

Unlike other creatures, humans must learn to traffic in very large numerosities. In the work done with infants and lower animals, the numerosities must be kept relatively small or performance breaks down. There seems to be an upper limit on the number of objects in a grouping that can be perceptually discriminated. It's relatively easy to discriminate two objects from three objects visually. In fact, in certain brain disorders, the ability to discriminate numerosities up to four remains intact, but the ability to discriminate larger numerosities is lost.[46] But how about discriminating sixty-two objects from sixty-three objects visually? To make that discrimination, you must either transform the task to allow you to detect some other perceptual attribute (e.g., line them up to see which is longer) or you must count them and compare your final answers.

There lies the rub: To go beyond the quantity-detecting limits of the perceptual system, humans must learn to coordinate a *verbal* counting system with a *numerical* system. This, as it turns out, is extremely difficult and time-consuming. As we saw in chapter 8 on language, *Homo sapiens sapiens* were communicating verbally for thousands of years before an abstract counting system was developed, and that system piggybacked on our capacity for language. Counting is not a biologically *evolved* system, like language, but an *invented* one. It should come as no surprise, then, to discover that it is extremely difficult to learn.

Although we can discriminate small numerosities shortly after birth, we usually don't completely master the verbal counting system until we are about three or four years old. And then the process is fraught with errors that belie our appreciation of abstract number. For example, if you ask three-year-olds to count a group of objects, they'll often leave a number or two out (e.g., 1, 2, 4, 5, . . .) or get them in the wrong order (e.g., 1, 2, 4, 3, . . .). But if you have them watch a puppet count the objects and ask them to tell you when the puppet makes a mistake, they'll cry, "He left out '3' " when the puppet says "1, 2, 4, 5," and "She mixed them up" when the puppet says "1, 2, 4, 3."[47] Kids understand more than their counting performance suggests.

The number-language coordination problem just gets tougher as one advances in math. Elementary school children typically misinterpret statements such as "Mary and John have 5 marbles altogether" as "Mary and John have 5 marbles EACH." They also misinterpret comparative statements such as "How many more birds are there than worms?" as meaning "How many birds are there?" These misunderstandings don't stem from deficiencies in their mathematical abilities because they can readily solve problems based on sentences like these when number sentences are given to them instead, such as "5 − 3 = ?" Their difficulties also disappear if the problems are reworded to avoid conjunctions and comparatives, such as "There are 5 marbles altogether" and "How many birds won't get a worm?"[48]

Confusions between math language and natural language continue right on through high school and college. For example, consider the following problem: "In a particular college, there are five students for every professor. Write an equation that captures the meaning of that statement." Try it. Did you write "5S = P"? If so, you performed like the majority of students in a study of mathematical reasoning.[49] Unfortunately, you performed wrongly. In the language of math, that equation means that the number of professors (P) is equal to five times the number of students (5S), or that there are five times as many professors as there are students. Some college! Or how about this one: "A twelve-inch board is cut in half. One piece is one-third the length of the other. What are the lengths of the boards?" Did you notice that this is an insoluble problem? Why? Because you can't cut a board *in half* and end up with two boards of unequal lengths. You lost track of how the semantics of English correspond to the semantics of algebra.

But, there is an important key to demystifying math: Treat is as though it were a foreign language. We've evolved considerable brain structures for processing language. Let them crunch away at the language of mathematics. Here's how:

Take algebra for example. It is a language in itself, a symbol system that has its own meanings. Consider this algebraic expression:

$$\sum_{i=1}^{N} X_i / N$$

Imagine your algebra teacher gives you this expression along with a list of numbers. What are you supposed to do? Simple: Try to understand the expression as though it were a sentence in the imperative mood, that is, a command. Here is the same sentence in French: *Totalisez les chiffres sur la liste et divisez la somme par le nombre des chiffres sur la liste.*

How would you go about figuring out what the French sentence said? You'd probably look up the words and try to make sense of them in terms of verbs, nouns, and, of course, context. Let's try the same thing with the algebra sentence using any basic algebra text. "Σ" and "/" mean "sum up" and "divide," respectively, so they are verbs. "X" and "N" are tricky; they are nouns, but they are also variables. The concept of an algebraic variable is difficult for most people to grasp first time around, but in fact, we deal with variables everyday in natural language.

Whenever you fill out a form that has things like "Name"

and "Address" followed by blank lines for you to fill in, you're dealing with a variable. "Name" is a variable that takes on different values depending on who's filling the form out; my name is different than yours, but they're both names. The *variable* "Name" takes on the *value* "Denise Cummins" when I fill out the form, and takes on the value "John Smith" when John Smith fills it out. Same thing with "address"; it too is a variable that takes on different values for each person who fills out the form. In the mathematical expression above, "X" is a variable that takes each number in the list (in turn) as values; "N" is a variable that takes the number of numbers as its value. The subscript "i = 1" means "start with the first number in the list." The superscript "N" means "end with the last number in the list."

Putting it all together, the algebraic sentence says "Add up all of the numbers in this list ($\sum_{i=1}^{N} \kappa$) and divide (/) the sum by the total number of numbers in the list (N)." And that's exactly what the French sentence says. We got there by doing the same things we'd do to understand the French sentence. Simple, but I'll bet dollars to doughnuts no one ever explained the *semantics of mathematics* to you this way. (Did you also notice that this is the formula for computing an average?)

We could go on having fun like this all day, but I'm sure you get the picture. Mathematics is hard because you need to learn a new language to do it, and it is not always clear how the symbol meanings of math language map onto the word meanings of English. Math language is not an evolved language, it is a designed one. Designed languages don't always map onto natural languages very well, which makes them hard to learn.

Just as designed languages collide with our evolved, natural language processes, so does formal reasoning often collide with our evolved categorization processes. This occurs most frequently when our proclivities for categorizing things collides with the need for formal, quantitative reasoning. For example, consider the following reasoning problem:

> A panel of psychologists have interviewed and administered personality tests to 70 engineers and 30 lawyers, all successful in their respective fields. On the basis of

this information, thumbnail descriptions of the 70 engineers and 30 lawyers have been written. You will find on your forms five descriptions, chosen at random from the 100 available descriptions. *For each description, please indicate your probability that the person described is an engineer, on a scale from 0 to 100.*

1. Jack is a 45-year-old man. He is married and has four children. He is generally conservative, careful, and ambitious. He shows no interest in political and social issues, and spends most of his free time on his many hobbies, which include home carpentry, sailing, and mathematical puzzles.

2. Dick is a 30-year-old man. He is married with no children. A man of high ability and motivation, he promises to be quite successful in his field. He is well liked by his colleagues.

Did you decide that Jack was an engineer, and that Dick could be either an engineer or a lawyer? So did most of the people who served as volunteers in a study using materials like these.[50] But this is really very sloppy reasoning. Why? Reread the introduction. Notice that the base rate information tells you that there are more than twice as many engineer descriptions than lawyer descriptions. Two randomly selected descriptions are more likely to have been lawyers than engineers. Yet you ignored the base rates in giving your answers.

You might argue that regardless of the base rates, the first description is more likely to be of a lawyer than an engineer. It is less *probable* given the base rates, but still *possible*. That's perfectly reasonable. But what about Dick? Given the base rates, he has a 70 percent chance of being an engineer, yet most people put it at 50 percent. Why? Clearly, most people just ignore the base rate information and simply ask whether the description is diagnostic of our stereotypes (i.e., categories) for lawyers and engineers. Since it isn't, we say we can't tell what Dick is, so he has a 50 percent chance of being either.

Why do we ignore base rates? Probably because in real life, we never know what they are. The more usual task for humans at large is generalizing some aspect of a small sample to an entire population, not the other way around. That is what happens in stereotypes. We have a bad experience with a dog or two, and conclude that all dogs are vicious. Or we have both good and bad experiences and conclude that not all dogs are vicious. Or we decide not to buy a certain make of car because we know someone who bought one and had nothing but trouble with it. We take our small sample of experiences and make conclusions about entire classes of objects, creatures, or events because we can never hope to sample every member of the entire class. Because we rarely know what the characteristics of an entire population are, we have very little experience in using base rate information during decision making. This is one reason why it is so hard to combat stereotypes and prejudice with factual in-formation. Only greater experience with the members of the maligned population helps—assuming those experiences are good!

We rely so much on our categorical knowledge because, quite simply, we're lost without it. Statistical reasoning problems are extraordinarily difficult for us *unless they can be correctly reduced to judgments about category membership*. To bring this point home a little more, I'd like you to consider the following more hum-drum reasoning problem. I'm going to be a little long-winded here because I have a very important point to make: It can be shown that if you are not *Bayesian* in your reasoning, Dutch book can be made against you. What is Dutch book? It is a set of bets, each of which seem entirely reasonable, that *you cannot win*. It is logically impossible. Unless you are Bayesian, some-one can make a sucker out of you very easily. Let's see what "Bayesian" means:

> Three cards are in a hat. One is red on both sides (the red-red card), one is white on both sides (the white-white card), and one is red on one side and white on the other (the red-white card). A card is selected at ran-dom, tossed into the air, and lands showing a red side up.
>
> (a) What is the probability that the red-red card was drawn?

(b) What is the probability that the drawn card lands with a red side up?
(c) What is the probability that the card lands red–side–up, if the red–red card was the one tossed?
(d) What is the probability that the red–red card was drawn, assuming that the drawn card lands with a red side up?

If you are like most people, you answered these questions as follows:

(a) p(RR) = one out of three
(b) p(R–up) = one out of two
(c) p(R–upIRR) = one
(d) p(RRIR–up) = one out of two

The problem is the answer to (d). Using Bayes theorem, the answer turns out to be two out of three, as follows:

$$p(RRIR) = \frac{p(RIRR)p(RR)}{p(R)} = \frac{(1)\ (1/3)}{1/2} = 2/3$$

As your answer to (d) shows, your reasoning was not Bayesian; hence it is theoretically possible to make Dutch book against you.

People generally believe the answer to (d) is one out of two because they know there are two cards that could produce a red-side-up landing, and they believe each was equally likely to have been chosen. But consider the question in another way: Which is more likely to produce a red-side-up landing, tossing the red-white card or tossing the red-red card? When put this way, it seems more likely that it was the red-red card that produced the red-side-up landing. In other words, given that a red–side–up landing was observed, it seems more likely that the red-red card was the one tossed. Our intuitions can also be brought more into line with Bayesian analysis if one thinks of the problem this way: There are three red *sides* in the hat, and two of them belong to the red-red card, so the chances that the tossed card is the red–red card, *given that a red side is showing,* are . . . two out of three.

As the typical answer to the red–white card problem shows, when problems are put to us in probability format, we just don't reason very well. Hence, Las Vegas and all of its splendor. If we reasoned well with probabilities, Las Vegas wouldn't exist because the casino owners could never win against us. We'd just compute the probabilities as we went along, and make the right bets. But as the reworded versions of the problem show, we are capable of rational decision making, especially when the problem format avoids talk of probabilities and other symbolic forms of expression.

Like our understanding of gravity and inertia, it took centuries of development of mathematical thought and the genius of a few to work out the subtleties of the Bayesian aspects of our world. Except for language, we are dismally poor symbolic reasoners. Instead, humans and other animals are first and foremost pattern recognizers and classifiers; our cognition is shot through with pattern recognition and classification processes, from elementary perception to higher-order reasoning. Anything else requires a good deal of effort on our part, and a great deal of reliance on the abstract representations afforded us by language. Without such abstract representations and the systems developed for manipulating them, we could not have discovered the laws of gravity and inertia, nor the probabilistic characteristics of events in the world. Because of the power afforded us by our language ability, we've invented ever more sophisticated formalisms that allow us to solve problems of enormous complexity and to create masterpieces of sublime expressiveness. Combining basic pattern-recognition and classification processes with the capacity for language produced a creative capacity of such power and breadth that it enabled *Homo sapiens sapiens* to build skyscrapers, launch satellites, create nuclear weapons, design computers, invent penicillin, control its own population growth, construct gas chambers, write symphonies, engage in three millennia of warfare, and . . . well, you get the picture. Think of that the next time you hear a two-year-old do something no other species can do: babble.

Notes

Notes citations refer to complete title information in the References section that follows.

Prologue

1. Helmholtz (1853; reprinted 1962), p. 40.
2. Kant, I. (1786).
3. Fancher (1979), pp. 100–101.
4. Donders (1868/1969).
5. Freud and Breuer (1895/1976), p. 672.
6. Locke, (1700), bk. 2, chap. 1, sec. 10.

Chapter 1

1. Milgram (1974).
2. Berkowitz (1962); Berkowitz, Green, and Macaulay (1962); Buss (1961).
3. Asch (1955; 1958).
4. Schacter (1951).
5. Nemeth (1986).
6. Latané and Rodin (1969).
7. Darley and Latané (1968).
8. Bickman (1971).
9. Schwartz and Clausen (1970).
10. Cialdini (1985), p. 118.
11. Schein (1956).
12. Festinger and Carlsmith (1959).
13. Cialdini (1985), p. 78.
14. Nel, Helmreich, and Aronson (1969).
15. Festinger and Carlsmith (1959).
16. Freedman (1965).
17. Walster, Aronson, Abrahams, and Rottman (1966).

18. Sigall and Aronson (1969).
19. Efran (1974).
20. Stewart (1980).
21. Touhy (1974a).
22. Touhy (1974b).
23. Johnson (1986).
24. Lewin, Lippett, and White (1939).
25. Rosenbaum and Rosenbaum (1971).

Notes to Chapter 2

1. Bahill and LaRitz (1984); DeLucia & Cochran (1985).
2. Reynolds and Weiss (1992).
3. Thompson (1985), pp. 234–235.
4. Ibid., pp. 141–144, 300–302.
5. Hoebel and Teitelbaum (1976).
6. Miller, Bailey, and Stevenson (1950).
7. Teitelbaum and Stellar (1954).
8. Stricker and Zigmond (1976); Friedman and Stricker (1976).
9. Churchland (1986), pp. 224–230.
10. Ibid., pp. 230–232.
11. Bogen (1969).
12. Penfield and Rasmussen (1950).
13. Parks, Lowenstein, Dodrill, Barker, Yoshii, Change, Emran, Apicella, Sheramata, and Duara (1988); Haier, Siegel, Neuchterlein, Hazlett, Wu, Paek, Browning, and Buchsbaum (1988).
14. Dobkin (1986), pp. 160–172.

Notes to Chapter 3

1. Treisman (1960).
2. Gregory (1978), p. 100.
3. Goren, Sarty, and Wu (1975).
4. Sacks (1985).
5. Gardner (1983).
6. Thompson, P., as cited in Parks and Cross (1986).
7. Wertheimer (1961).
8. Meltzoff and Borton (1979).
9. Spelke (1976).
10. Gregory (1978), pp. 161–162.
11. Locke (1690; reprinted), *Essay on Human Understanding,* bk. 2, chap. 9, sec. 8.

12. Gregory (1978), pp. 194–200.
13. Wiesel (1982).
14. Ibid.
15. Hubel (1963); Hubel (1988); Hubel and Wiesel (1959).
16. Hubel (1963), Rauscheker and Singer (1981); Blakemore (1974).
17. Hirsh and Spinelli (1970); Blakemore and Cooper (1970).
18. Held (1965); Held and Hein (1963).
19. Halpern, Blake, and Hillenbrand (1986).

Notes to Chapter 4

1. Kunst-Wilson and Zajonc (1980).
2. Shlomo and Moscovitch (1990).
3. Schacter (1983); Squire (1992a; 1992b).
4. Schacter and Graf (1989); Graf and Mandler (1984); Graf, Mandler, and Haden (1982); Graf, Shimamura, and Squire (1985); Jacoby and Dallas (1981); Roediger and Blaxton (1987).
5. Jacoby and Dallas (1981).
6. Kolers (1975); Roediger and Blaxton (1987); Roediger and Weldon (1987).
7. Squire, Ojemann, Miezen, Petersen, Videen et al., (1992); Paller and Kutas (1992).
8. Schacter (1987).
9. Kinsbourne and Wood (1975); Squire (1992a).
10. Weiskrantz and Warrington (1979).
11. Johnson, Kim, and Risse (1985).
12. Crovitz, Harvey, and McClanahan (1979).
13. Brooks and Baddeley (1976).
14. Glisky (1992).
15. See note 10 above.
16. See note 10 above.
17. Nissen and Bullemer (1987).
18. Milner (1966).
19. Milner, Corkin, and Teuber (1968).
20. Hostetler (1988).
21. Squire (1992a; 1992b).
22. Nadel and Zola-Morgan (1984).
23. Sperling (1960).
24. Averbach and Coriell (1961); Loftus, Johnson and Shimamura (1985).
25. Crowder and Morton (1969); Darwin, Turvey, and Crowder (1972).

26. Miller (1956), p. 81.
27. Johnson (1965); Miller (1956).
28. Ericsson, Chase, and Faloon (1980).
29. Murdock (1962).
30. Hintzman and Block (1970); Madigan (1969); Melton (1970); Underwood (1970).
31. Light and Carter-Sobell (1970).
32. Glucksberg and McCloskey (1981).

Notes to Chapter 5

1. Beech, Powell, McWilliams, and Claridge (1989); Frith (1979).
2. Cherry (1953).
3. Moray (1959).
4. MacKay (1973).
5. Gazzaniga (1967).
6. Wada (1949); Wada and Rasmussen (1960).
7. Hilgard (1977).
8. Putnam (1986).
9. See note 7 above.
10. White (1944); Levine (1951).
11. Lindsley (1960).
12. See Deutsch and Deutsch (1973), pp. 397–399.
13. Rechtschaffen, Hauri, and Zeitlan (1966).
14. Koella (1967).
15. Rechtschaffen and Kales (1968).
16. Pessah and Roffwarg (1972).
17. Wolpert and Trosman (1958).
18. Anch, Browman, Mitler, and Walsh (1988), p. 45.
19. Allison and van Twyer (1970).
20. Work by Henley and Morrison and Jouvet and Delorme as cited in Anch et al. (1988), pp. 99 and 142.
21. Patterson (1979); Patterson (1981).
22. Webb (1969).
23. Dement (1960).
24. Anch, et al. (1988), pp. 157–160.
25. Body clocks keep insomniacs wide awake, *Science News* 135 (July 1, 1989): 13.
26. Hartmann (1973); Adam and Oswald (1977); work by Moruzzi (1972) as cited in Anch et al. (1988), p. 18.
27. Shapiro, Bortz, Mitchell, Bartel, and Jooste (1981).
28. Fishbein, McGaugh, and Swarz (1971); Fishbein (1971).

29. DuJardin, Guerrien, and LeConte (1990).
30. Hennevin, Hars, and Bloch (1989).
31. Shashoua (1985); Drucker-Colin, Bowersox, and McGinty (1982).
32. Work by Levental, Susic, Rusic, and Rakic as cited in Anch et al. (1988), p. 146.
33. Smith, Tenn, and Annett (1991).
34. Wood, Bootzin, Kihlstrom, and Schacter (1992).
35. Ekstrand, Barrett, West, & Maier (1977).
36. Kihlstrom and Schacter (1990).
37. Kihlstrom and Couture (1992).
38. Cheek (1959); Cheek (1964); Bennett (1988).
39. Levinson (1965).
40. Bonke, Schmitz, Verhage, and Zwaverling (1986); Evans and Richardson (1988); McClintock, Aitken, Downie, and Kenny (1990).
41. Bennett, Davis, and Giannini (1985).
42. Cork, Kihlstrom, and Schacter (1992); Kihlstrom, Schacter, Cork, Hunt, and Behr (1990); work by Stolzy, Couture, and Edmonds as cited in Kihlstrom and Couture (1992), pp. 412–414.
43. Work by Couture and Edmonds as cited in Kihlstrom and Couture (1992), p. 415.
44. Danion, Zimmerman, Willard-Schroeder, Grange, et al. (1989; 1990).

Notes to Chapter 6

1. Olds, (1956); Olds and Milner (1954).
2. Gregory (1987), p. 527.
3. Ibid., p. 529.
4. Wasman and Flynn (1962); Egger and Flynn (1963).
5. Hutchinson and Renfew (1966).
6. Valenstein (1973), pp. 49–50 and 107–108.
7. Thatcher and John (1977), pp. 130–134.
8. Davidson (1992).
9. Davidson, Ekman, Saron, Senulis, and Friesen (1990).
10. Ley and Bryden (1979).
11. Bowers, Blonder, Feinberg, and Heilman (1991).
12. Fox and Davidson (1986).
13. Davidson and Fox (1982).
14. Bringing up baby: Emotion's early role, *Science News* 131 (February 14, 1987): 104.
15. Ekman (1973); Ekman, Levenson, and Friesen (1983).

16. Darwin (1872).
17. Erwin, Gur, Gur, Skolnick, Mawhinney, and Smailis (1992).
18. Gainotti (1972).
19. Robinson, Kubox, Starr, Rao, and Price (1984).
20. Wechsler (1973); Heilman, Bowers, Speedied, and Coslett (1984) and Blonder, Bowers, and Heilman (1991); Bihrle, Brownell, Powelson, and Gardiner (1986); Bloom, Borod, Obler, and Gerstman (1992).
21. Bloom, Borod, Obler, and Gerstman (1992).
22. Pettersen (1991); Lalande, Braun, Charlebois, and Whitaker (1992).
23. Reiman, Raichle, Butler, Hercovitch, and Robins (1984).
24. Henriques and Davidson (1991).
25. Davidson, Finman, Straus, and Kagan (1992).
26. Davidson, 1992, p. 147.
27. Harlow (1958); Harlow and Zimmerman (1959).
28. Harlow and Harlow (1972); Suomi and Harlow (1971); Harlow and Novak (1973).
29. Suomi, Harlow, and McKinney (1972); Novak and Harlow (1975).
30. Seay, Alexander, and Harlow (1964).
31. Goldfarb (1955); Yarrow (1961); Skeels (1966).
32. Skeels (1966).
33. Kotelchuk (1976).
34. Rebelsky and Hanks (1971).
35. Lamb (1981).
36. Zigler and Hall (1989).
37. Hoffman (1974).
38. Cycle of child abuse can be broken, say scholars, *Yale Weekly Bulletin and Calendar* 16 (4) (September 21–28, 1987): p. 1; Kaufman and Zigler, (1988); Martin and Elmer, (1992).
39. Loeber and Dishion (1984); Patterson (1980).
40. Weiss, Dodge, Bates, and Pettit (1992).
41. Speisman, Lazarus, and Mordokoff (1964).
42. Dutton and Aron (1974).
43. Ibid.
44. White, Fishbein, and Rutsein (1981).
45. Plotnik, (1974); Plotnik, Mir, and Delgado (1971); Delgado (1966).
46. Green and Berkowitz (1967).
47. Berkowitz and LePage (1967).
48. Baron (1971) (a) and (b).
49. Shortell, Epstein, and Taylor (1970); Baron (1971).
50. A convict's view: People don't want solutions, *Time* (August 23, 1993): p. 33.

51. Weissberg, Roger, 1988, personal communication on research program, Yale University.
52. Huesman, Lagerspetz, and Eron (1984); Eron (1972; 1982).
53. Thomas, Horton, Lippincott, and Drabman (1977).
54. Drabman and Thomas (1974a and b); Drabman and Thomas, (1975).
55. Thomas and Drabman (1975).
56. Thomas (1982).
57. Donnerstein (1980).
58. Donnerstein and Berkowitz (1981).
59. Malamuth (1989a and 1989b).
60. Nadler (1988).
61. Hokanson and Edelman (1966).
62. Dembroski, MacDougall, Williams, Haney, and Blumenthal (1985).
63. Schill (1972).
64. Hokanson and Shetler (1961).
65. Hokanson (1961).
66. Dengerink and Covey (1983).

Notes to Chapter 7

1. Pavlov (1927).
2. Moore (1972).
3. Harvey (1981).
4. Siegel (1983); Siegel and MacRae (1984).
5. Hunt, Barnett, and Branch (1971).
6. Phillips (1991), pp. 418–424.
7. O'Brien, Testa, O'Brien, and Greenstein (1974).
8. O'Brien (1976).
9. Sideroff and Jarvik (1980).
10. Ludwig and Stark (1974); Ludwig, Cain, Wikler, Taylor, and Bendfeldt (1977).
11. Robins, Helzer, and Davis (1975).
12. O'Brien, Nace, Mintz, Meyers, and Ream (1980).
13. Siegel, Hinson, Krank, and McCully (1982).
14. Siegel, Hinson, and Krank (1978).
15. Siegel (1975).
16. Thompson and Ostlund (1965).
17. Schwartz (1986), pp. 13–30.
18. Watson and Rayner (1920).

19. This case study was described in a class I took as an undergraduate. Unfortunately, I have not been able to track down a citation, but you must admit the case is not one you're likely to forget.
20. Skinner (1938).
21. Gambling, *The encyclopedia Americana: International edition* (Danbury, CT: Grolier, 1991) 12: 264–266.
22. Kendall (1989).
23. Weinstock (1954); Reynolds (1968), p. 77.
24. Ibid.
25. Beatty (1977).
26. Miller and Banuazizi (1968).

Notes to Chapter 8

1. Crichton (1990).
2. Descartes R. (1637), Discourse on method, pt. 5.
3. Chomsky (1959).
4. Chomsky (1965; 1980; 1986).
5. Broca (1861); Broca (1863); Luria (1966).
6. Wernicke (1874).
7. Galaburda and Kemper (1979).
8. Sasanuma (1975); Sasanuma and Fujimura (1971).
9. Bloom and Lazerson (1985), pp. 287–288.
10. Curtiss (1977).
11. Brown (1958).
12. Newport (1991).
13. Johnson and Newport (1989).
14. Gopnik (1990).
15. Berko (1958).
16. The clues in idle chatter, *U.S. News and World Report* (August 19, 1991): 61–62.
17. See Pinker (1990) and Bloom (in press) for review.
18. Example taken from Bellugi (1971).
19. Mehler, Jusczyk, Lambertz, Halsted, Bertoncini, and Amiel-Tison (1988).
20. Birnholz (1983).
21. Gleitman (1986), p. 498.
22. Eimas, Siqueland, Jusczyk, and Vigorito (1971).
23. Oller and Eilers (1988).
24. Pettito and Marentette (1991).
25. de Boysson-Bardies and Vihman (1991).

26. Lenneberg (1967).
27. See Pinker (1990) and Bloom (in press) for reviews; Slobin (1973); Petitto and Marentette (1991).
28. Example taken from Bickerton (1990).
29. Clark and Clark (1977), pp. 348–351.
30. Example taken from McNeill (1966), p. 69.
31. Brown and Hanlon (1970).
32. Example taken from Neisser (1967), pp. 244–245.
33. Naigles (1990).
34. Meyer and Schvanevelt (1971), experiment 1, table 1, p. 229.
35. Swinney (1979).
36. Garrett, Bever, and Fodor (1966).
37. Haberlandt, Berian, and Sandson (1980).
38. Grice (1975).
39. Conti and Camras (1984).
40. Suls (1972).
41. Sarich and Wilson (1967).
42. Summary of human evolution based on Corballis (1991), pp. 30–48, and "Putting our oldest ancestors in their proper place." *Science* (1994), *265*, 2011–2012.
43. Falk (1983; 1987a and b); Tobias (1987).
44. Bower, B. (1989) A 'handy' guide to primate evolution. *Science News, 135*, 10–12.
45. Deacon, T. (as cited in note 48 below).
46. Corballis (1991), pp. 232–238.
47. Summary of larynx position and descent based on Laitman (1984).
48. "Talk of ages: A tiny bone rekindles arguments over the roots of speech and language." *Science News, 136*, 24–26; also Pinker and Bloom (1990).
49. Corballis (1991), p. 40.
50. Premack (1985), p. 276.
51. "Tokens of plenty: How an ancient counting system evolved into writing and the concept of abstract numbers." *Science News* (1988), *134*, 408–410.

Notes to Chapter 9

1. Popper, K., as cited in Dennett (1978, p.77).
2. Tronick, Als, Adamson, Wise, and Brazelton (1978).
3. Scaife and Bruner (1975).
4. Campos and Stenberg (1981).
5. Murray and Trevarthen (1985).

6. Gelman and Markman (1986; 1987).
7. Keil (1986), pp. 143–144.
8. Carey (1985), pp. 111–161.
9. Rips (1989).
10. Turiel (1983); Turiel (1989); Turiel, Edwards, and Kohlberg (1978); Turiel, Killen, and Helwig (1987).
11. Ibid.
12. Cummins (1995).
13. Cheng and Holyoak (1985); Griggs and Cox (1982); Griggs and Cox (1983).
14. Griggs and Cox (1982).
15. Baillargeon, Spelke, and Wasserman (1985); Baillargeon (1987); Spelke (1991).
16. Leslie and Keeble (1987).
17. Hume, D. (1777) *Enquiry concerning human understanding*. Section vii, Pt. 1.
18. Kant, I. (1781) *The critique of pure reason*. Second analogy.
19. See note 15 above.
20. Walk and Gibson (1961).
21. McCloskey (1983).
22. Cummins (in press); Cummins, Lubart, Alksnis, and Rist (1991).
23. "Aristotle." *The encyclopedia americana: International edition*, 1991, vol. 2, pp. 290–291. Danbury, CT: Grolier.
24. van Heuvelen (1982), p. 35.
25. Newton, I. (1687) as cited in van Heuvelen (1982), p. 107.
26. Asimov (1989), pp. 172–174.
27. Rumelhart and McClelland (1986).
28. Posner and Keele (1968), Experiment 3, Table 5.
29. Knapp and Anderson (1984).
30. Rosch (1973); Rosch and Mervis (1975).
31. Garcia and Koelling (1966).
32. Feynman (1985), pp. 191–192.
33. Chi, Feltovich, and Glaser (1981).
34. This is the Rutherford model of the atom. See Cummins (1994) and Gentner (1983).
35. Duncker (1945).
36. Cited in Wertheimer (1945), pp. 108–142.
37. Quoted in Humphrey (1951), p. 53.
38. Gick and Holyoak (1980; 1983).
39. Cummins (1992).
40. Köhler (1925); also see Gleitman (1986), pp. 127–129.
41. Beck (1980).

42. "Biting flies flee elephants' swatters". *Science News*, 7/31/93, Vol. 144, p.70; Corballis (1991).
43. Antell and Keating (1983); Starkey, Spelke, and Gelman (1983; 1990).
44. Wynn (1992a).
45. Wynn (1991).
46. "Small amounts go down for the count." *Science News*, 1994, Vol. 146, p. 293.
47. Gelman and Meck (1983); Wynn (1990; 1992b).
48. Cummins (1991b); Cummins, Kintsch, Reusser, and Weimer (1988); Dellarosa (1986).
49. Hinsley, Hayes, and Simon (1977).
50. Kahneman and Tversky (1973).
51. Bar-Hillel and Falk (1982).

References

Adam, K., and Oswald, I. 1977. Sleep is for tissue restoration. *Journal of the Royal College of Physicians* 11: 376–388.

Allison, T., and van Twyer, H. 1970. The evolution of sleep. *Natural History* 79: 56–65.

Anch, A. M., Browman, C. P., Mitler, M. M., and Walsh, J. K. 1988. *Sleep: A scientific perspective.* Englewood Cliffs, NJ: Prentice-Hall.

Antell, S., and Keating, D. P. 1983. Perception of numerical invariance in neonates. *Child Development* 54: 695–701.

Asch, S. E. 1955. Opinions and social pressure. *Scientific American* 193: 31–35.

————. (1958) Effects of group pressure upon the modification and distortion of judgments. In *Readings in social psychology,* edited by E. E. Maccoby, T. M. Newcomb, and E. L. Hartley, 174–181. New York: Henry Holt.

Asimov, I. 1989. *Asimov's chronology of science and discovery.* New York: Harper and Row.

Averbach, E., and Coriell, A. S. 1961. Short term memory in vision. *The Bell System Technical Journal* 40: 309–328.

Bahill, A. T., and LaRitz, T. 1984. Why can't batters keep their eyes on the ball? *American Scientist* 72: 249–253.

Baillargeon, R. 1987. Object permanence in 3½- and 4½-month-old infants. *Developmental Psychology* 23: 655–664.

Baillargeon, R., Spelke, E. S., and Wasserman, S. 1985. Object permanence in five-month-old infants. *Cognition* 20: 191–208.

Bar-Hillel, M., and Falk, R. 1982. Some teasers concerning conditional probabilities. *Cognition* 11: 109–122.

Baron, R. A. 1971a. Magnitude of victim's pain cues and level of prior anger arousal as determinants of adult aggressive behavior. *Journal of Personality and Social Psychology* 17: 236–243.

————. 1971b. Aggression as a function of the magnitude of victim's pain cues, level of prior anger arousal and aggressor-victim similarity. *Journal of Personality and Social Psychology* 18: 48–54.

Beatty, J. 1977. Learned regulation of the human electroencephalogram. In *Biofeedback: Theory and research*, edited by G. Schwarz and J. Beatty, 351–370. New York: Academic Press.

Beck, B. B. 1980. *Animal tool behavior: The use and manufacture of tools by animals.* New York: Garland STPM Press.

Beech, A., Powell, T., McWilliams, J., and Claridge, G. 1989. Evidence of reduced "cognitive inhibition" in schizophrenia. *British Journal of Clinical Psychology* 28: 109–116.

Bellugi, U. 1971. Simplification in children's language. In *Language acquisition: Models and methods,* edited by R. Huxley and E. Ingram. New York: Academic Press.

Bennett, H. L. 1988. Perception and memory for events during adequate general anesthesia for surgical operations. In *Hypnosis and memory*, edited by H. M. Pettinati, 193–231. New York: Guilford.

Bennett, H. L., Davis, H. S., and Giannini, J. A. 1985. Non-verbal response to intraoperative conversation. *British Journal of Anaesthesia* 57: 174–179.

Berko, J. 1958. The child's learning of English morphology. *Word* 14: 150–177.

Berkowitz, L. 1962. *Aggression: A social psychological analysis.* New York: McGraw-Hill.

Berkowitz, L., Green, J. A., and Macaulay, J. R. 1962. Hostility catharsis as the reduction of emotional tension. *Psychiatry* 25: 23–31.

Berkowitz, L., and LePage, A. 1967. Weapons as aggression-eliciting stimuli. *Journal of Personality and Social Psychology* 7: 202–207.

Bickerton, D. 1990. *Language and species.* Chicago: University of Chicago.

Bickman, L. 1971. The effect of another bystander's ability to help on bystander intervention in an emergency. *Journal of Experimental Social Psychology* 7: 367–379.

Bihrle, A. M., Brownell, H. H., Powelson, J., and Gardiner, H. 1986. Comprehension of humorous and non-humorous materials by left and right brain-damaged patients. *Brain and Cognition* 5: 388–412.

Birnholz, J. C. 1983. The development of human fetal hearing. *Science* 222: 516–518.

Blakemore, C. 1974. Developmental factors in the formation of feature extracting neurons. In *The neurosciences, 3rd study program*, edited by F. G. Worden and F. O. Smith. Cambridge, MA: MIT Press.

Blakemore, C., & Cooper, G. F. 1970. Development of the brain depends on visual environment. *Nature* 228: 477–478.

Blonder, L. X., Bowers, D., and Heilman, K. M. 1991. The role of the right hemisphere in emotional communication. *Brain* 114: 1115–1128.

Bloom, F. W., and Lazerson, A. 1985. *Brain, mind, and behavior.* 2nd ed. New York: W. H. Freeman.

Bloom, P. In press. Recent controversies in the study of language acquisition. In *Handbook of psycholinguistics,* edited by M. A. Gernsbacher. San Diego, CA: Academic Press.

Bloom, R. L., Borod, J. C., Obler, L. K., and Gerstman, L. J. 1992. Impact of emotional content on discourse production in patients with unilateral brain damage. *Brain and Language* 42: 153–164.

Bogen, J. E. 1969. The other side of the brain II: An appositional mind. *Bulletin of the Los Angeles Neurological Societies* 34: 135–162.

Bonke, B., Schmitz, P. I. M., Verhage, F., and Zwaverling, A. 1986. Clinical study of so-called unconscious perception during general anaesthesia. *British Journal of Anaesthesia* 58: 957–964.

Bowers, D., Blonder, L. X., Feinberg, T., and Heilman, K. M. 1991. Differential impact of right and left hemisphere lesions on facial emotion and object imagery. *Brain* 114: 2593–2610.

de Boysson-Bardies, B., and Vihman, M. M. 1991. Adaptation to language: Evidence from babbling and first words in four languages. *Language* 67: 297–319.

Broca, P. 1861. Remarques sur le siège de la faculté du langage articulé; suivies d'une observation d'aphemie (perte de la parole). *Bulletin de la société anatomique de Paris* 36: 330–357.

———. 1863. Localisation des fonction cerebrales: Siège du langage articulé. *Bulletin de la société d'anthropologie, Paris* 4: 200–202.

Brooks, D. N., and Baddeley, A. 1976. What can amnesic patients learn? *Neuropsychologia* 14: 111–122.

Brown, R. 1958. *Words and things.* New York: Free Press.

Brown, R., and Hanlon, C. 1970. Derivational complexity and order of acquisition in child speech. In *Cognition and the development of language,* edited by J. R. Hayes. New York: Wiley.

Buss, A. H. 1961. *The psychology of aggression.* New York: Wiley.

Campos, J. J., and Stenberg, C. 1981. Perception, appraisal, and emotion: The onset of social referencing. In *Infant social cognition: Empirical and theoretical considerations,* edited by M. Lewis and L. Rosenblum. Hillsdale, NJ: Erlbaum.

Carey, S. 1985. *Conceptual change in childhood.* Cambridge, MA: MIT Press.

Cheek, D. B. 1959. Unconscious perception of meaningful sounds during surgical anesthesia as revealed under hypnosis. *American Journal of Clinical Hypnosis* 1: 101–113.

———. 1964. Surgical memory and reaction to careless conversation. *American Journal of Clinical Hypnosis* 6: 237.

Cheng, P. W., and Holyoak, K. J. 1985. Pragmatic reasoning schemas. *Cognitive Psychology* 17: 391–416.

Cherry, E.C. 1953. Some experiments upon the recognition of speech, with one and with two ears. *Journal of the Acoustical Society of America* 25: 975–979.

Chi, M. T. H., Feltovich, P. J., and Glaser, R. 1981. Categorization and representation of physics problems by experts and novices. *Cognitive Science* 5: 121–152.

Chomsky, N. 1959. Review of Skinner's *Verbal Behavior. Language* 35: 26–58.

———. 1965. *Aspects of a theory of syntax.* Cambridge, MA: MIT Press.

———. 1980. *Rules and representations.* New York: Columbia.

———. 1986. *Knowledge of language: Its nature, origin, and use.* New York: Praeger.

Churchland, P. S. 1986. *Neurophilosophy: Toward a unified science of mind-brain.* Cambridge, MA: Bradford/MIT Press.

Cialdini, R. B. 1985. *Influence: Science and practice.* Glenview, IL: Scott, Foresman.

Clark, H. H., and Clark, E. V. 1977. *Psychology and language.* New York: Harcourt Brace Jovanovich.

Conti, D. J., and Camras, L. A. 1984. Children's understanding of conversational principles. *Journal of Experimental Child Psychology* 38: 456–463.

Corballis, M. C. 1991. *The lopsided ape: Evolution of the generative mind.* Oxford: Oxford University Press.

Cork, R. C., Kihlstrom, J. F., and Schacter, D. L. 1992. Absence of explicit or implicit memory in patients anesthetized with sufentanil/nitrous oxide. *Anesthesiology* 76: 892–898.

Crichton, M. 1990. *Jurassic Park.* New York: Knopf.

Crovitz, H. F., Harvey, M. T., and McClanahan, S. 1979. Hidden memory: A rapid method for the study of amnesia using perceptual learning. *Cortex* 17: 273–278.

Crowder, R. G., and Morton, J. 1969. Precategorical acoustic storage (PAS). *Perception and Psychophysics* 5: 365–373.

Cummins, D. D. 1991. Children's interpretations of arithmetic word problems. *Cognition & Instruction,* 8: 261–289.

———. 1992. The role of analogical reasoning in the induction of problem categories. *Journal of Experimental Psychology: Learning, Memory, and Cognition*, 18: 1103–1124.

———. 1994. Analogical reasoning. *The Encyclopedia of Human Behavior*. New York: Academic Press.

———. 1995. Pragmatic schemas in the reasoning of 3- and 4-year-olds. Under review.

———. (in press) Naive theories and causal deduction. *Memory & Cognition*.

———, Kintsch, W., Reusser, K., and Weimer, R. 1988. The role of understanding in solving word problems. *Cognitive Psychology*, 20: 405–438.

———, Lubart, T., Alksnis, O., and Rist, R. 1991. Conditional reasoning and causation. *Memory & Cognition*, 19: 274–282.

Curtiss, S. 1977. *Genie: A psycholinguistic study of a modern day "wild child."* New York: Academic Press.

Danion, J. M., Zimmerman, M. A., Willard-Schroeder, D., Grange, D., et al. 1989. Diazepam induces a dissociation between explicit and implicit memory. *Psychopharmacology* 99: 238–243.

———. 1990. Effects of scopolamine, trimipramine, and diazepam on explicit memory and repetition priming in healthy volunteers. *Psychopharmacology* 102: 422–424.

Darley, J. M., and Latane, B. 1968. Bystander intervention in emergencies: Diffusion of responsibility. *Journal of Personality and Social Psychology* 8: 377–383.

Darwin, C. 1872. *The expression of the emotions in man and animals.* London: Appleton.

Darwin, C. J., Turvey, M. T., and Crowder, R. G. 1972. An auditory analogue of the Sperling partial report procedure: Evidence for brief auditory storage. *Cognitive Psychology* 3: 255–267.

Davidson, R. J. 1992. Anterior cerebral asymmetry and the nature of emotion. *Brain and Cognition* 20: 125–151.

Davidson, R. J., Ekman, P., Saron, C. D., Senulis, J. A., and Friesen, W. V. 1990. Approach/withdrawal and cerebral asymmetry: Emotional expression and brain physiology: I. *Journal of Personality and Social Psychology* 58: 330–341.

Davidson, R. J., Finman, R., Straus, A., and Kagan, J. 1992. Childhood temperament and frontal lobe activity: Patterns of asymmetry differentiate between wary and outgoing children. Cited in Davidson, 1992.

Davidson, R. J., and Fox, N. A. 1982. Asymmetrical brain activity discriminates between positive versus negative affective stimuli in human infants. *Science* 218: 1235–1237.

Delgado, J. M. R. 1966. Aggressive behavior evoked by radio stimulation in monkey colonies. *American Zoologist* 6: 669–681.

Dellarosa, D. 1986. A computer simulation of children's arithmetic word-problem solving, *Behavior Research Methods, Instruments, and Computers*, 18, 147–154.

DeLucia, P. R., and Cochran, E. L. 1985. Perceptual information for batting can be extracted throughout a ball's trajectory. *Perceptual and Motor Skills* 61: 143–150.

Dembroski, T. M., MacDougall, J. M., Williams, R. B., Haney, T. L., and Blumenthal, J. A. 1985. Components of Type A, hostility, and anger-in: Relationship to angiographic findings. *Psychosomatic Medicine* 47: 218–233.

Dement, W. C. 1960. The effect of dream deprivation. *Science* 131: 1705–1707.

Dengerink, H. A., and Covey, M. K. 1983. Implication of an escape-avoidance theory of aggressive responses to attack. In *Aggression: Theoretical and empirical reviews*, Vol. 1, *Theoretical and methodological issues*, edited by R. G. Geen and E. I. Donnerstein, 163–188. New York: Academic Press.

Dennett, D. 1978. *Brainstorms*. Cambridge, MA: MIT.

———. 1991. *Consciousness explained*. Boston: Little, Brown.

Deutsch, J. A., and Deutsch, D. 1973. *Physiological Psychology*. Homewood, IL: Dorsey Press.

Dobkin, B. H. 1986. *Brain matters*. New York: Crown.

Donders, F. C. 1868. Reprinted 1969. On the speed of mental processes. *Acta Psychologica* 30: 412–431.

Donnerstein, E. 1980. Aggressive erotica and violence against women. *Journal of Personality and Social Psychology* 39: 269–277.

Donnerstein, E., and Berkowitz, L. 1981. Victim reactions in aggressive erotic films as a factor in violence against women. *Journal of Personality and Social Psychology* 41: 710–724.

Drabman, R. S., and Thomas, M. H. 1974a. Exposure to filmed violence and children's tolerance of real-life aggression. *Personality and Social Psychology Bulletin* 1: 198–199.

———. 1974b. Does media violence increase children's toleration of real-life aggression? *Developmental Psychology* 10: 418–421.

———. 1975. Does TV violence breed indifference? *Journal of Communication* 25: 88–89.

Drucker-Colin, R., Bowersox, S., and McGinty, D. 1982. Sleep and medial reticular unit response to protein synthesis inhibitors: Effects of chloramphenicol and thiamphenicol. *Brain Research* 252: 117–127.

DuJardin, J., Guerrien, A., and LeConte, P. 1990. Sleep, brain activation, and cognition. *Physiology and Behavior* 47: 1271–1278.

Duncker, K. 1945. On problem solving. *Psychological Monographs* 58, whole no. 270.

Dutton, D. G., and Aron, A. P. 1974. Some evidence for heightened sexual attraction under conditions of high anxiety. *Journal of Personality and Social Psychology* 30: 510–517.

Efran, M. G. 1974. The effect of physical appearance on the judgment of guilt, interpersonal attraction, and severity of recommended punishment in a simulated jury task. *Journal of Experimental Research in Personality* 8: 45–54.

Egger, M. D., and Flynn, J. P. 1963. Effect of electrical stimulation of the amygdala on hypothalamically elicited behavior in cats. *Journal of Neurophysiology* 26: 705–720.

Eimas, P. D., Siqueland, E. R., Jusczyk, P., and Vigorito, J. 1971. Speech perception in infants. *Science* 171: 303–306.

Ekman, P. 1973. Cross-cultural studies in facial expression. In *Darwin and facial expression*, edited by P. Ekman, 169–222. New York: Academic Press.

Ekman, P., Levenson, R. W., and Friesen, W. V. 1983. Emotions differ in autonomic nervous system activity. *Science* 221: 1208–1210.

Ekstrand, B. R., Barrett, T. R., West, J. N., and Maier, W. G. 1977. The effects of sleep on human long-term memory. In *Neurobiology of sleep and memory*, edited by R. Drucker-Colin and J. L. McGaugh, 419–438. New York: Academic Press.

Ericsson, K. A., Chase, W. G., and Faloon, S. 1980. Acquisition of a memory skill. *Science* 208: 1181–1182.

Eron, L. D. 1972. Does television violence cause aggression? *American Psychologist* 27: 253–263.

———. 1982. Parent child interaction, television violence, and aggression of children. *American Psychologist* 37: 197–211.

Erwin, R. J., Gur, R. C., Gur, R. W., Skolnick, B., Mawhinney, H. M., and Smailis, J. 1992. Facial emotion discrimination: I. Task construction and behavioral findings. *Psychiatry Research* 42: 231–240.

Evans, C., and Richardson, P. H. 1988. Improved recovery and reduced post operative stay after therapeutic suggestions during general anaesthesia. *Lancet* 8609: 491–493.

Falk, D. 1983. Cerebral cortices of East African early hominids. *Science* 222: 1072–1074.

———. 1987a. Brain lateralization in primates and its evolution in hominids. *Yearbook of Physical Anthropology* 30: 107–125.

————. 1987b. Hominid paleoneurology. *Annual Review of Anthropology* 16: 13–30.

Fancher, R. E. 1979. *Pioneers of psychology.* New York: W.W. Norton.

Festinger, L., and Carlsmith, J. M. 1959. Cognitive consequences of forced compliance. *Journal of Abnormal and Social Psychology* 58: 203–210.

Feynman, R. P. 1985. *Surely you're joking, Mr. Feynman!: Adventures of a curious character.* New York: Bantam Books.

Fishbein, W. 1971. Disruptive effects of rapid-eye-movement sleep deprivation on long-term memory. *Physiology and Behavior* 6: 279–282.

Fishbein, W., McGaugh, J. L., and Swarz, J. R. 1971. Retrograde amnesia: Electroconvulsive shock effects after termination of rapid-eye-movement sleep deprivation. *Science* 172: 80–82.

Fox, N. A., and Davidson, R. J. 1986. Taste-elicited changes in facial signs of emotion and the asymmetry of brain electrical activity in newborns. *Neuropsychologia* 24: 417–422.

Freedman, J. L. 1965. Long-term behavioral effects of cognitive dissonance. *Journal of Experimental Social Psychology* 1: 145–155.

Freud, S., and Breuer, J. 1895. Reprinted 1976. Studies on hysteria. In *The complete psychological works*, Vol. 2, translated and edited by J. Strachey. New York: Norton.

Friedman, M. I., and Stricker, E. M. 1976. The physiological psychology of hunger: A physiological perspective. *Psychological Review* 83: 409–431.

Frith, D. C. 1979. Consciousness, information processing, and schizophrenia. *British Journal of Psychiatry* 134: 225–235.

Gainotti, G. 1972. Emotional behavior and hemispheric side of lesion. *Cortex* 8: 41–55.

Galaburda. A. M., and Kemper, T. M. 1979. Cytoarchitectonic abnormalities in developmental dyslexia: A case study. *Annals of Neurology* 6: 94–100.

Garcia, J., and Koelling, R. A. 1966. The relation of cue to consequence in avoidance learning. *Psychonomic Science* 4: 123–124.

Gardner, M. 1983. Illusions of the third dimension. *Psychology Today* 17 (August): 62–67.

Garrett, M. F., Bever, T. G., and Fodor, J. A. 1966. The active use of grammar in speech perception. *Perception and Psychophysics* 1: 30–32.

Gazzaniga, M. S. 1967. The split brain in man. *Scientific American* 217: 24–29.

Geen, R. G., and Berkowitz, L. 1967. Some conditions facilitating the occurrence of aggression after the observation of violence. *Journal of Personality* 35: 666–676.

Gelman, S. A., and Markman, E. M. 1986. Categories and induction in young children. *Cognition* 12: 183–209.

Gelman, S. A., and Markman, E. M. 1987. Young children's inductions from natural kinds: The role of categories and appearances. *Child Development* 58: 1532–1541.

Gelman, R., and Meck, E. 1983. Preschoolers' counting: Principle before skill. *Cognition* 13: 343–359.

Gentner, D. 1983. Structure mapping: A theoretical framework for analogy. *Cognitive Science* 7: 155–170.

Gick, M. L., and Holyoak, K. J. 1980. Analogical problem solving. *Cognitive Psychology* 12: 306–355.

———. 1983. Schema induction and analogical transfer. *Cognitive Psychology* 15: 1–38.

Gleitman, H. 1986. *Psychology.* 2nd ed. New York: Norton.

Glisky, E. L. 1992. Acquisition and transfer of declarative and procedural knowledge of memory-impaired patients: A computer data-entry task. *Neuropsychologia* 30: 899–910.

Glucksberg, S., and McCloskey, M. 1981. Decisions about ignorance: Knowing that you don't know. *Journal of Experimental Psychology: Human Learning and Memory* 7: 311–325.

Goldfarb, W. 1955. Emotional and intellectual consequences of psychological deprivation in infancy: A reevaluation. In *Psychopathology of childhood*, edited by P. Hock and H. Zubin. New York: Grune and Stratton.

Gopnik, M. 1990a. Feature blindness: A case study. *Language Acquisition: A Journal of Developmental Linguistics* 1: 139–164.

———. 1990b. Feature blind grammar and dysphasia. *Nature* 344: 715.

Goren, C. C., Sarty, M., and Wu, P. Y. K. 1975. Visual following and pattern discrimination of face-like stimuli by newborn infants. *Pediatrics* 59: 544–549.

Graf, P., and Mandler, G. 1984. Activation makes words more accessible, but not necessarily more retrievable. *Journal of Verbal Learning and Verbal Behavior* 23: 553–568.

Graf, P., Mandler, G., and Haden, P. E. 1982. Simulating amnesic symptoms in normal subjects. *Science* 218: 1243–1244.

Graf, P., Shimamura, A. P., and Squire, L. R. 1985. Priming across modalities and priming across category levels: Extending the domain of preserved function in amnesia. *Journal of Experimental Psychology: Learning, Memory, and Cognition* 11: 385–395.

Gregory, R. L. 1978. *Eye and brain: The psychology of seeing*. New York: McGraw-Hill.

———, ed. 1987. *The Oxford Companion to the Mind*. Oxford: Oxford University Press.

Grice, H. P. 1975. Logic and conversation. In *Syntax and Semantics*, Vol. 3, edited by Cole and Morgan, 41–58. New York: Academic Press.

Griggs, R. A., and Cox, J. R. 1982. The elusive thematic-materials effect in Wason's selection task. *British Journal of Psychology* 73: 407–420.

———. 1983. The effects of problem content and negation on Wason's selection task. *Quarterly Journal of Experimental Psychology*. 35A: 519–533.

Haberlandt, K., Berian, C., and Sandson, J. 1980. The episode schema in story processing. *Journal of Verbal Learning and Verbal Behavior* 19: 635–650.

Haier, R. J., Siegel, B., Jr., Neuchterlein, K. H., Hazlett, W., Wu, J. C., Paek, J., Browning, H. L., and Buchsbaum, M. S. 1988. Cortical glucose metabolic rate correlates of reasoning and attention studied with positron emission tomography. *Intelligence* 12: 199–217.

Halpern, L., Blake, R., and Hillenbrand, J. 1986. Primal screech. *Psychology Today* 20: (September): 68.

Harlow, H. F. 1958. The nature of love. *American Psychologist* 13: 673–685.

Harlow, H. F., and Harlow, M. K. 1972. The young monkeys. *Readings in Psychology Today*. Albany, NY: Delmar Publications, CRM Books.

Harlow, H. F., and Novak, M. A. 1973. Psychopathological perspectives. *Perspectives in Biology and Medicine* 16: 461–478.

Harlow, H. F., and Zimmerman, R. R. 1959. Affectional responses in the infant monkey. *Science* 130: 421–432.

Hartmann, E. 1973. *The functions of sleep*. New Haven: Yale University.

Harvey, J. G. 1981. Drug-related mortality in an inner city area. *Drug and Alcohol Dependence* 7: 239–247.

Heilman, J. M., Bowers, D., Speedied, L., and Coslett, H. B. 1984. Comprehension of affective and nonaffective prosody. *Neurology* 34: 917–921.

Heilman, K. M., Watson, R. R., Valenstein, E., and Damasio, A. R. 1983. Localization of lesions in neglect. In *Localization in neuropsychology*, edited by A. Kertesz, 471–492. New York: Academic.

REFERENCES

Held, R. 1965. Plasticity in sensory-motor systems. *Scientific American* 211: 84–94.

Held, R., and Hein, A. 1963. Movement-produced stimulation in the development of visually-guided behavior. *Journal of Comparative Physiological Psychology* 56: 872–876.

Helmholtz, H. von 1853. Reprinted 1962. On Goethe's scientific researches, translated by H. W. Eve. In *Popular scientific lectures by Hermann von Helmholtz*, edited by M. Kline. New York: Dover.

Hennevin, E., Hars, B., and Bloch, V. 1989. Improvement of learning by mesencephalic reticular stimulation during postlearning paradoxical sleep. *Behavioral and NeuralBiology* 51: 291–306.

Henriques, J. B., and Davidson, R. J. 1991. Left frontal hypoactivation in depression. *Journal of Abnormal Psychology* 100: 535–545.

Hernandez-Peon, R. 1955. Central mechanisms controlling conduction along central sensory pathways. *Acta Neurologia Latinoamerica* 1: 256.

van Heuvelen, A. 1982. *Physics: A general introduction*, Vol. 2, 89–195. New York: Academic Press.

Hilgard, E. R. 1977. *Divided consciousness: Multiple controls in human thought and action.* New York: John Wiley.

Hinsley, D. A., Hayes, J. R., and Simon, H. A. 1977. From words to equations: Meaning and representations in algebra word problems. In *Cognitive processes in comprehension*, edited by M. A. Just and P. A. Carpenter, 89–108. Hillsdale, NJ: Erlbaum.

Hintzman, D. L., and Block, R. A. 1970. Memory judgments and the effects of spacing. *Journal of Verbal Learning and Verbal Behavior* 9: 561–566.

Hirsh, H. V. B., and Spinelli, D. N. 1970. Visual experience modifies distribution of horizontally and vertically oriented receptive fields in cats. *Science* 168: 869–871.

Hoebel, B. G., and Teitelbaum, P. 1976. Weight regulation in normal and hyperphagic rats. *Journal of Physiological and Comparative Psychology* 61: 189–193.

Hoffman, L. W. 1974. Effects of maternal employment on the child. A review of research. *Developmental Psychology* 10: 204–228.

Hokanson, J. E. 1961. The effect of frustration and anxiety on overt aggression. *Journal of Abnormal and Social Psychology* 62: 346–351.

Hokanson, J. E., and Edelman, R. 1966. Effects of three social responses on vascular processes. *Journal of Personality and Social Psychology* 3: 442–447.

Hokanson, J. E., and Shetler, S. 1961. The effect of overt aggression on physiological arousal. *Journal of Abnormal and Social Psychology* 63: 446–448.

Hostetler, A. J. 1988. Exploring the "gatekeeper" of memory: Changes in the hippocampus seen in aging, amnesia, and Alzheimer's. *APA Monitor* (April).

Hubel, D. H. 1963. The visual cortex of the brain. *Scientific American* 209: 54–62.

———. 1988. *Eye, brain, and vision.* New York: W. H. Freeman.

Hubel, D. H., and Wiesel, T. N. 1959. Receptive fields of single neurones in the cat's visual cortex. *Journal of Physiology* 148: 574–591.

Huesman, L. R., Lagerspetz, K., and Eron, L. D. 1984. Intervening variables in the TV violence-aggression relation: Evidence from two countries. *Developmental Psychology* 20: 746–775.

Humphrey, G. 1951. *Thinking: An introduction to its experimental psychology.* New York: Wiley.

Hunt, W. A., Barnett, L. W., and Branch, L. G. 1971. Relapse rates in addiction programs. *Journal of Clinical Psychology* 27: 455–456.

Hutchinson, R. R., and Renfew, J. W. 1966. Stalking attack and eating behaviors elicited from the same sites in the hypothalamus. *Journal of Comparative and Physiological Psychology* 61: 360–367.

Jacoby, L. L., and Dallas, M. 1981. On the relationship between autobiographical memory and perceptual learning. *Journal of Experimental Psychology: General* 110: 306–340.

Johnson, D. C., and Newport, E. L. 1989. Critical period effects in second-language learning: The influence of maturational state on the acquisition of English as a second language. *Cognitive Psychology* 21: 60–99.

Johnson, M. K., Kim, J. K., and Risse, G. 1985. Do alcoholic Korsakoff's syndrome patients acquire affective reactions? *Journal of Experimental Psychology: Learning, Memory, and Cognition* 11: 27–36.

Johnson, N. F. 1965. The psychological reality of phrase structure rules. *Journal of Verbal Learning and Verbal Behavior* 5: 469–475.

Johnson, R. D. 1986. The influence of gender composition on evaluation of professions. *Journal of Social Psychology* 126: 161–167.

Kahneman, D., and Tversky, A. 1982. Variants of uncertainty. *Cognition* 11: 143–158.

Kant, I. 1786. Reprinted 1974. Metaphysische Anfangsgrunde der Naturwissenschaft. Excerpted in *The roots of psychology: A sourcebook in the history of ideas,* edited by S. Diamond. New York: Basic Books.

Kaufman, J., and Zigler, E. F. 1988. Do abused children become abusive parents? *Annual Progress in Child Psychiatry and Child Development* 29: 591–600.

Keil, F. 1986. The acquisition of natural kind and artifact terms. In *Language learning and concept acquisition: Foundational issues*, edited by W. Demopoulos and A. Marras, 133–153. Norwood, NJ: Ablex.

Kendall, S. B. 1989. Risk-taking behavior of pigeons in a closed economy. *The Psychological Record* 39: 211–220.

Kihlstrom, J. F., and Couture, L. J. 1992. Awareness and information processing in general anesthesia. *Journal of Psychopharmacology* 6: 410–417.

Kihlstrom, J. F., and Schacter, D. L. 1990. Anaesthesia, amnesia, and the cognitive unconscious. In *Memory and awareness in anaesthesia*, edited by B. Bonke, W. Fitch, and K. Miller, 21–44. Amsterdam: Swets & Zeitlinger.

Kihlstrom, J. F., Schacter, D. L., Cork, R. C., Hurt, C. A., and Behr, S. E. 1990. Implicit and explicit memory following surgical anesthesia. *Psychological Science* 1: 303–306.

Kinsbourne, M., and Wood, F. 1975. Short term memory and the amnesic syndrome. In *Short term memory*, edited by D. D. Deutsch and J. A. Deutsch, 258–291. New York: Academic Press.

Knapp, A. G., and Anderson, J. A. 1984. Theory of categorization based on distributed memory storage. *Journal of Experimental Psychology: Learning, Memory, and Cognition* 10: 616–637.

Koella, W. P. 1967. *Sleep: Its nature and physiological organization*. Springfield, IL: Charles C. Thomas.

Köhler, W. 1925. *The mentality of apes*. New York: Harcourt.

Kolers, P. A. 1975. Memorial consequences of automatized encoding. *Journal of Experimental Psychology: Human Learning and Memory* 1: 689–701.

Kotelchuk, M. 1976. The infant's relationship to the father: Some experimental evidence. In *The role of the father in child development*, edited by M. Lamb. 1st ed. New York: Wiley.

Kunst-Wilson, R., and Zajonc, R. B. 1980. Affective discrimination of stimuli that cannot be recognized. *Science* 207: 557–558.

Laitman, J. T. 1984. The anatomy of human speech. *Natural History* (August 20–27).

Lalande, S., Braun, C. M. J., Charlebois, N., and Whitaker, H. A. 1992. Effects of right and left hemisphere cerebrovascular lesions on discrimination of prosodic and semantic aspects of affect in sentences. *Brain and Language* 42: 165–186.

Lamb, M. E. 1981. The development of father-infant relationships. In *The role of the father in child development*, edited by M. E. Lamb, 459–488. New York: John Wiley.

Latane, B., and Rodin, J. 1969. A lady in distress: Inhibiting effects of friends and strangers on bystander intervention. *Journal of Experimental Psychology* 5: 189–202.

Lenneberg, E. H. 1967. *Biological foundations of language*. New York: Wiley.

Leslie, A. M., and Keeble, S. 1987. Do six-month-old infants perceive causality? *Cognition* 25: 265–288.

Levine, S. A. 1951. *Clinical heart disease*. 4th ed. Philadelphia: Saunders.

Levinson, B. W. 1965. States of awareness during general anaesthesia: Preliminary communication. *British Journal of Anaesthesia* 37: 544–546.

Lewin, K., Lippett, R., and White, R. 1939. Patterns of aggressive behavior in experimentally created social climates. *Journal of Social Psychology* 10: 271–299.

Ley, R. G., and Bryden, M. P. 1979. Hemispheric differences in processing emotions and faces. *Brain and Language* 7: 127–138.

Light, L. L., and Carter-Sobell, L. 1970. Effects of changed semantic context on recognition memory. *Journal of Verbal Learning and Verbal Behavior* 9: 1–11.

Lindsley, D. B. 1960. Attention, consciousness, sleep, and wakefulness. In *Handbook of physiology*. Vol. 3, *Neurophysiology*. Washington, DC: American Physiological Society.

Loeber, R., and Dishion, T. J. 1984. Boys who fight at home and school: Family conditions influencing cross-setting consistency. *Journal of Consulting and Clinical Psychology* 52: 759–768.

Loftus, G. R., Johnson, C. A., and Shimamura, A. P. 1985. How much is an icon worth? *Journal of Experimental Psychology* 11: 1–13.

Ludwig, A. M., Cain, R. B., Wikler, A., Taylor, R. M., and Bendfeldt, F. 1977. Physiologic and situational determinants of drinking behavior. In *Alcohol Intoxication and Withdrawal—IIIb: Studies in Alcohol Dependence*, edited by M. M. Gross, 589–600. New York: Plenum.

Ludwig, A. M., and Stark, L. H. 1974. Alcohol caving: Subjective and situational aspects. *Quarterly Journal of Studies of Alcohol* 35: 899.

Luria, A. R. 1966. *Higher cortical functions in man*. New York: Basic Books.

MacKay, D. G. 1973. Aspects of the theory of comprehension, memory, and attention. *Quarterly Journal of Experimental Psychology*, 25: 22–40.

Madigan, S. A. 1969. Intraserial repetition and coding processes in free recall. *Journal of Verbal Learning and Verbal Behavior* 8: 828–835.

Maier, N. 1930. Reasoning in humans. I. On direction. *Journal of Comparative Psychology* 10: 15–43.

Malamuth, N. M. 1989a. The attraction to sexual aggression scale: Part one. *Journal of Sex Research* 26: 26–49.

———. 1989b. The attraction to sexual aggression scale: Part two. *Journal of Sex Research* 26: 324–354.

Martin, J. A., and Elmer, E. 1992. Battered children grown up: A follow-up study of individuals severely maltreated as children. *Child Abuse and Neglect* 16: 75–88.

McClintock, T. T., Aitken, H., Downie, C. F. A., and Kenny, G. N. C. 1990. Postoperative analgesia requirements in patients exposed to positive intraoperative suggestions. *British Medical Journal* 301: 788–790.

McCloskey, M. 1983. Naive theories of motion. In *Mental models*, edited by D. Gentner and A. L. Stevens, 299–324. Hillsdale, NJ: Erlbaum.

McNeill, D. 1966. Developmental psycholinguistics. In F. Smith and G. A. Miller (eds.) *The Genesis of Language*. Cambridge, MA: MIT.

Mehler, J., Jusczyk, P. W., Lambertz, G., Halsted, N., Bertoncini, J., and Amiel-Tison, C. 1988. A precursor of language acquisition in young infants. *Cognition* 29: 143–178.

Melton, A. W. 1970. The situation with respect to the spacing of repetitions and memory. *Journal of Verbal Learning and Verbal Behavior* 9: 596–606.

Meltzoff, A. N., and Borton, R. W. 1979. Intermodal matching by human neonates. *Science* 198: 75–78.

Meyer, D. E., and Schvanevelt, R. W. 1971. Facilitation in recognizing pairs of words: Evidence of a dependence between retrieval operations. *Journal of Experimental Psychology* 90: 227–234.

Milgram, S. 1974. *Obedience to authority*. New York: Harper and Row.

Miller, G. A. 1956. The magical number seven, plus or minus two: Some limits on our capacity for processing information. *Psychological Review* 63: 81–97.

Miller, N. E., Bailey, C. J., and Stevenson, J. A. F. 1950. Decreased "hunger" but increased food intake resulting from hypothalamic lesions. *Science* 112: 256–259.

Miller, N. E., and Banuazizi, A. 1968. Instrumental learning by curarized rats of a specific visceral response, intestinal or cardiac. *Journal of Comparative and Physiological Psychology* 65: 1–7.

Milner, B. 1966. Amnesia following operation on the temporal lobes. In *Amnesia*, edited by C. W. M. Whitty and D. L. Zangwill, 109–133. London: Butterworth.

Milner, B., Corkin, S., and Teuber, H. L. 1968. Further analysis of the hippocampal syndrome: 14-year follow-up study of H. M. *Neuropsychologia* 6: 215–234.

Moore, J. W. 1972. Stimulus control: Studies of auditory generalization in rabbits. In *Classical conditioning II: Current research and theory*, edited by A. H. Black and W. F. Prokasy, 206–230. New York: Appleton-Century-Crofts.

Moray, N. 1959. Attention in dichotic listening: Affective cues and the influence of instructions. *Quarterly Journal of Experimental Psychology* 11: 56–60.

Murdock, B. 1962. The serial position effect of free recall. *Journal of Experimental Psychology* 64: 482–488.

Murray, L., and Trevarthen, C. 1985. Emotional regulation of interactions between two-month-olds and their mothers. In *Social perception in infants*, edited by T. M. Field and N. Fox. Norwood, NJ: Ablex.

Nadel, L., and Zola-Morgan, S. 1984. Infantile amnesia: A neurobiological perspective. In *Infant memory*, edited by M. Moscovitch, 145–172. New York: Plenum.

Nadler, R. 1988. Sexual aggression in the great apes. *Annals of the New York Academy of Sciences* 528: 154–162.

Naigles, L. 1990. Children use syntax to learn verb meanings. *Journal of Child Language* 17: 357–374.

Neisser, U. 1967. *Cognitive Psychology*. Englewood Cliffs, NJ: Prentice-Hall.

Nel, E., Helmreich, R., and Aronson, E. 1969. Opinion change in the advocate as a function of the persuasibility of his audience: A clarification of the meaning of dissonance. *Journal of Personality and Social Psychology* 12: 117–124.

Nemeth, C. J. 1986. Differential contributions of majority and minority influence. *Psychological Review* 91: 23–32.

Newport, E. L. 1991. Contrasting concepts of the critical period for language. In *The epigenesis of mind: Essays on biology and cognition*, edited by S. Carey and R. Gelman. Hillsdale, NJ: Erlbaum.

Nissen, M. J., and Bullemer, P. 1987. Attentional requirements of learning: Evidence from performance measures. *Cognitive Psychology* 19: 1–32.

Novak, M. A., and Harlow, H. F. 1975. Social recovery of monkeys isolated for the first year of life: I. Rehabilitation and therapy. *Developmental Psychology* 11: 453–465.

O'Brien, C. P. 1976. Experimental analysis of conditioning factors in human narcotic addiction. *Pharmacological Reviews* 27: 533–543.

O'Brien, C. P., Nace, E. P., Mintz, J., Meyers, A. L., and Ream, N. 1980. Follow-up of Vietnam veterans. I. Relapse to drug use after Vietnam service. *Drug and Alcohol Dependence* 5: 333–340.

O'Brien, C. P., Testa, T., O'Brien, T. J., and Greenstein, R. 1974. Systematic extinction of addiction-associated rituals using narcotic antagonists. *Psychosomatic Medicine* 36: 458.

Olds, J. A. 1956. A preliminary mapping of electrical reinforcing effects in the rat brain. *Journal of Comparative Physiology and Psychology* 49: 281–285.

Olds, J., and Milner, P. 1954. Positive reinforcement produced by electrical stimulation of septal areas and other regions of rat brains. *Journal of Comparative and Physiological Psychology* 47: 419–427.

Oller, D. K., and Eilers, R. E. 1988. The role of audition in infant babbling. *Child Development* 59: 441–449.

Osborne, R. E., and Gilbert, D. T. 1992. The preoccupational hazards of social life. *Journal of Personality and Social Psychology* 62: 219–228.

Paller, K. A., and Kutas, M. 1992. Brain potentials during memory retrieval: Neurophysiological support for the distinction between conscious recollection and priming. *Journal of Cognitive Neuroscience* 4: 375–393.

Parks, T. E., and Coss, R. G. 1986. Prime illusion. *Psychology Today* (October): 6–7.

Parks, R. W., Lowenstein, D. A., Dodrill, K. L., Barker, W. W., Yoshii, F., Change, J. Y., Emran, A., Apicella, A., Sheramata, W. A., and Duara, R. 1988. Cerebral metabolic effects of a verbal fluency test: A PET scan study. *Journal of Clinical and Experimental Neuropsychology* 10: 565–575.

Patterson, F. G. 1979. The gesture of the gorilla: Language acquisition in another pongid. *Brain and Language* 5: 72–97.

———. 1981. Ape language. *Science* 221: 87–88.

Patterson, G. R. 1980. Mothers: The unacknowledged victims. *Monographs of the Society for Research in Child Development.* no. 45.

Pavlov, I. 1927. *Conditioned reflexes.* Oxford: Oxford University Press.

Penfield, W., and Rasmussen, T. 1950. *The cerebral cortex of man.* New York: Macmillan.

Pessah, M., and Roffwarg, H. 1972. Spontaneous middle ear muscle activity in man: A rapid eye movement sleep phenomenon. *Science* 178: 773–776.

Petitto, L. A., and Marentette, P. F. 1991. Babbling in the manual mode: Evidence for the ontogeny of language. *Science* 251: 1493–1495.

Pettersen, L. 1991. Sensitivity to emotional cues and social behavior in children and adolescents after head injury. *Perceptual and Motor Skills* 73: 1139–1150.

Phillips, J. 1991. *You'll never eat lunch in this town again*, 418–424. New York: Signet.

Pinker, S., and Bloom, P. 1990. Natural language and natural selection. *Behavioral and Brain Sciences* 13: 707–784.

Pinker, S. 1990. Language acquisition. In *An invitation to cognitive science: Language*, Vol. 1, edited by D. N. Osherson and H. Lasnik, 199–242. Cambridge, MA: MIT Press.

———. 1994. *The language instinct*. New York: W. Morrow.

Plotnik, R. 1974. Brain stimulation and aggression: Monkeys, apes, and humans. In *Primate aggression, territoriality, and xenophobia: A comparative perspective*, edited by R. L. Holloway. New York: Academic.

Plotnik, R., Mir, D., and Delgado, J. M. R. 1971. Aggression, noxiousness, and brain stimulation in unrestrained rhesus monkeys. In *The physiology of aggression and defeat*, edited by B. E. Eleftheriou and J. P. Scott, 143–222. New York: Plenum Press.

Posner, M. I., and Keele, S. W. 1968. On the genesis of abstract ideas. *Journal of Experimental Psychology* 77: 353–363.

Premack, D. 1985. "Gavagai!" or the future history of the animal language controversy. *Cognition* 19: 207–296.

Putnam, F. W. 1986. The scientific investigation of multiple personality disorder. In *Split minds/split brains*, edited by J. M. Quen, 109–125. New York: New York University.

Rauscheker, J. P., and Singer, W. 1981. The effects of early visual experience on the cat's visual cortex and their possible explanation by Hebb synapses. *Journal of Physiology* 310: 215–239.

Rebelsky, F., and Hanks, C. 1971. Father's verbal interaction with infants in the first three months of life. *Child Development* 42: 63–68.

Rechtschaffen, A., Hauri, P., and Zeitlan, M. 1966. Auditory awakening thresholds in REM and NREM sleep stages. *Perceptual and Motor Skills* 22: 927–942.

Rechtschaffen, A., and Kales, A. 1968. *A manual of standardized terminology, techniques, and scoring system for sleep stages of human sleep subjects*. Washington, DC: U.S. Government Printing Office.

224

Reiman, E. M., Raichle, M. E., Butler, F. K., Hercovitch, P., and Robins, E. 1984. A focal brain abnormality in panic disorder, a severe form of anxiety. *Nature* 310: 684–685.

Reynolds, B. A., and Weiss, S. 1992. Generation of neurons and atrocytes from isolated cells of the adult mammalian central nervous system. *Science* 225: 1707–1710.

Reynolds, G. S. 1968. *A primer of operant conditioning.* Glenview, IL: Scott, Foresman.

Rips, L. J. 1989. Similarity, typicality, and categorization. In *Similarity and analogical reasoning,* edited by S. Vosniadou and A. Ortony, 21–60. Cambridge: Cambridge University Press.

Robins, L. N., Helzer, J. E., and Davis, D. H. 1975. Narcotic use in southeast Asia and afterwards. *Archives of General Psychiatry* 32: 955–961.

Robinson, R. G., Kubos, K. L., Starr, L. B., Rao, K., and Price, T. R. 1984. Mood disorders in stroke patients: Importance of location of lesion. *Brain* 107: 81–93.

Roediger, H. L., III, and Blaxton, T. A. 1987. Effects of varying modality, surface features, and retention interval on priming in word-fragment completion. *Memory & Cognition* 15: 379–388.

Roediger, H. L., III, and Weldon, M. A. 1987. Reversing the picture superiority effect. In *Imagery and related mnemonic processes,* edited by M. A. McDaniel and M. Pressley, 151–174. New York: Springer-Verlag.

Rosch, E. H. 1973. Natural categories. *Cognitive Psychology* 4: 328–350.

Rosch, E. H., and Mervis, C. B. 1975. Family resemblances: Studies on the internal structure of categories. *Cognitive Psychology* 7: 573–605.

Rosenbaum, L. L., and Rosenbaum, W. B. 1971. Morale and productivity consequences of group leadership style, stress, and type of task. *Journal of Applied Psychology* 55: 343–348.

Ross, B. H. 1984. Remindings and their effects in learning a cognitive skill. *Cognitive Psychology* 16: 371–416.

———. 1990. Distinguishing types of superficial similarities: Different effects on the access and use of earlier problems. *Journal of Experimental Psychology: Learning, Memory, & Cognition* 15: 456–468.

Rumelhart, D. E., and McClelland, J. L. 1986. *Parallel distributed processing: Explorations in the microstructure of cognition.* Cambridge, MA: MIT Press.

Sacks, O. 1985. *The man who mistook his wife for a hat and other clinical tales.* New York: Peter Smith.

Sarich, V. M., and Wilson, A. C. 1967. Immunological time scale for hominid evolution. *Science* 158: 1200–1203.

Sasanuma, S. 1975. Kana and Kanji processing in Japanese aphasics. *Brain and Language* 2: 369–383.

Sasanuma, S., and Fujimura, O. 1971. Selective impairment of phonetic and non-phonetic transcription of words in Japanese aphasic patients: Kana vs. Kanji in visual recognition and writing. *Cortex* 7: 1–18.

Scaife, M., and Bruner, J. 1975. The capacity for joint visual attention in the infant. *Nature* 253: 265–266.

Schacter, D. L. 1983. Amnesia observed: Remembering and forgetting in a natural environment. *Journal of Abnormal Psychology* 92: 235–242.

———. 1987. Implicit memory: History and current status. *Journal of Experimental Psychology: Learning, Memory, and Cognition* 13: 501–518.

Schacter, D. L., and Graf, P. 1989. Modality specificity of implicit memory for new associations. *Journal of Experimental Psychology: Learning, Memory, and Cognition* 15: 3–12.

Schacter, S. 1951. Communication, deviation, and rejection. *Journal of Abnormal and Social Psychology*, 46: 190–207.

Schein, E. 1956. The Chinese indoctrination program for prisoners of war: A study of attempted "brainwashing." *Psychiatry* 19: 149–172.

Schill, T. R. 1972. Aggression and blood pressure responses of high- and low-guilt subjects following frustration. *Journal of Consulting and Clinical Psychology* 38: 461.

Schwartz, S. 1986. *Classic studies in psychology*. Palo Alto, CA: Mayfield Publishing Co.

Schwartz, S. H., and Clausen, G. 1970. Responsibility, norms, and helping in an emergency. *Journal of Personality and Social Psychology* 16: 299–310.

Seay, B., Alexander, B. K., and Harlow, H. F. 1964. Maternal behavior of socially deprived rhesus monkeys. *Journal of Abnormal and Social Psychology* 69: 345–354.

Shapiro, C. M., Bortz, R., Mitchell, D., Bartel, P., and Jooste, P. 1981. Slow wave sleep: A recovery period after exercise. *Science*, 214: 1253–1254.

Shashoua, V. 1985. The role of extracellular proteins in learning and memory. *American Scientist* 73: 364–370.

Shlomo, B., and Moscovitch, M. 1990. Psychophysiological indices of implicit memory performance. *Bulletin of the Psychonomic Society*. 28: 346–352.

Shortell, J., Epstein, S., and Taylor, S. P. 1970. Instigation to aggression as a function of degree of defeat and the capacity for massive retaliation. *Journal of Personality* 38: 313–328.

Sideroff, S. I., and Jarvik, M. E. 1980. Conditioned responses to a videotape showing heroin related stimuli. *International Journal of Addiction* 15: 529.

Siegel, S. 1975. Evidence from rats that morphine tolerance is a learned response. *Journal of Comparative Physiological Psychology* 89: 498–506.

———. 1983. Classical conditioning, drug tolerance, and drug dependence. In *Research advances in alcohol and drug problems,* Vol. 7, edited by Y. Israel, F. B. Glaser, H. Kalant, R. E. Popham, W. Schmidt, and R. Smart, 207–246. New York: Plenum.

Siegel, S., Hinson, R. W., and Krank, M. D. 1978. The role of predrug signals in morphine analgesic tolerance: Support for a Pavlovian conditioning model of tolerance. *Journal of Experimental Psychology: Animal Behavior Processes* 4: 188–196.

Siegel, S., Hinson, R. W., Krank, M. D., and McCully, J. 1982. Heroin "overdose" death: Contribution of drug-associated environmental cues. *Science* 216: 436–437.

Siegel, S., and MacRae, J. 1984. Environmental specificity of tolerance. *Trends in Neuroscience* 7: 140–143.

Sigall, H. and Aronson, E. 1969. Liking of an evaluator as a function of her physical attractiveness and nature of the evaluations. *Journal of Experimental Social Psychology* 5: 93–100.

Skeels, H. 1966. Adult status of children with contrasting early life experiences. *Monograph of the Society for Research in Child Development.* no. 3.

Skinner, B. F. 1938. *The behavior of organisms.* New York: Appleton-Century-Crofts.

Slobin, D. I. 1973. Cognitive prerequisites for the development of grammar. In *Studies of child language development,* edited by C. Ferguson and D. Slobin, 175–208. New York: Holt, Reinhart, and Winston.

Smith, C., Tenn. C., and Annett, R. 1991. Some biochemical and behavioral aspects of the paradoxical sleep window. *Canadian Journal of Psychology* 45: 115–124.

Speisman, J. C., Lazarus, R. S., Mordokoff, A. 1964. Experimental reduction of stress based on ego-defense theory. *Journal of Abnormal and Social Psychology* 68: 367–380.

Spelke, E. S. 1976. Infants' intermodal perception of events. *Cognitive Psychology* 8: 553–560.

———. 1991. Physical knowledge in infancy: Reflections on Piaget's theory. In *The epigenesis of mind*, edited by S. Carey and R. Gelman, 133–160. Hillsdale, NJ: Erlbaum.

Sperling, G. (1960) The information available in brief visual presentations. *Psychological Monographs* 74, whole no. 498.

Squire, L. R. 1992a. Declarative and nondeclarative memory: Multiple brain systems supporting learning and memory. *Journal of Cognitive Neuroscience* 4: 232–242.

———. 1992b. Memory and the hippocampus: A synthesis from findings with rats, monkeys, and humans. *Psychological Review* 99: 195–231.

Squire, L. R., Ojemann, J. G., Miezen, F. M., Petersen, S. E., Videen, T. O., et al. 1992. Activation of the hippocampus in normal humans: A functional anatomical study of memory. *Proceedings of the National Academy of Sciences USA* 89: 1837–1841.

Starkey, P., Spelke, E. S., and Gelman, R. 1983. Detection of intermodal numerical correspondences by infants. *Science* 222: 179–181.

Stewart, J. E. 1980. Defendant's attractiveness as a factor in the outcome of criminal trials: An observational study. *Journal of Applied Social Psychology* 10: 348–361.

Stricker, E. M., and Zigmond, M. J. 1976. Recovery of function after damage to catecholamine-containing neurons: A neurochemical model for the lateral hypothalamic syndrome. In *Progress in psychobiology and physiological psychology*, Vol. 6, edited by J. M. Sprague and A. N. Epstein, Vol. 6, 121–188. New York: Academic Press.

Suls, J. M. 1972. A two-stage model for the appreciation of jokes and cartoons: An information processing analysis. In *The psychology of humor*, edited by J. H. Goldstein and P. E. McGhee, 81–100. New York: Academic Press.

Suomi, S. J., and Harlow, H. F. 1971. Abnormal social behavior in young monkeys. In *Exceptional infants: Studies in abnormalities*, Vol. 2, edited by J. Helmuth 483–529. New York: Brunner/Mazel.

Suomi, S. J., Harlow, H. F., and McKinney, W. T. 1972. Monkey psychiatrist. *American Journal of Psychiatry* 128: 41–46.

Swinney, D. A. 1979. Lexical access during sentence comprehension: (Re)consideration of context effects. *Journal of Verbal Learning and Verbal Behavior* 18: 645–659.

Teitelbaum, P., and Stellar, E. 1954. Recovery from failure to eat produced by hypothalamic lesions. *Science* 120: 894–895.

Thatcher, R. W., and John, E. R. 1977. *Functional neuroscience: Volume*

I, Foundations of Cognitive Processes, 130–134. Hillsdale, NJ: Erlbaum.

Thomas, M. H. 1982. Physiological arousal, exposure to a relatively lengthy aggressive film, and aggressive behavior. *Journal of Research in Personality* 16: 72–81.

Thomas, M. H., and Drabman, R. S. 1975. Toleration of real life aggression as a function of exposure to televised violence and age of subject. *Merrill-Palmer Quarterly* 21: 227–232.

Thomas, M. H., Horton, R. W., Lippincott, E. C., and Drabman, R. S. 1977. Desensitization to portrayals of real-life aggression as a function of exposure to television violence. *Journal of Personality and Social Psychology* 35: 450–458.

Thompson, R. F. 1985. *The brain: An introduction to neuroscience.* New York: W. H. Freeman.

Thompson, T., and Ostlund, W. 1965. Susceptibility to readdiction as a function of the addiction and withdrawal environments. *Journal of Comparative Physiological Psychology* 60: 388.

Tobias, P. V. 1987. The brain of *Homo habilis:* A new level of organization in cerebral evolution. *Journal of Human Evolution* 16: 741–761.

Touhy, J. C. 1974a. Effects of additional women professionals on ratings of occupational prestige and desirability. *Journal of Personality and Social Psychology* 29: 86–89.

———. 1974b. Effects of additional men on prestige and desirability of occupations typically performed by women. *Journal of Applied Social Psychology* 4: 330–335.

Tranel, D., and Damasio, A. R. 1985. Knowledge without awareness: An autonomic index of facial recognition by prosopagnosics. *Science* 228: 1453–1454.

Triesman, A. M. 1960. Contextual cues in selective listening. *Quarterly Journal of Experimental Psychology* 12: 242–248.

Tronick, E. Z., Als, H., Adamson, L., Wise, S., and Brazelton, T. B. 1978. The infant's response to entrapment between contradictory messages in face-to-face interaction. *Journal of the American Academy of Child Psychiatry* 17: 1–13.

Turiel, E. 1983. *The development of social knowledge: Morality and convention.* Cambridge: Cambridge University Press.

———. 1989. Domain-specific social judgments and domain ambiguities. *Merrill-Palmer Quarterly* 35: 89–114.

Turiel, E., Edwards, C. P., and Kohlberg, L. 1978. Moral development in Turkish children, adolescents, and young adults. *Journal of Cross-Cultural Psychology* 9: 75–86.

Turiel, E., Killen, M., and Helwig, C. C. 1987. Morality: Its structure, functions, and vagaries. In *The emergence of moral concepts in young children*, edited by J. Kagan and S. Lamb. Chicago: Chicago University Press.

Underwood, B. J. 1970. A breakdown of the total-time law in free-recall learning. *Journal of Verbal Learning and Verbal Behavior* 9: 573–580.

Valenstein, E. S. 1973. *Brain control: A critical examination of brain stimulation and psychosurgery*, pp. 49–50. New York: Wiley.

Wada, J. 1949. A new method for the determination of the side of cerebral speech dominance: A preliminary report on the intracarotid injection of sodium amytal in man. *Medical Biology* 14: 221–222.

Wada, J., and Rasmussen, T. 1960. Intracarotid injection of sodium amytal for the lateralization of cerebral speech dominance. Experimental and clinical observations. *Journal of Neurosurgery* 17: 266–282.

Walk, R. D., and Gibson, E. J. 1961. A comparative and analytical study of visual depth perception. *Psychological Monographs* 75, Whole no. 519.

Walster, E., Aronson, E., Abrahams, D., and Rottman, L. 1966. The importance of physical attractiveness in dating behavior. *Journal of Personality and Social Psychology* 4: 508–516.

Warrington, E. K., and Weiskrantz, L. 1968. New method of testing long-term retention with special reference to amnesic patients. *Nature* 217: 972–974.

Wasman, M., and Flynn, J. P. 1962. Directed attack elicited from the hypothalamus. *Archives of Neurology* 6: 220–227.

Watson, J. B., and Rayner, R. 1920. Conditioned emotional reactions. *Journal of Experimental Psychology* 3: 1–14.

Webb, W. B. 1969. Partial and differential sleep deprivation. In *Sleep: Physiology and pathology*, edited by A. Kales, 221–231. Philadelphia: Lippincott.

Wechsler, A. F. 1973. The effect of organic brain disease on recall of emotionally charged versus neutral narrative text. *Neurology* 23: 130–135.

Weinstock, S. 1954. Resistance to extinction of a running response following partial reinforcement under widely spaced trials. *Journal of Comparative and Physiological Psychology* 47: 318–322.

Weiskrantz, L., and Warrington, E. K. 1979. Conditioning in amnesic patients. *Neuropsychologia* 17: 187–194.

Weiss, B., Dodge, K. A., Bates, J. E., and Pettit, G. S. 1992. Some consequences of early harsh discipline: Child aggression and a maladaptive social information processing style. *Child Development* 63: 1321–1335.

Wernicke, C. 1874. *Der Aphasische Symptomenkomplex*. Breslau: Cohn and Weigart.

Wertheimer, M. 1945. Reprinted 1982. *Productive thinking*. Chicago: University of Chicago.·

———. 1961. Psychomotor coordination of auditory and visual space at birth. *Science* 134: 1692.

White, G. L., Fishbein, S., and Rutsein, J. 1981. Passionate love and the misattribution of arousal. *Journal of Personality and Social Psychology* 41: 56–62.

White, P. D. 1944. *Heart disease*. New York: MacMillan.

Wiesel, T. N. 1982. Postnatal development of the visual cortex and the influence of the environment. *Nature* 299: 583–591.

Wolpert, E. A., and Trosman, H. 1958. Studies in psychophysiology of dreams: I. Experimental evocation of sequential dream episodes. *Archives of Neurology and Psychiatry* 79: 603–606.

Wood, J. M., Bootzin, R., Kihlstrom, J. F., and Schacter, D. L. 1992. Implicit and explicit memory for verbal information presented during sleep. *Psychological Science* 3: 236–239.

Wynn, K. 1990. Children's understanding of counting. *Cognition* 36: 155–193.

———. 1991. Psychological evidence against empiricist theories of mathematical knowledge. *Mind and Language* 7: 315–332.

———. 1992a. Addition and subtraction by human infants. *Nature*, *358*, 749–750.

———. 1992b. Children's acquisition of the number words and the counting system. *Cognitive Psychology* 24: 220–251.

Yarrow, L. 1961. Maternal deprivation: Toward an empirical and conceptual reevaluation. *Psychological Bulletin* 58: 459–490.

Zigler, E., and Hall, N. 1989. Day care and its effects on children: An overview for pediatric health professionals. *Annual Progress in Child Psychiatry and Child Development* 30: 543–560.

Index

Biological distinctions, development of, 161–164
Blindness denial, 38
Blindsight, 38
Blood pressure
aggression and, 109–110
biofeedback and, 127–128
manipulation of, 112–113
Body awareness, 39
Boredom
biofeedback and, 127
intermittent reinforcement and, 126
Brain, structure and function of, 28–43
cerebral cortex, *36, 130*
language acquisition and, 130–132, 150–159
lobes of cerebral hemispheres, 37
"three brains," view of, 33
Brain Matters (Dobkin), 41
Breakthrough dreaming, 82
Breuer, Josef, 4
Broca, Paul, 131
Broca's area, 130–132, 153
Brutality, obedience to authority and, 6–12
Bystander apathy, 15–17

Careers, obedience and, 11
Carlsmith, James, 21
CAT scan, 42–43
Catastrophic depression syndrome, 93
Category restructuring, 174–187, *175*, 191–195
Causation, notion of, 168, 177
Cerebellum, 32–33
Cerebral cortex
emotions, processing of, 90–95, 103
sleep and, 79–80
structure of the brain, 35–39, *36*

Child abuse, emotional development and, 99–100
Childhood
emotional development during, 95–100
humor and, 150
language development during, 132–146
See also Innate knowledge
Chomsky, Noam, 10
Cialdini, Robert, 20
Cigarette addiction, 120. *See also* Addiction
Classical conditioning, 111–123
drug addiction and, 111, 114–120
phobias and, 111, 120–123
See also Operant conditioning
Clinical psychology, 3
Cognition. *See* Thinking
Cognitive dissonance theory, 18–24
"Cold-blooded killer" response, 89–90
Coma, RAS and, 79
Communication and cooperation, 129, 155–156
Compulsive gambling, 124–126
Computers
connection machines, 174
natural-language-processing, 148
Computing, brain activity of, 28. *See also* Mathematics
Conditioning. *See* Classical conditioning; Operant conditioning
Conformity
bystander apathy, 15–17
power of, 12–14
Connection machines, 174
Consciousness
anesthesia and, 83–87
sleeping, 78–83
waking, 71–78

Plasticity of brain cells, 56
Plato, 87
Pleasant surprise, processing of, 90
Pluralistic ignorance, 16–17
Pornography, aggression and, 107
Positive reinforcement, 123
Positron emission tomography (PET), 40–41, 62
Possible vs. impossible events, attention and, *166*
Pragmatic knowledge, language and, 146–150
Prejudice, 25
Primacy-recency effect, 69
Problem stellung, 181–183, *182*
Productivity, leadership styles and, 27
Professions, obedience and, 11
Prototypes, category restructuring and, 176
Psychology. *See* Clinical psychology; Experimental psychology
Punishment
    discipline and, 106
    operant conditioning and, 123–124
    threat of and attitude shifts, 22–24

Questions, formation of, 140

Rabies, 90
Rage response, 90
Rayner, Rosalie, 121, 123
Reaction-time task, 64
Reasoning. *See* Thinking
Recursion, brain evolution and, 153–157
Reduplicative babbling, 138–139
Reinforcement schedules, 126–128
REM sleep, 80–83

Representational thinking, evolution of, 157–158
Restructuring. *See* Category restructuring
Retaliation, fear of and aggression, 104–105
Reticular activating system (RAS), 79, 82
Reward. *See* Positive reinforcement
Right vs. left hemispheres (brain), 39, 42, 74–76, 90–95
Rodin, Judy, study by, 15–16
Rolandic fissure, *37*
Romantic arousal, 102–103

Sacks, Oliver, 49
Sadness, processing of, 90
Scapegoating, 26, 110
Schein, Edgar, 19
Schizophrenia, 72
Secure attachment, 98
Sensation and perception, 44–58
Septum, 89–90
Sequencing, 39
Sexuality
    aggression and, 107–109
    Freud's notion of, 4
    pleasure of, 89
Shyness, brain asymmetry and, 94–95
Sight and sound, relationship between, 51. *See also* Vision
Skill learning, 61
Skin stress responses. *See* Galvanic skin response (GSR)
Skinner, B. F., 123, 130
Sleep, consciousness and, 78–83
Social
    concepts, development of, 164–166
    environment, impact on emotional state, 100–104
    interactions, operant learning and, 123